KNOWLEDGE, COMPETENCE
and
COMMUNICATION

KNOWLEDGE, COMPETENCE and COMMUNICATION

Chomsky, Freire, Searle, and Communicative Language Teaching

William H. Walcott

BLACK
ROSE
BOOKS

Montreal/New York/London

Black Rose Books No. JJ351

National Library of Canada Cataloguing in Publication Data

Walcott, William Henry

Knowledge, competence and communication : Chomsky, Freire, Searle, and communicative language teaching / William H. Walcott

Includes bibliographical references and index.

ISBN: 1-55164-287-5 (bound)   ISBN: 1-55164-286-7 (pbk.)
(alternative ISBNs 9781551642871 [bound]   9781551642864 [pbk.])

1. Communicative competence. 2. Communication in education. 3. Critical pedagogy. 4. Freire, Paulo, 1921-. 5. Chomsky, Noam. 6. Searle, J.R. I. Title.

LC196.W33 2006   370.11'5   C2006-902798-6

Cove image unitiled; aritst unknown.

Book design and Cover design by L.G. Barton

C.P. 1258	2250 Military Road	99 Wallis Road
Succ. Place du Parc	Tonawanda, NY	London, E9 5LN
Montréal, H2X 4A7	14150	England
Canada	USA	UK

To order books:

In Canada: (phone) 1-800-565-9523 (fax) 1-800-221-9985
email: utpbooks@utpress.utoronto.ca

In the United States: (phone) 1-800-283-3572 (fax) 1-651-917-6406

In the UK & Europe: (phone) 44 (0)20 8986-4854 (fax) 44 (0)20 8533-5821
email: order@centralbooks.com

Our Web Site address: http://www.blackrosebooks.net

A publication of the Institute of Policy Alternatives of Montréal (IPAM)

Printed in Canada

Contents

for Maisie and Cathryne

Tobal

We muse in horror, as Tobal's terror soiled the sacred serge on Sabina's marooning mariners. They shield their woolen waste in our bleeding bosoms and preen their salted shores in thorny

trails of debtor demons. They plague our chieftain's crown with gems of pillaged pride and maim our union rites. They groom the grandeur of their pirate passages to mate the silence of our missing mother.

We are artists and angels whose virtues have been charmed by curses of the colonials.

We are choruses and choirs whose moods have been cradled by the churchman's chimes.

We are priests and pundits lured by the luck of liberty.

We are schools and scholars whose wisdom has been wrenched from riches of the wary.

We are West Indians bathed in the beauty of baneful babble.

We are West Indians drenched in the rights of darkest dawns.

We are West Indians orphaned on the blight of Tobal's Bounty.

We are West Indians festering on dreams of fatherless fortunes.

We are West Indians shackled in the cent of Tobal's treasures.

We are West Indians championed by the lore of princely purses.

—*William H. Walcott*

Acknowledgments

In 2001, I submitted a paper for publication to the journal, *Radical Pedagogy*. The chief editor, Professor Tim McGettigan (Colorado State University), who had examined the paper, encouraged me towards a deeper analysis of the subject matter. To him I am very grateful, as the foundation for this book was laid in that paper and in those words of encouragement.

For having taken the time to shepherd me along complicated language pathways, I also want to thank: James Heap, Dean of Education, Brock University; Jim Cummins, Professor of Education, Ontario Institute for Studies in Education, University of Toronto; Vito Signorile, Professor of Sociology, University of Windsor; and Barry Adam, Chair of the Sociology Department, Univeristy of Windsor.

Thanks, as well, to Linda Barton at Black Rose Books, for her patience, discretion, and tactful guidance, and to Joseph Stephen, of Seneca College, who helped me appreciate some of the technical intricacies and requirements of contemporary publishing.

I also want to express my gratitude to my mother, who taught me in my teenage years that it was far more profitable to be reading my textbooks than to be immersed in imagining the elegance of late afternoon cover drives on the cricket feild, and to my cousin, V.A.D. Ogle, a self-taught intellectual who used his jazz sensibility to make me aware of ideas emanating from the writing of that sociological genius, C. Wright Mills.

Introduction

How is the interchange of roles between the areas of teaching and learning managed within target language instructional settings so that persons might be prepared to interact in societies awash with diversity? I suppose this is an issue which has occupied the mind of many a promoter of communicative language teaching. For well over thirty years, they have been addressing themselves to it by using learner acquisition of communicative competence as a strong foundation to actualising exchange. My analytical interest in their work stems from acceptance of role exchange as a crucial basis to preparation.

I, however, do not consider it to be reasonable or valid for promoters of communicative language teaching to depend upon communicative competence within which they incorporate or subsume linguistic competence, a seminal idea of the psycholinguist, Noam Chomsky. It is true that communicativists, like Chomsky (but very much unlike the highly discredited behaviourists who once dominated language teaching) regard mind as important to language acquisition. However, the innate mentalistic operations Chomsky strongly associates with linguistic competence are incompatible with the externally mediated interactive practices communicativists extol as viable routes to acquisition. Significantly, in the link established between linguistic and communicative competence, communicativists disregard Chomsky's aversion to communication as an essential function of language. They also ignore implications behind his claims about the uselessness of language teaching practices.

While it may appear that the link can be sustained by developing semantic competence within instructional settings careful examination reveals the opposite. The idea of semantic competence clearly emanates from work on speech acts of leading philosophers of language such as John Langshaw Austin and student, John Searle. It is precisely because they regard speech as action and their claims about speech acts are eminently driven by interaction that semantic competence should not be linked to or fused with linguistic competence.

I am, in no way, offering a suggestion that communicative language teaching should be discredited. I think what is needed of it is significant modification in the form of replacing communicative competence by the Freireian idea, *conscientizacao*. This is an idea well suited to pursuit of the query I identified as central to communicative language teaching. It is rooted in searches to relieve learners of illiteracy. It encapsulates the interactive within the very diverse contexts which define lives of those language learners who are, and are not, being taught. It is noticeably humanistic in its inseparable links to freeing those who have been disadvantaged by injustices of inequality. This, I emphasise, is the very inequality which seems to be timeless in its entrapment of several language learners far too numerous to be counted. It is with a deep interest in these individuals, many of whom I regard as little people,[1] that I begin my exploratory journey.

Several years ago, when I was a senior high school student in British Guiana, the sole British colonial possession on the Latin American mainland, I read numerous works about slavery. This is a phenomenon which the brilliant historian, Fisher described as marking a special note of European infamy, a terrible commentary on Christian civilisation. What was so terrible? Fisher says the longest period of slave raiding known to history was initiated by the actions of Spain, Portugal, France, Holland, and Britain after the Christian faith had—for more than a thousand years—been the established religion of Western Europe.

These actions, clearly motivated by European demand for sugar, tobacco, and cotton, were fed by the labour of African slaves "…herded in barracks, working in gangs, and regimented, as they had been recruited, by soulless and mercenary violence" (Fisher, 1949: 1030). The historian contends that the inability of the Protestant religion to ameliorate the horrific nature of the traffic in slaves is all the more serious, because the British were the most successful and, thus, the most guilty of the European traders.

The guilt could not be divorced from the eighteenth century, a period in which Fisher notes no colonies were so valuable as the British West Indian islands. He adds that since they were cultivated by African slave labour, the entire West Indian interest was arrayed against any proposal to abate or destroy the traffic upon which its profits depended. From readings in my high school days, I was well aware that the interest was strongly represented by the white plantocracy whose members adopted the views: at the beginning of the eighteenth century the British West Indian possessions were jewels in the English crown. Sugar was established as King and he was a wealthy monarch.

Britain abolished the slave trade in 1806 and slavery itself in 1834 but like its European competitors, continued its illegal ownership and dominance in African, Asian, and Caribbean colonies. Much of the dominance was defined by the imposition of European languages on these foreign lands, most of which are no longer colonies. The languages were usually taught by Europeans who boasted openly about the cultural superiority of their societies. Today, the former illegal occupiers prefer, and use, routes of economic, rather than physical power to maintain domination within the ex-colonies.

A powerful correlate of such use is existence of a profitable enterprise commonly known as foreign and second language teaching which takes place in the ex-colonies, as well as, large cities of previous colonising powers. Britain's Liverpool and Bristol, whose prosperity Fisher says was based largely on the slave trade, come to mind, immediately. So do capitals in other countries which traded in, and used, slaves. Foreign and second language teaching is also profitable in large urban areas of Canada (a former dominion possession of Great Britain), and the USA, the world's most massive economic giant whose corporate prevalence and cultural hegemony in Latin America are indisputable.

My principal goal, in this work, is to examine one of the current and most popular approaches to language teaching, the communicative approach, whose proponents, in my view, pursue the following important major objectives: (1) assisting learners to produce language as a central feature of their social interaction for the purpose of performing tasks which are important or essential to their everyday existence; (2) assisting learners to construct sequentially organised discourse and helping them to figure out how it is constructed; (3) providing contexts within which learners could be helped from states where their displays of target language use depend on analysis of material with great care, difficulty, and reflection to positions at which displays are not indicative of difficulty, careful or reflective analysis: how can learners be helped to replace their explicit displays of target language by tacit displays; (4) using the real world of target language production outside classrooms as important reference points for fostering effective language use in classrooms.

Brumfit (2001) identifies, at least, nine features which are central to principles of communicative language teaching:

(a) Emphases on identifying needs of language learners;
(b) Stressing conceptual structures and speech acts in syllabus design;

(c) Tolerating variation within classrooms partially exemplified by mixing of target and first languages;

(d) A concern for individualisation and autonomy in learning;

(e) Learner support partly signified as reducing roles of teachers as the only decision makers of appropriate language;

(f) Acceptance of error production as an unavoidable aspect of language acquisition practices;

(g) Contextualising the delivery of language teaching items;

(h) Authenticating of material presented in classrooms;

(i) Promoting strategies that foster 'natural' language performance, particularly in oral form through activities such as group and pair work, role playing, and information-gap exercises.

He notes, quite logically, that all nine features are interconnected and they embody the tripartite claim:

(a) Variant social settings require different language use;

(b) Learner needs in language will differ because persons experience different settings;

(c) Allowing learners to devise their own linguistic systems instead of subjecting them to strict reproduction of target models as a way of assisting them to produce flexibility in language tailored to unpredictable settings.

Brumfit is, however, clear that syllabus design is the one feature unique to communicative language teaching. The crucial point to be grasped in the history of language teaching "…may not be these [nine] features in themselves so much as the justifications that have been produced in support of them" (2001: 49).

Anyone who accepts Brumfit's view about syllabus design and justifications cannot ignore the early work by Wilkins (1976, 1978, 1981) on notional-functional syllabuses and his communicative justification for these syllabuses. It is, therefore, to his ideas that I direct my attention.

Let me be explicit from the outset that Wilkins and Brumfit, British trained linguists, use the term 'syllabus,' in a very specific sense. This is a sense which Stern (1981) correctly describes as referable to the curriculum content of a language course, as well as, criteria of selecting and arranging course content. Hence, language syllabi are not necessarily based on criteria of grammatical sequencing, but have their foundation, also, in thematic, situational or semantic criteria.

Wilkins (1981) says syllabuses are specifications of the content of language teaching and they are structured or ordered, for the purpose of making the processes of teaching and learning more effective. He adds that content should be understood as the linguistic and nonlinguistic categories used to describe characteristics of the linguistic skills which language teaching attempts to develop. It therefore forms the objectives of teaching; and in addition, is a selection from the totality of language.

Further, syllabuses differ according to the manner of selection and types of criteria used to provide an appropriate ordering of language selected. One such syllabus is the notional syllabus:

> In drawing up a notional syllabus, instead of asking how speakers of the language express themselves, or when and where they use language, we ask what it is they communicate through language. We are then able to organise language teaching in terms of the content rather than the form of language. (Wilkins, 1976: 18)

To Wilkins a syllabus counts as notional, if the content of what is to be learnt is derived from learners' needs which represent the different aspects of communication in which learners may engage (1981).

Wilkins (1976) also distinguishes synthetic from what he terms analytic approaches to language teaching, the second of which are indicative of notional syllabi. A synthetic strategy is one in which different aspects of language are taught separately and progressively to promote gradual approximation of language mastery until the entire structure of language has been built. Language to be learnt is segmented into restricted lists of vocabulary items and syntactic structures which are carefully ordered. The job of the language learner is that of resynthesising language which has been segmented into smaller pieces to encourage ease of learning.

An analytic approach is not indicative of deliberate linguistic control of what is learnt. Aspects of language are not offered to learners as building blocks to be progressively accumulated. From the outset, learners are exposed to great variety of language structure and are assisted, via gradual approximation, to pattern their language performance more closely to global target language. Wilkins emphasises that structural considerations are not primary to decision making about language to be presented for learning

It seems evident as to what is to be granted priority in a notional syllabus. Wilkins appears to indicate this forcefully when he says it is after those aspects of language which learners should most usefully be able to communicate in using foreign languages have been chosen that a decision about the language forms appropriate to those aspects may be made. And granting priority to communication requires that the units of language in a notional syllabus are to be primarily semantic (1981).These units make up three categories: communicative function, which express the social purpose of language; semantico-grammatical categories, which indicate the meaning relations expressed by the forms of sentences; and modal categories, indicators of features of language which express a speaker's attitude and degree of certainty (1981).

I shall return to the issue of the notional-functional syllabus, when I address myself to the matter of fluency, another significant feature of communicative language teaching. My current concern is communicative competence. It is to this topic that I direct my focus.

A principal foundation to fulfilling the objectives of communicative language teaching (CLT) is development of communicative competence, which is presented as more representative of the learner's language capabilities than Noam Chomsky's linguistic competence. According to Brumfit, the term, 'communicative competence,' "still provides the most widely accepted metaphor in current foreign language teaching theory" (Brumfit, 2001: 47).

I argue that if proponents of CLT are to fulfil their objective legitimately or validly, they should not do so by employing communicative competence as their basis. I propose, instead, that they use the Freireian approach, *conscientizacao*, for the purpose of helping learners acquire foreign and second languages. In order for me to perform my tasks appropriately, I must examine two views of competence, Noam Chomsky's linguistic competence, as well as, applied linguistic views of communicative competence. Once my examination is complete, I shall make my case for *conscientizacao*.

Note

1. A term I borrowed from the extraordinarily brilliant West Indian cricketer, Garfield St. Auburn Sobers, who never forgot the humble roots from which his sporting genius sprang.

Chapter One
Linguistic And Communicative Competence

I shall show that because of the significant incompatibility between Chomsky's and communicative views of language, the communicativists should not employ communicative competence as a legitimate basis to helping students produce target language effectively. Let me immediately state some of the prominent and enduring applied linguistic views of communicative competence.

It is to ideas of Savignon's and Canale and Swain's that I turn, in order to perform my initial task. Savignon views communicative competence as:

> ...the ability to function in a truly communicative setting—that is a dynamic exchange in which linguistic competence must adapt itself to the total information input, both linguistic and paralinguistic of one or more interlocutors. (Savignon, 1985: 130)

Communicative competence includes grammatical competence (sentence level grammar), sociolinguistic competence (an understanding of the social context in which language is used), discourse competence (an understanding of how utterances are strung together to form a meaningful whole), and strategic competence (a language user's employment of strategies to make the best use of what s/he knows about how a language works, in order to interpret, express, and negotiate meaning in a given context).

Canale and Swain (1980) say communicative competence is composed minimally of grammatical competence, sociolinguistic competence, and communication strategies or strategic competence. The first includes knowledge of the lexical items and rules of morphology, syntax, sentence grammar, semantics, and phonology. The second consists of two sets of rules, sociocultural rules of use and rules of discourse, knowledge of both of which, is crucial to interpreting utterances for social meaning particularly when there is a low level of transparency between the literal meaning of an utterance and the speaker's intention.

Strategic competence consists of verbal and non-verbal strategies of communication that may be employed to compensate for communication breakdown attributable to performance variables or to insufficient competence. Communication strategies are of two kinds: those that are relevant, mainly to grammatical competence, and those that relate more to sociolinguistic competence. An example of the first kind is paraphrasing of grammatical forms that a person has not mastered or cannot recall, momentarily, while examples of the second would be the various role playing strategies such as how a stranger should be addressed by someone who is uncertain about the stranger's social status.

Bachman and Palmer (1997) regard strategic competence as a set of metacognitive devices or tactics which serve to provide cognitive management functions in language use and almost all cognitive activity. They add that as language users construct and interpret discourse in situationally suitable ways, they integrate affective categories with grammatical, textual, pragmatic, sociolinguistic, and topical, knowledge. Bachman and Palmer emphasise that metacognition is always central to language production. This is so, even in circumstances that are not very interactive.

They argue that there are three broad areas within which metacognition operates: goal setting, assessing, and planning. The first consists of three components: (a) identification of language use tasks; (b) choice of specific tasks based on consideration of possibilities; (c) deciding whether to complete task performance. Included in assessing are: (a) evaluating features of task performance in language to determine the value of attaining it; (b) analysing topical and linguistic knowledge to ascertain if it contains the necessary components; (c) monitoring and appraising the correctness and suitability of language use. Planning covers three areas. They are: (a) choosing particular elements from topical and linguistic knowledge, e.g., concepts, words, structures, functions; (b) devising strategies whose materialisation stands as a response to the requirement for task performance; (c) selecting a specific plan to be actually employed as a response to the requirement.

In what is obviously an application of his views about communicative competence, Canale (1985) makes reference to problem posing education. He associates his example of problem posing education, which approximates a natural target setting, with the acts of figuring out and meaningful task performance. What is his example of problem posing education? His particular interest is in problem posing activities in language development. He looks at projects which involve the creation of interactive adventure stories. Part of one such project is an "oral interactive activity" in which groups of target language learners are required to locate and remove a treasure hidden on an imaginary farm.

The groups consist of persons whose oral language proficiency varies. Members of each group are provided with a map of the farm and each is given a different clue about the location of treasure. Now, all clues are necessary to locating the treasure and all communication must take place by means of target language use or gestures. Canale infers that each person, therefore, has a specific responsibility and all must aid one another to attain a common goal. Consequently, learners must interpret, express, and negotiate meaning, at affective, cognitive, linguistic, and social levels, i.e., create and use a variety of representations and strategies, at each level. Finally, he states, very clearly, that his view of problem posing activities and language use strategies is that they are important to learners' development of interactional and critical thinking skills which are, also, crucial to academic achievement.

Other applied linguists, notably, Bachman (1990) and Blum-Kulka and Levenston (1983), have offered additional extensions to communicative competence. Blum-Kulka and Levenston view semantic competence as consisting of: (1) awareness of hyponymy, antonymy, converseness, and other possible systematic links between lexical items, by means of which, the substitution of one lexical item for another can be explained in particular contexts; (2) ability to avoid using specific lexical items by means of circumlocution and paraphrase;. (3) ability to recognise degrees of paraphrasic equivalence. Bachman has posited two core aspects of linguistic competence, organisational competence which subsumes grammatical and discourse competence, as well as, pragmatic competence which encompasses illocutionary and sociolinguistic competence.

In describing what she regards as a conceptual expansion, Kasper notes that strategic competence operates at the levels of pragmatic and organisational competence but in a broader sense than that proposed by Canale and Swain.

> While the ability to solve receptive and productive problems due to lack
> of knowledge or accessibility remains an aspect of strategic competence,
> it is now more generally thought of as the ability to use linguistic
> knowledge efficiently. (Kasper: 345)

She adds that the extension is compatible with the view that language use, a version of goal-oriented behaviour, is always strategic.

At an institutional level, some of the most ambitious work to extend conceptions broaden categories, and specify aspects of competence, comes from the Council of Europe, a sociopolitical organisation committed to attaining greater unity among European societies by adopting common action within the cultural field. I shall describe significant portions of this work as it is laid out in a Council document, "The Common European Framework in Its Political and Educational Context."

In line with its sociopolitical interests, the Council has reaffirmed the political objectives of its actions within the area of modern languages. Some of these objectives are stated: (1) to promote mutual understanding and tolerance, respect for identities and cultural diversity through more international communication; (2) to maintain and further develop the richness and diversity of European cultural life through greater mutual knowledge of national and regional languages, including those less widely taught; (3) to meet the needs of a multilingual and multicultural Europe by appreciably developing the ability of Europeans to communicate with each other across linguistic and cultural boundaries, which requires a sustained, lifelong effort to be encouraged, put on an organised footing and financed at all levels of education by the competent bodies.

Beyond its interest in advancing multilingualism, the Council wants to promote plurilingualism within a pan-European context. It notes that multilingualism may be accomplished through diversifying languages to be taught within specific educational settings, reducing the dominant status of English in international communication or by supporting persons to gain more than one foreign language. Plurilingualism is grounded in the idea that as one's experience of language in their cultural context grows from language of the home to that of wider society and languages of other peoples, all the languages and attendant cultures are not subject to rigid mental segmentation. Instead, one builds communicative competence whose growth is derived from interaction of all forms of knowledge and experience in languages.

The Framework consists of a common foundation for matters such as elaboration of language syllabuses, curriculum guidelines, examinations, and textbooks within Europe. It represents comprehensive description of what language learners must learn to produce language for communication, as well as, the knowledge and skills they must develop in order to be effective users. Description also encompasses proficiency levels which are to be assessed at all stages of learning on a life-long basis.

Appropriate implementation of the Framework depends upon three important criteria: transparency, coherence, and comprehensiveness. To be comprehensive, the framework must specify as full a range as is possible of linguistic knowledge, skills, and uses. Transparency covers clear and explicit formulation of information which must be readily apprehended by learners. Coherence represents harmonious connections among such things as identification of needs, evaluation, testing and measurement, selection of teaching items, content definition, and determination of objectives.

Among other matters central to the Framework are statements about language learning, language users, and language learners. The latter two are formulated as social agents who perform tasks under particular circumstances, within specific settings, specific fields of action. Importantly, language learning, subsumed by language use, is made up of actions performed by agents who develop a range of competence, parts of which, are specified as features of communicative competence.

Agents also apply their general and communicative competence range within different contexts under varied constraints to participate in language activities by means of which they activate strategies suitable to accomplishing tasks they set out to complete. Further, the practice of monitoring actions contributes to alteration and reinforcement of competence.

The features of communicative competence are identified as linguistic, sociolinguistic, pragmatic, general, and existential. General competence or knowledge of the world includes sociocultural awareness, knowledge of societies and cultures of communities where languages are spoken. It is knowing about locations, organisations, persons, objects, events, and processes exemplified: the home, public spaces, occupational areas, educational settings, families, strangers, co-workers, teachers, doing business transactions, playing. General competence also covers intercultural awareness, knowledge, awareness and understanding of similarities and differences between target language communities and native language communities.

Existential competence is the totality of personal characteristics, personality features, attitudes, motivations, beliefs, and cognitive styles indicative of someone's views about others and readiness to participate with others in social interaction. Though this type of competence emerges from acculturation, it is subject to modification.

Linguistic competence includes lexical, grammatical, semantic, phonological, orthographic, and orthoepic competence. The last covers ability to read prepared texts aloud, and utter words initially recognised in writing. It involves ability to use context for resolving ambiguity, ascertaining links among written forms, punctuation, and intonation, knowing about spelling conventions, and how to use dictionaries. Lexical competence involves knowledge of, and ability to use, lexical and grammatical elements such as phrasal idioms, phrasal verbs, proverbs, fixed collocations, single word forms, question words, demonstratives, articles, possessives, and auxiliary verbs. Grammatical competence, ability to understand and express meaning by producing and recognising well formed sentences and phrases, entails the practice of organising various features. Some of these features are morphemes, roots and affixes, words, tense forms, clauses, sentences, valency, concord, and government.

Semantic competence, the awareness and control of the organisation of meaning, is indicative of lexical, grammatical, and pragmatic components. Lexical semantics is concerned with matters of word meaning in areas such as connotation, collocation, hyponymy, and synonymy/antonymy. Grammatical semantics conveys the meaning of grammatical elements, categories, structures and processes while pragmatic semantics covers logical connections in matters such as implicature and presupposition.

Phonological competence, is knowledge of, and skill in, perception and production of features such as different phonemes, varied syllabic structures, and prosody. Orthographic competence is conveyed as knowledge of, and ability to perceive and produce, printed and cursive letter forms, appropriate word spellings, punctuation marks, and logographic signs which are regularly used.

Sociolinguistic competence is constituted by knowledge and skills needed for handling social dimensions of language production which feature as markers of social intercourse, politeness strategies, expressions of folk-wisdom, register variations, as well as, accent and dialect distinctions. Social intercourse can be indicated as use of greeting exchanges, address forms, turn-taking conventions, and expletives. Politeness takes the forms of impoliteness, and positive and negative politeness. Folk-wisdom can be conveyed in proverbs, idioms, and familiar quotations while register differences can be offered as variation in formality and informality. Some notable distinctions are intimacy, formality, neutrality, and familiarity. Dialect and accent are marked linguistically in social class, regions, ethnicity, and occupation via phonological, paralinguistic, grammatical, lexical, and body language variations.

Pragmatic competence is represented as functional and discourse competence. Discourse competence is concerned with the sequential arrangement of sentences for producing coherent stretches of language. Functional competence, which includes conversational competence, deals with ways in which spoken discourse and written texts are used interactively, for the purposes of initiating, developing, and concluding exchanges.

It is the American anthropologist, Dell Hymes, in the early seventies, who first put forth the idea of communicative competence. For Hymes (1971a: 47–93), an adequate approach to competence must differentiate among four elements of competence: systematic potential, appropriateness, occurrence, and feasibility. The first encompasses the possibility that an act can be accomplished, as well as, the extent to which it can be attained, once it is possible. Appropriateness includes the possibility, degree, and effectiveness to which an act is suitable within a particular context. Occurrence accounts for the possibility of performing an act and the extent to which the act is performed. Feasibility accounts for the possibility that an act can be performed. Hymes is also interested in rules of speaking, ways in which language users establish links between specific modes of speaking and topics or message forms, on the one hand, and particular contexts and activities, on the other.

Further, Hymes (1972) says an interest in determining ways of speaking must be based on four other forms of information: (a) the linguistic resources available to speaker/hearers or the various speech styles from which they can choose; (b) supra-sentential structuring, recognition of various ways in which language events such as trials, religious ceremonies, and songs are structured; (c) rules of interpretation applied with the aim of attaching communicative value to language items; (d) norms which govern different forms of interaction.

Schacter (1990) notes that the model of communicative competence proposed initially by Hymes gave tremendous impetus to linguists frustrated by a principal focus on grammatical competence. Two of those linguists, identify a major shift in perspective within the second language teaching profession:

> In relatively simple terms, there has been a change of emphasis from presenting language as a set of forms (grammatical, phonological, lexical) which have to be learned and practised, to presenting language as a functional system which is used to fulfil a range of communicative purposes. This shift in emphasis has largely taken place as a result of fairly convincing arguments, mainly from ethnographers and others who study language in its context of use, that the ability to use a language should be described as communicative competence.
> (Tarone and Yule, 1989: 17)

The principal ethnographer is, of course, Hymes (1971a, 1972, 1977, 1988) whom Ellis and Roberts (1987) claim was interested in what degree of competence speaker/hearers needed, in order to give themselves membership of particular speech communities. He examined what factors—particularly sociocultural ones—in addition to grammatical competence are required for speaker/hearers to participate in meaningful interaction.

Ellis and Roberts add that not only did Hymes give initial impetus to the sociocultural idea, but he also demonstrated how language variation correlated with social and cultural norms of speech events or certain defined public interactions. And in one of his earliest statements about the broad version of competence Hymes says the purpose of the linguist is to account for the fact that a "normal child" acquires much more than grammatical knowledge of sentences. In one of his clearest statements, he observes:

> The linguist's problem is to explain how the child comes rapidly to be able to produce and understand (in principle) any and all of the grammatical sentences of a language. If we consider a child actually capable of producing all possible sentences, he would probably be institutionalised, particularly if not only the sentences but also speech or silence were random or unpredictable. We then have to account for the fact that a normal child acquires knowledge of sentences not only as grammatical but also as appropriate. This is not accounted for in a transformational grammar which divides linguistic theory into two parts: linguistic competence and linguistic performance.
> (Hymes, 1971b: 5)

Hymes adds that children acquire repertoires of speech acts and are capable of participating in the performance of speech acts, as well as, evaluating the speech acts of others.

Hymes is talking about competence which is integral to attitudes and values concerning language and other codes of communication. Here is reference to social features which he exemplifies as positive productive aspects of linguistic engagement in social life: there are rules of use without which rules of grammar would be useless.

Criper and Widdowson (1978), two principal protagonists of communicative language teaching, adopt a similar stance. They note Chomsky's distinction between competence (the ideal language user's knowledge of grammatical rules) and performance (actual realisation of the knowledge in utterances) and add that he has made the former a prime object of linguistic study. Such choice —they claim—has allowed him to define linguistics by restricting the kind of information about language which has to be accounted for within his theoretical framework.

They characterise the choice as a necessary investigative step in confronting limited problems and achieving their partial or complete solutions prior to increasing the complexity of data studied. This approach is, however, too limited for the language teacher who is concerned, simultaneously, with competence in describing or contrasting language systems and ways of using the systems. In a particular reference to language learning, they say it means learning rules of use, as well as, rules of formal linguistic systems.

Until learners know how to use grammatical resources for sending meaningful messages in real life situations, they cannot be said to know a language. It is essential that they know: what varieties of language are used in specific situations, how to vary styles according to their addressees, when they should speak or be silent, what types of gestures are needed for different forms of speech. They insist that the very essence of language is that it serve as a means of communication. Language use involves social interaction.

Thus, knowing a language means knowing how it fulfils communicative function. And in what is, surely expression of preference for the broad version of competence, they state that it is inadequate for persons to possess knowledge about rules of sentence formation, they must also know how to utilise rules for the purpose of producing appropriate utterances.

The Hymesian position is endorsed, also, by Hudson (1980) who regards communicative competence as much more broadly based than linguistic competence within Chomskyan linguistics. Communicative competence includes knowledge of linguistic forms, and ability to use the forms appropriately.

If all of the aforementioned references to competence are appropriate indicators of the broad version, then it would appear that this version could be of dual significance to communicativists. Not only is there indication, within this version, that action is meaningful, it seems, also, to be a version which is entirely compatible with the communicative aim of assisting students to produce target language as a central feature of their social interaction. Hence, the broad version could be employed to help learners.

According tho Stern, interest in communicative language teaching has grown and spread since the late nineteen seventies. "Communication or communicative competence has come to be viewed as the main objective of language teaching; at the same time, communication has increasingly been seen as the instrument, the method, or way of teaching" (Stern: 94-95). In what I deem a very explicit stance, Kehe and Kehe (1994) claim that the communicative approach seems to be firmly established within the language teaching profession.

They add that it is difficult to argue against the communicative approach, for the purpose of language does seem to be communication. Further, the link between the term, 'communication,' and the idea of competence implies that there are identifiable abilities and skills which communicators must master. Kehe and Kehe argue that no difficulty exists in recognising linguistic competence but they acknowledge the existence of another area, strategic competence, which needs to be learnt and taught.

French Immersion, the Natural, 'L' and 'P' Approaches

While addressing himself to the significance of French Immersion education, Stern (1990) writes the immersion movement served to enhance the belief in communicative-experiential teaching through the weight it attached to content and message oriented teaching. It is clear that one version of communicative language teaching which has grown, spread, and taken strong roots within the target language field is French Immersion education. According to Swain and Lapkin (1981), immersion education in schools, a Canadian innovation, is based on the principle that learners receive the same type of education as they would in a regular English language programme, but the medium of instruction, the language through which materials are presented and discussed, is French. In immersion programmes, the second language is acquired in much the same way as children learn their first language by using authentic settings of communication.

Lambert (1990), one of the two pioneers of immersion education, states that immersion programmes are intended principally for English speaking children who, as members of the major Canadian linguistic group (English), are ready to add a second language, French, without losing their footing in the first language.

From their first day in kindergarten or grade 1, they find themselves with a teacher who speaks only some foreign language...and who starts conversing and interacting, slowly and considerately, in that language. The foreign language (L2) is used as the sole medium of instruction for kindergarten and grade 1 and 2, and only then is English introduced, in the form of English arts. By grade 5 and 6, half of the curriculum is taught via L2 and half via L1. (Lambert, 1990: 216)

Lambert also offers what he terms are descriptions of immersion success which he says is rather dramatic.

At the end of elementary school, immersion students develop a functional bilinguality in L2 gained mainly in an incidental manner through its use as language of instruction. Functional bilinguality acquired by grades 5 and 6 does not —in any way—impair development of L1 skills. Degrees of L1 competence are enriched, when examined in relation to carefully matched non-immersion control groups. Immersion students who learn to read via L2 keep up with the controls in English language reading and other aspects of this language, i.e., skills in subject areas such as mathematics, social studies and science. Immersion students meet L2 requirements of their programme "...with all the thinking and language abilities they have and this apparently promotes a continuous, mutually beneficial interplay between L2 (the instructional code) and L1 (the basic language of thought and expression for the children at the start of their experience)" (Lambert, 1990: 217).

Other proponents of French immersion education who advocate communicative competence as a strong basis to target language development are Stern and Swain (1973). In findings from a pilot investigation, they refer to strategies used by bilingual teachers in French immersion kindergarten classes. Particular attention was given to language behaviour of child learners and their teachers, as well as, the general conduct of classes.

Stern and Swain point to three strategies employed, commonly as ways of indicating what teachers do, when children speak to them in English. In the first strategy, the teacher repeats the child's statement or question in French, then responds appropriately:

Child 1: Madame, can I paint?

Teacher: Est-ce que tu peux peindre?

Child 2: I want to show you something.

Teacher: Tu veux me montrer quelque chose? Qu'est-ce que c'est?

In the second, the teacher simply responds appropriately to the child's questions or statements:

Child: We made a train.

Teacher: Avec la neige?

Child: No, with people.

Teacher: Que fait le train?

Child: Choo choo!

And in the third, the teacher responds by attempting to have the child repeat, in French, what he has expressed in English:

Child 1: It's snowing.

Teacher: En Français?

Child 1: Neiges.

Child 2: No, it's raining.

Teacher: Il...?

Child 2: Pleut.

Stern and Cummins (1981) point to student and teacher strategies or interactions of elaboration, expansion, digression, and repetition employed in immersion classes which enhance linguistic progress of immersion students. In a reference —albeit implied—to the greater usefulness of discourse strategies employed by teachers in immersion classes, rather than those where French is learnt within a conventional class, Stern and Cummins say the French immersion teacher elaborates, expands, and digresses, thereby "...using language in a natural and expanded manner. In a conventional class, the teacher's language is restricted to a minimal level, because of the students' basic level of competence" (Stern and Cummins, 1981: 227). The teacher's sentence structure is simple and without digressions. Questions are brief, and are followed, frequently, by a single-word response and exact repetition. The following "interactions" exemplify the foregoing teacher strategies:

Immersion

Teacher positive evaluation: Oui, c'est très bien.

Disciplinary directive: Je répète, James, pour que l'enregistrement soit utile, on évite d'e faire des bruits comme tu es en train d'en faire. Tu n'as pas touché à ton cahier.

Teacher positive evaluation: Oui, Anne. Anne a absolument raison.

Comment: Andréa à répète la dernière phrase qui était copiée au tableau. C'est "soudain le feu est passé au vert" et Andréa a continué en disant "le feu est passé au vert, quand le vieux monsieur a lâché le poteau. Il a...

Implicit correction: Ah, c'est pas...

Student response: Oh..."aussitôt qu'il a lâché le poteau."

Teacher accept: Oui, c'est ca.

Conventional Class

Teacher specific information: Qu'est ce que c'est? Jason (picture cue).
Student response: Matin.
Teacher explicit correction: Le matin.
Student repetition: Le matin.
Teacher accept: Oui.

Teacher specific information: Et ça? Danny (picture cue).
Student response: L' après-midi.
Teacher accept: Uh huh (nodding).

There is no doubt that French immersion education has been extremely successful. Its success stems from efforts to develop five features among learners which I think are highly consistent with what Brumfit (1981, 1982) regards as fluency. Let me, therefore, address myself to both of these matters. Brumfit regards fluency as the learner's use of language—albeit with "an inadequate dialect"—without fear of being corrected and with a concern for the message or purpose of her language use. To encourage fluency, a teacher—for the most part—interacts with learners as a "communicator," so that they might become autonomous users of whatever language they are acquiring. Further, learners should be allowed to behave with whatever inadequate dialect they have developed in the same way as they behave in their first language.

With clear attachment of greater weight to fluency, rather than accuracy, Finocchiaro and Brumfit (1983) situate fluency within the notional-functional syllabus, which they say is principally based on students' needs and purposes. They emphasise that such learners should be granted opportunities for language use and expressing purposes which teachers do not foresee. As such, the learners would be able to accomplish what persons do in natural settings, express themselves through whatever linguistic means are available to them, despite their production of mistakes. Finocchiaro and Brumfit are making a plea for what they call adaptation to, and improvisation of, features in the notional-functional syllabus.

Significantly, they claim that the argument for these two qualities is accepted—albeit in varying forms—within the communicative movement: (a) while formal teaching should not be abolished, greater emphasis ought to be given to improvisation; (b) genuine learning will not occur unless there is much improvisation and invention by students from the very start of the learning process; (c) learning target languages through engagement with subject matter knowledge and problem solving is effective, because improvisation and adjustment will be natural and goal-oriented.

They are emphatic that too much accuracy is a barrier to fluency. When decisions are made to promote accuracy, probable consequences are the production of linguists and language testers, rather than language users.

Brumfit's view of fluency is compatible with an exemplification of competence offered by Paulston (1980) who states that competence in a language is demonstrated as fluency to express one's own opinions in appropriate situations.

The five features in French immersion education are: (1) the learners' production of French as a major feature of their social interaction for the purpose of performing actions that are important or essential to their lives; (2) the learners' use of a task-oriented education whose problem posing component[1] they can employ as a central basis to meaningful French language use outside instructional settings; (3) the learners' meaningful construction of sequentially organised discourse; (4) the learners' replacement of their tacit display of L1 or native language knowledge by a tacit[2] display of French target language knowledge; (5) employing the real world of French target language use outside classrooms as an important reference point for fostering effective French language production within classrooms.

All five of these features are very significant components of communicative language teaching (CLT) which Stern (1981, 1990) offers in two guises, the 'L' or linguistic approach, and the 'P' or pedagogical approach. Immersion education lies within the P approach. For Stern, immersion education demonstrates a radical version of a communicative approach to language learning. Emphasis is placed on the message in, rather than, the medium of language use. Stern thus describes immersion education as the deliberate and artificial creation of a second language environment in which language has to be used for communication with the expectation that it offers close approximation to conditions learners would face in a natural target setting.

The L approach, which is analytic and formal, is concerned with deliberate study and systematic practice, typically occurs in classrooms, but can take place in the field. Some major features of this approach are: (1) isolation of specific language features, thereby making them salient for the learner; (2) a necessary decontextualisation of linguistic features; (3) provision of opportunities for the learner to cope with specific language features by means of practice; (4) attention to accuracy and error correction in a form deemed as appropriate for a given group of learners.

The P approach, which operates in a psychological and pedagogical frame-work, is an experiential approach. Here is a clear statement which embodies underlying assumptions of the P approach:

> In ordinary language use…when we talk to someone, read a letter or the newspaper, listen to news on the radio, our attention is usually focused on the message itself, not on its formal linguistic properties. We are involved in communication, and are not paying much attention, if any, to the forms of language or the "code" in which we communicate. This intuitive use of a language for communication is characteristic of the full competence of the native speaker. Indeed for a native speaker it may be difficult to focus on isolated formal features of the code. (Stern, 1981: 136–137)

The P approach emphasises "ego involvement" of learners in communicative activities and production of language in real life situations through which the learners interact with target language users.

When Stern uses the world of ordinary language to highlight the P approach, he should be regarded as grounding his focus in communicative competence. This is quite obvious in the accounts he offers of what knowing a language means. Stern says that in learning a new language learners aim to approximate the native speaker's knowledge. He uses research from psycholinguistics and sociolinguistics as his basis to making his claim. He makes specific reference to the concept of competence devised by Chomsky and reinterpreted by Hymes. Stern goes on to list four features of competence: form, meaning, communication, creativity. Form is not analytical; it is universal and intuitive. "We master our native language; we can unfailingly distinguish right from wrong; we feel at home in it; and its rules are self evident to us. But we cannot explain it" (Stern, 1980: 55).

Meaning, displayed affectively, socioculturally, cognitively, and linguistically, emanates from persons taking it for granted, focusing on it, rather than form. In listening or reading, for instance, persons are intent on conveying meaning. Communication is the ability to produce language through maximum focus on meaning and minimal attendance to form. Persons are usually absorbed in what they want to do with language. They are barely aware of language, when they perform tasks such as reading or listening to news. They are engrossed in events. While listing several different communicative acts, Stern associates them with what he deems second nature. They are greeting, leave-taking, small talk, enquiring, teaching, learning, letter writing, poetry reading, promising, persuading, betting, requesting, commanding, threatening, joking, declaring, arguing, swearing, apologising, and making excuses. These are creative aspects of competence which indicates that competence is dynamic and active, rather than mechanical or static. Language use is flexible and inventive. It is geared to productive thinking.

Major features of the P approach are: (1) focusing activities of target language classes on a substantive topic or theme which is not arbitrary or trivial but motivated by identified educational or personal need; (2) arrangement of classroom activities in a manner through which the learner is engaged in purposeful enterprises; (3) creation of conditions for real language use and, more importantly, real conversation; (4) encouragement of learners to convey meaning in their language production, without worrying greatly about absolute correctness.

> One [the L approach] is teaching about communication (i.e., the analysis of communication through the study of speech acts, discourse analysis and sociolinguistics).This analytic treatment of communication derives mainly from the work of European linguists such as Widdowson, Wilkins, Brumfit, and others, and the Council of Europe project. The other [the P approach] is the concept of communicative teaching as teaching through communication by involving the learner as a participant. In North America this approach is mainly represented by Savignon and Krashen and the advocates of immersion education; in Britain, Candlin and Breen have adopted this point of view.
> (Stern, 1990: 96)

Candlin (1979a) is, of course, one of the earliest advocates of using "real" language, within communicative settings. He points to a distinction between the sentence and the utterance. This is a distinction which he claims should be grasped by the second language teaching profession: the sentence is a theoretical term which refers to well formed strings produced by grammar, whereas the utterance a unit of discourse. In implying that the distinction has not been grasped, he claims that language teaching materials make use of the sentence as unit of grammar, rather than the utterance as unit of discourse.

What this results in is that language learnt by foreign language learners is unlike "real" language, since what sentences exemplify exclude the proper communicative purpose of language as an illustrator of language users' roles. Conceptual grounding for the foregoing position resides in a Hymesian view which Candlin conveys, in a forthright manner.

It is significant that in a desire to establish a framework within which to interrelate linguistic form, semantic interpretation and pragmatic use for the more complete understanding of communicative competence, we are driven outside the narrow confines of linguistic structure. (Candlin, 1979b: ix)

He acknowledges that learners have to display the ability to construct grammatically well formed sentences and be aware of intrasentential semantic equivalence. He adds that they must also manage pragmatic values which sentences assume in discourse. A requirement for this dual ability is the devising of encounter syllabuses whose use sensitises learners to Hymesian aspects of speech events. This requirement is necessitated for the purposes of analysing and comparing ways in which different types of interpersonal encounters are accomplished within settings where target language users interact with each other and with first language users.

Sensitisation occurs, when meanings of specific communicative strategies are negotiated. Candlin wants language learners to become discourse analysts of target language, with a teacher's assistance, which promotes their application of existing conversational awareness in first languages at the same time as they are being equipped with feasible models for analysing target language. Breen and Candlin (1980) also state that a reference to language as communication is tantamount to regarding its users as involved in negotiating meaning, on the basis of their social interaction.

Krashen's contribution to the P approach takes the form of the Natural Approach whose development he says was influenced by ideas about acquisition. Four principles underlie this approach. Class time is used principally to provide input for acquisition. Secondly, while students may use either first or second language, the teacher's classroom language is exclusively in the target language. Error correction is employed by the teacher, only if communication is seriously impeded. Thirdly, students are assigned homework which may include formal grammar work. Error correction is used in correcting homework. The fourth principle is that course objectives are semantic activities, by means of which, students talk about ideas, solve problems, and engage in meaningful task performance.

Acquisition and Communication (CS) Strategies

There is no doubt in my mind that if immersion education resides within the P approach, one of its important premises is communicative competence. I advance my claim, in view of the fact that it bears all the marks of the stamp (acquisition) of target language. This is a stamp imprinted by Krashen (1980, 1981, 1987) who has placed competence at its core. I shall explore his placement and follow my examination by looking at the work of some theorists and practitioners who have used Krashen's views. These are views which indicate distinctions between learning and acquisition, the second of which, he clearly favours. He claims that fluency in second language performance is owed to what persons acquire, rather than what they have learnt.

He says language learning is conscious knowledge about language, the everyday term for which, is 'grammar.' Equivalent terms for learning are formal and explicit knowledge. Persons learn by consciously apprehending form, by reading about, or listening to, or figuring out explanations of rules and benefiting from correction of their errors.

According to Krashen, acquisition refers to the manner in which linguistic abilities are internalised "naturally" without conscious focusing on linguistic forms. A minimal requirement for its occurrence is participation in natural communication situations and is also the way children gain knowledge of, and develop abilities in, first and second languages. Acquisition is different to learning, conscious, explicit, or formal knowledge of language. A necessary condition for acquisition is that acquirers understand, through reading or hearing, input language which consists of structure slightly beyond levels of competence they possess. Thus, if an acquirer's competence resides at stage or level i, then input language for his understanding should contain i+1. What does Krashen mean when he refers to an acquirer's understanding? To understand means focusing on message—not form—in language use. Acquisition is realised, when persons strive for meaning, initially, and acquire structure, as a consequence of understanding message. Such a state of affairs is possible, because in the act of understanding, persons utilise knowledge of the world, as well as, extralinguistic information. In addition, acquisition, which requires meaningful and communicative language use, is a subconscious process. Acquirers are not usually aware that they use language for communication.

Acquired competence, the result of language acquisition, is subconscious, as well. Acquired competence is also responsible for utterance initiation. In suggesting that acquired competence exemplifies application of linguistic rules, Krashen adds that persons are not generally aware, or conscious of, the rules they acquire. They have a "feel" for correctness. Grammatically appropriate sentences, for instance, "sound" or "feel" right and errors feel wrong, although persons do not consciously know what rules are violated.

Among the theorists and practitioners who have accepted Krashen's views of acquisition and place communicative competence at the root of their ideas are Pica and Doughty (1985), Long (1980, 1981, 1983,), Yule and Tarone (1997), Rampton (1997), Wilkes-Gibbs (1997), Poulisse (1997), Kasper and Kellerman (1997), Wagner and Firth (1997) as well as Williams, Inscoe and Tasker (1997). All of the linguists noted above make use of what can be termed communication strategies (CS), for the purpose of exemplifying the foundational significance of communicative competence.

There is no single account of what constitutes CS. However, these strategies can be classified under two broad categories: those derived from psycholinguistic, as well as, interactional views of communication. The psycholinguistic or "intra-individual" perspective is neatly summarised by Kasper and Kellerman (1997) who state that its proponents locate CS in models of speech production or cognitive organisation and processing. While addressing themselves to speech production and analytic aspects, two of those proponents, Kellerman and Bialystock (1997), state that any effort to account for a taxonomy of communication strategies must satisfy three requirements: parsimony, generalisability, and psychological plausibility.

Meeting the first requirement means that analysts must be guided by the principle of offering a minimum number of explicit strategy types to classify data. Generalisability encompasses the use of taxonomy which is equally referable to all regularly endowed speakers who display strategic behaviour, regardless of proficiency stages or any particular joint configuration of native and non-native language use. Psychological plausibility entails that any taxonomy should be based on contemporary knowledge about language processing, cognition and problem solving behaviour. Further, language proficiency is made up of two aspects of processing: analysis of knowledge and control of processing. Both aspects are employed for mental representations, the entire spectrum of intellectual attainment.

They are parts of a broader mechanism responsible for enabling progress in proficiency. Control of processing, or selective attention, means that in the performance of any cognitive task, persons concentrate only on specific segments of information available to them, at a particular time. The justification for this claim rests on the argument that cognition occurs as continual choice from more knowledge than persons can process. In addition, persons apply perceptual or experiential inclinations to make certain segments of information pertinent to themselves. In conversational engagement, it is usually meaning to which persons direct their attention. On some occasions, it is the identity of language itself—syntax, gestures, or phonology—that attract persons' attention. In other instances, when native speakers converse with nonnative speakers, specific direction is given to lexical choices.

Proponents of the interactive approach, on the other hand, locate CS within the social and contextually contingent aspects of language production which covers features of use characterised as problematic. In their focus on the interactive, Wagner and Firth (1997), say that what is crucial to understanding problematic features of use is knowing about markers which indicate that speakers experience difficulty in expressing talk. Such speakers "flag" problems in discourse encoding, thus signalling the imminence of a CS. Flagging provides speaker/hearers with information about how utterances are to be interpreted and acted upon and can be exemplified by such phenomena as pausing, change of voice quality, or intonation contour and rhythms.

Crucial to the interactional approach is investigating how communication is attained as a situated, contingent, accomplishment. Interactionists regard CS as things displayed publicly and made visible to an analyst via participants' actions. Emphasis is on the social, rather than individual, or cognitive processes, underlying talk.

> An interactional approach defines instances of talk as CS if, and only if, the participants themselves make public in the talk itself an encoded related problem and by so doing engage—individually or conjointly—in attempts to resolve the problem. CS, then, are available to the analyst only to the extent that they have been produced and reacted upon by the parties to the talk. The encoding problem may either be a purely linguistic one or a combined linguistic and conceptual one. (Wagner and Firth, 1997: 325-326)

Rampton (1997), another notable proponent of the interactional approach, claims that the study of CS should be central to L2 research. He adds that the full weight of such investigation can be appreciated, only if CS research is not restricted to psycholinguistic exploration.

While citing the value of his own analysis, he notes that CS research must give total consideration to interpersonal and social meaning. Adopting such a stance, he adds, displays how a sense of linguistic difficulty is integrally linked to not just a psychologically, but also, an interactionally active sense of the learner. Links between language learner identity and communicative problems are reciprocal. The presence of problems evokes identity and identity generates problems, as well. Identity is also closely intertwined with other social relations. It can be stigmatised, at the same time, by L1 and L2 users or L2 users can stigmatise it while L1 users grant it high status. Wagner and Firth take the further step of claiming that the interactional approach is best served by divesting itself of any connections with the psycholinguistic issue, language acquisition.

Quite apart from the positions of Stern and CS theorists, Canale and Swain (1980) imply, very strongly, that communicative competence could be used as a significant basis to helping students produce target language as a central feature of their social interaction. They state that one of the many aspects of communicative competence which must be investigated, more rigorously, before a communicative approach can be implemented fully in the areas of second language teaching and testing, is development of administratively feasible classroom activities that can be used to encourage meaningful action in target language use. Some of these activities have been developed by Tarone and Yule (1989). They analyse and discuss means, as well as instruments, classroom teachers can utilise to determine students' abilities within areas of grammatical, sociolinguistic, and strategic competence.

The Bilingual Proficiency Project

It is these very areas which are analysed as some of the significant components in a Bilingual Proficiency Project, a highly ambitious effort to provide what Schacter (1990) views as empirical justification for a model of linguistic proficiency. This five year research project was conducted in the nineteen eighties at the Modern Language Centre, Ontario Institute for Studies in Education, Toronto, Canada. The main purpose of this project was to examine a group of educationally relevant issues concerned with the second language development of school age children. Three of the issues were: the effect of classroom treatment on second language learning; the relation of social-environmental factors to bilingual proficiency; and the relation between age and language proficiency (Allen, Cummins, Harley, and Swain, 1990).

While Schacter does express reservations about adequacy and clarity of the concept, communicative competence, as well as its exemplification in the project, she does not recommend its rejection. She—in fact—endorses Chomsky's grammatical or linguistic competence, although she notes two issues of special relevance to the project. They are: what are the major constitutive components of communicative competence, whether—and to what extent—the components can be delineated clearly.

In responding to her concerns, not only do project researchers (Allen, Cummins, Harley, and Swain, 1990) accept Chomsky's linguistic competence, but they also claim to be demonstrating a broadening of competence. An exchange between the two parties about competence is quite revealing.

Schacter says that beyond the level of isolated sentences, confusion, disagreement and fragmentation are reflected in the general state of knowledge about communicative competence. On the other hand, the researchers emphasise that grammar, discourse, and sociolinguistic constructs are not indicative of everything that is involved in communicative competence. They, however, express their research aims: isolate aspects of communicative competence they consider to be educationally relevant, and test the hypothesis that these aspects would emerge as distinct components and would be differentially manifested under different task conditions and under different circumstances of learning.

Synthesising 'L' and 'P' Approaches

All the linguists named above and the Council of Europe are, doubtless, proponents of communicative language teaching. From Stern's standpoint, their work would lie within either the L or P approaches. Stern did commit himself to synthesising the two approaches. I wish to complete my discussion of the heavy communicative dependence on competence by dealing with Stern's views of synthesis.

An L and P synthesis consists of a three level curriculum of communicative competence. Allen (1980) proposes a way of attaining linkage. The three levels are structural (analytic, functional) analytic, and experiential. He also indicates that at level 1, practice is medium-oriented, at level 2, it is medium and message-oriented while at level 3 it is message-oriented.

The main characteristics of his curriculum are summarized as follows:

LEVEL 1 STRUCTURAL	LEVEL 2 RHETORICAL	LEVEL 3 INSTRUMENTAL
Focus on language (formal features)	Focus on language (discourse features)	Focus on the use of language
a. STRUCTURAL CONTROL	a. DISCOURSE CONTROL	a. SITUATIONAL OR TOPICAL CONTROL
b. MATERIALS SIMPLIFIED STRUCTURALLY	b. MATERIALS SIMPLIFIED FUNCTIONALLY	b. AUTHENTIC LANGUAGE
c. MAINLY STRUCTURAL PRACTICE	c. MAINLY DISCOURSE PRACTICE	c. FREE PRACTICE

In as much as he is committed to a synthesis, Stern is concerned with two other matters: how should the three components be sequenced and insufficient attention that has been paid by proponents of L and P approaches to the sociocultural element in language use. In regard to the first, he suggests:

> Perhaps with a clearer understanding of the relationships between language study, language practice and language use, between classroom and field, between structural-functional and experiential aspects, it should be possible to gain a better understanding and more effective handling of the relative advantages of ordering these different components. (Stern, 1981: 143)

In remarks about the second, he says that despite advantages in sociolinguistics and cultural anthropology, culture still remains a somewhat unintegrated appendage to language teaching. Language use—whether sociolinguistically analysed or lived as a personal experience— always occurs in a sociocultural context.

He, therefore, calls for the incorporation of sociocultural awareness as a necessary expansion of conceptualisations about communicative language teaching. To this end, he has modified the three level curriculum:

STRUCTURAL ASPECT	FUNCTIONAL ASPECT	SOCIOCULTURAL ASPECT	EXPERIENTIAL ASPECT
[Language	study and	practice]	Language use in authentic contexts

> ...we are saying that language teaching can and should approach language learning objectively and analytically through the study and practice of structural, functional and sociocultural aspects and it should offer opportunities to live the language as a personal experience through direct language in contact with the target language community. (Stern, 1981: 144)

I have sought to explore some of the earlier, as well as, more recent views of communicative competence. None of these positions is peripheral to communicative language teaching, as it is practised today. I would take the bold step of claiming that the current proponents of communicative language teaching see communicative competence as inseparable from communicative language teaching.

While I do wish to see communicative language teaching progress, I hold the view that its practice should be free of associations with communicative competence. In very simple, but realistic terms, the communicative in communicative language teaching emerges from traditions of knowledge that are very different to the traditions of knowledge from which the competence in linguistic competence emanates. I, therefore, submit that it is methodologically unsound to fuse the competence in linguistic competence with the communicative in communicative language teaching. I offer my submission, despite my inclination to concede that some North American roots of communicative language teaching are traceable to psychology. Let me build a general framework, here, for part of my submission which I shall follow by addressing myself to specific considerations of Noam Chomsky's views of language.

Krashen's claim that language acquisition is a subconscious process is most incompatible with Chomsky's idea that knowledge of language is unconscious. This point needs to be emphasised, because Krashen makes the bold statement that what he terms applied transformational grammar (TG) did not advance language teaching significantly. While expounding his view on TG he adds that its actual impact was, probably, to needlessly make numerous teachers feel unprepared because they had not been trained in the latest version of transformational theory. For him, transformational theory was not t theory of language acquisition. TG also failed, because it was not a theory of how adults got competence. It was merely a theory of the adult's competence,

Krashen obviously operates with a sense of what competence is. Whatever that sense is, it is not obvious to me that it is the same as Chomsky's linguistic competence, something integral to TG. Thus when proponents of communicative language teaching embrace the idea of language acquisition as central to target language teaching grounded in communicative competence that incorporates linguistic competence, their sense of competence cannot be the same as Krashen's. Hence, even before they hold on to the idea of communicative competence, they must make it transparently clear that their sense of competence is the same as or different to Krashen's. This they have not done.

Can the communicativists legitimately embrace the notion of communication which is pivotal to acquisition and link that notion with linguistic competence, when Chomsky is explicitly critical about communication? I offer a negative reply.

Let me also state that linguist, Chomsky, has neither held nor demonstrated any analytical interest in determining how children and adults placed within instructional settings gain knowledge of languages different to their first languages. It, therefore, seems to me that anyone who incorporates linguistic competence within communicative competence as a basis to explaining or accounting for what takes place among children and adults within these instructional settings is taking a huge leap of faith.

Assuming, however, that a cursory observation does not include my criticisms above and the Krashen view of competence were the same as that held by proponents of communicative language teaching, they, as well as, he would still face other criticisms.

If the Natural Approach, immersion education, preference for Communication Strategies, and the work of Breen and Candlin's all lie within the P approach to communicative language teaching, they would be underpinned by acquisition and not learning. Thus the engine of communicative competence which drives these positions would, in turn, be strongly intertwined with acquisition and not learning. Further, if the L approach is formal, deliberate, and teaches about communication, it would be underpinned by learning, rather than acquisition. Hence, the mechanism of communicative competence enabling the L approach would be intertwined with learning, rather than acquisition.

The points about differential learning and acquisition foundations to communicative competence are, by no means, trivial; there may be no convincing evidence that Hymes's understanding of communicative competence either parallels, or is identical to, Krashen's sense of the subconscious. When he offered communicative competence in response to Noam Chomsky's linguistic competence, Hymes was, in no way, proposing a learning foundation to communicative competence. To the extent that Hymes is central to communicative competence in communicative language teaching, the Council of Europe, a major player in the communicative game, is obliged to show, explicitly, that it bears no connections with a learning foundation. Such it has not, however, done, thereby running the risk of attracting the label: an organisation whose use of communicative competence is incompatible with Hymes's. Proponents of the P approach—including CS proponents of interaction—do much more than attract the label of incompatibility. To the extent that acquisition underpins their sense of communicative competence, that sense would not be compatible with Hymes's, whose work is not grounded in the subconscious. CS proponents of interaction cannot logically and legitimately express an interest in acquisition and claim that the communicative enterprise is best served if ideas of communicative strategies are freed of psycholinguistic perspectives.

The very important query I must pose at this point is whether a Stern synthesis of L and P approaches is legitimate? My response is unequivocally negative. The gel needed for this development, Hymes's communicative competence, is not compatible with an acquisition foundation to communicative competence. There is also no way of knowing whether that gel can be used by the Council of Europe, which is linked with a learning foundation to communicative competence, despite the fact that the Council is careful to distinguish learning and acquisition, as well as, avoid endorsing either of the two in connection with target language teaching.

Notes

1. My reference to the problem posing is derived from Canale (1985) "A Theory of Strategy Oriented Language Development." Draft paper prepared for presentation for the National Information Exchange on Issues in English language Development for Minority Language Education: Virginia.

2. My reference to the tacit is derived from Polyani, M. *The Study of Man*. Chicago: The University of Chicago Press (1959). See also Heap, J. L. "On Recollecting The Possible: A Critique of The Repair System in Conversation Analysis." Paper prepared for presentation at the Annual Meetings of the Society for Phenomenology and Existential Philosophy, West Lafayette, Indiana (1979).

Chapter Two
The Libertarian, Anti-Experiential Basis

I am now in a position to initiate my argument against use of communicative competence within the field of communicative language teaching. Let me, therefore, turn to Noam Chomsky's ideas. Chomsky wants persons to liberate themselves from the tyranny of forces external to them. There is a clear libertarian basis to his interest. That basis inheres in his interpretation of Bertrand Russell's views on education, René Descartes, on creativity, Jean Jacques Rousseau's, as well as, Wilhelm von Humboldt's on freedom from repressive authority. He seeks to concretise his interest by finding out what contribution the study of language can make to understanding human nature (Chomsky, 1972a). He deals with this issue by utilising his views of linguistic theory and language learning to explain what he terms the property of normal language use.

I want to address myself, initially, to the libertarian basis by attending to Chomsky's great appreciation of Bertrand Russell. Chomsky (1972b) claims that Russell occupies a particular position of honour in the twentieth century among a small group whose members have demonstrated the splendour human life can attain via individual creativeness and the battle for liberty. Russell, he notes, has been an inspiring personality to his (Chomsky's) generation through the problems he raised, causes for which he stood, and insightful views.

A clear picture of the great appreciation Chomsky has for Russell can be located in the linguist's direct reference to liberal education:

> The task of a liberal education, Bertrand Russell once wrote, is 'to give a sense of value to things other than domination, to help create wise citizens of a free community, and through the combination of citizenship with liberty in individual creativeness to enable men to give to human life that splendour which some few have shown it can achieve.' (Chomsky, 1972b: 9)

In turning my attention to Rousseau, let me note that according to Chomsky (1988), the libertarian ideas of Rousseau's were based strictly on Cartesian conceptions of body and mind. Not only did Rousseau accept that humans, who possess minds, are crucially distinct from machines and animals, he argued, also, that the properties of mind surpass mechanical determinacy. Rousseau concluded—so claims Chomsky—that any infringement on human freedom is illegitimate, and must be confronted and overcome.

Chomsky adds that the Cartesian conceptions were developed in the libertarian social theory of von Humboldt, that persons have essential human rights to carry out "productive and creative work" under their own control, in solidarity with others. Further, these rights were rooted in "human essence."

The Cartesian conception subject to the greatest exposition by Chomsky is the creative version of language use. He notes, with great approval, Descartes' observations: the normal use of language is apparently free from control by external stimuli or internal states, is unbounded and constantly innovative. In normal use, persons do not repeat what they have heard, they produce new linguistic forms and do so infinitely.

The Chomskyan position is, doubtless, against the experiential. This is shown in his presentation of Russell's question, "How comes it that human beings, whose contacts with the world are brief and personal and limited, are nevertheless able to know as much as they know?" For Chomsky (1972) this query is the principal issue of learning theory. More significantly, he adds that the study of psychology has been placed on the periphery of inquiry by a failure to deal with the issue, how experience is connected to knowledge and belief. Such an inquiry must give priority to examining structures of knowledge and belief. Its appropriate pursuit does not, however, occur, by applying principles governing stimuli and responses, as well as, habit structures. Knowledge systems forming the basis to "normal human behaviour" cannot be described via configurations of association, inclinations to respond, and habits. Such is true, in regard to language and other instances of cognitive processes.

And in a frontal assault on the experiential, he rejects the notion that words he understands derive their meaning from his experience.

> If I use language to express or clarify my thoughts, with the intent to
> deceive, to avoid an embarrassing silence, or in a dozen other ways, my
> words have a strict meaning and I can very well mean what I say, but
> the fullest understanding of what I intend my audience (if any) to be-

lieve or to do might give little or no indication of the meaning of my discourse. (Chomsky, 1972: 24)

This stance is consistent with one of his principal goals, elucidating the humanistic
conception of man's intrinsic nature and creative potential. In pursuing the goal,
he is not just strongly committed to highlighting the significance of Russell's
views on liberal education, he also expresses certainty that Russell and Wilhelm
von Humboldt would have established common ground about the human condition.

What is the commonality? As Chomsky (1972) describes it, inquiring and
creating are the focal points around which human endeavour revolves. In solidifying his point, he invokes von Humboldt to state that all moral culture emanates
exclusively and instantly from the soul, can only be enlivened in human nature,
and is never constructed as a result of external and artificial management. He adds
that what does not emerge from free choices and is dependent upon instruction
and guidance is not incorporated into persons' existence. Rather it is distant from
their true nature. It is, thus, with mechanical precision (not genuine human ener-
gies) that persons perform on the basis of instruction and guidance.

Chomsky's embracing of individual creativeness, citizenship with liberty, as
well as aversion to instruction, guidance, habits, and associations, is an important
feature of his views on systems of knowledge and beliefs which he says result
from interplay of innate mechanisms, genetically determined maturational processes, and interaction with the social and physical environment. The analyst's job
is to account for the systems as constructed by the mind in the course of interaction. Further, the particular system of human knowledge which has lent itself
most readily to the performance of such a task is the system of human language.

Chomsky (1974) presents the conditions for task performance, very forcefully, when he says the analyst interested in studying languages is faced with a
very definite empirical problem. He has to look at a mature adult speaker who has
acquired an amazing range of intricate and highly articulated abilities which enable him/her to use language in very creative and novel ways. Much of what
he/she says and understands bears no close resemblance to anything in experience. Chomsky regards the abilities as knowledge of language, which he characterises as instinctive or innate knowledge.

Persons possess instinctive knowledge, because they approach the learning
experience with very explicit and detailed schematisims which tell them what languages they are exposed to. As children, they do not begin with knowledge that

they are hearing particular languages such as English, Dutch, or French. They start with knowledge that they are hearing a human language of a very narrow and explicit type which permits a very small range of variation. The Chomskyan position on experience is expressed clearly when he claims what are revealed from serious study of a wide range of languages: remarkable limitations to the kinds of systems which emerge from the different types of experiences to which people are exposed.

The analyst who investigates these limitations must confront, as well, a well-delineated scientific problem, accounting for the gap between the small quantity of data presented to persons when they are children and the highly articulated, highly systematic, profoundly organised knowledge derived from the data. What is Chomsky's explanation of the gap? Persons, themselves, contribute overwhelmingly to the general schematic structure and, perhaps, to the specific content of knowledge they derive, ultimately, from the data, otherwise characterised by him as very scattered and limited experience.

Linguistic Competence and Generative Grammar

His primary concern in offering explanation of language learning is to account for linguistic or grammatical competence, grammar, and generative grammar. Let me, thus, provide interpretations of his versions of theory, linguistic competence, grammar, and generative grammar. He states that linguistic theory is concerned with an ideal speaker/listener in a completely homogeneous speech community who knows language perfectly and is not affected by factors such as memory limitations or distractions. He specifies his positions about the ideal speaker/listener in a statement that grammatical or linguistic competence is a cognitive state which "encompasses those aspects of form and meaning and their relations, including underlying structures that enter into that relation which are properly assigned to the specific sub-system of the human mind that relates representations of form and meaning " (Chomsky, 1980: 24–59).

For Chomsky, grammar, which describes sentences of a language, is the determinant of features within each sentence of that language. Grammar is the weak generator of sentences in a language, but a strong generator of structural descriptions of those sentences. In each sentence, it is grammar that sets constraints on much more than phonetic form and meaning.

In a statement about generative grammar, he says it is expressive of principles which determine the intrinsic correlation of sound and meaning in language.

It is also a theory of linguistic competence, a speaker's unconscious latent knowledge (1966a). He adds that serious investigation of generative grammars quickly reveals that rules which determine sentence forms and their interpretations are both intricate and abstract: the structures they manipulate are connected to physical fact only in a remote way by a lengthy chain of interpretive rules. And it is because of the abstractness of linguistic representations that the analytic procedures of modern linguistics (with their reliance on segmentation and classification, as well as, principles of association and generalisation in empiricist psychology) must be rejected.

This is, of course, clear rejection of phrase structure grammar which Chomsky (1957) finds inadequate and complex. It is also clear rejection of principles of operant conditioning in behaviourist psychology popularised in audiolingual approaches to target language learning. And it was partially, but significantly, in reaction to audiolingualism that communicative language teaching (CLT) arose. The Chomskyan opposition to behaviourism should not, however, be seen as compatible with negative reaction in communicative language teaching circles to audiolingualism. CLT, audiolingualism, and behaviourism, are all experientially based. Chomsky's views of generative grammar, linguistic competence, and language teaching are decidedly not. In fact, his general remarks about contemporary language teaching are not complimentary.

Consider his reasons for distinctions between the difficulty in teaching target language to adults and the ease of childhood language learning.

> Use your common sense and use your experience and don't listen too
> much to the scientists, unless you find that what they say is really of
> practical value and of assistance in understanding the problems you
> face, as sometimes it truly is. (Chomsky, 1988: 182)

He is, however, more explicit when he says persons involved in a practical activity such as language teaching should not take what are happening in the sciences seriously, because the capacity to carry out practical activities without much conscious awareness of what is being done is usually far more advanced than scientific knowledge.

Ideas in the modern sciences of linguistics and psychology, which are of little practical use to understanding the distinctions, are completely crazy and they may be responsible for trouble. He adds that modern linguistics has very little to contribute which is of practical value. Language, he says, is not learnt. It grows in the mind. It is, thus, wrong to think that language is taught, and misleading to think of it as being learnt (1982).

I, therefore, do not think it would be presumptuous of me to conclude, at this point, that communicativists have no legitimate grounds for utilising their broad version of competence, which includes Chomsky's linguistic competence, as a basis to fulfilling their aim. That aim is getting students to produce language as a central feature of their social interaction, in order to perform tasks which are essential or important to them. The communicativists are nowhere near to expressing a concern for analysing the issues: how the anti experiential Chomskyan view of linguistic competence emerges from his interpretation of Russell's, von Humboldt's, Rousseau's and Descartes' ideas, how such a view can be reconciled to the communicative position which is not anti-experiential.

Lest my conclusion be regarded as inappropriate, I must point out, for purposes of exemplification, that Chomsky (1966a) says a theory of generative grammar serves only as one component of a theory which can be made to accommodate the characteristic creative aspect of language use. He, himself, points out that whatever little attention Descartes devoted to language is subject to various interpretations and it should not be assumed that the various contributors to Cartesian linguistics necessarily regarded themselves as constituting a single tradition.

One of those interpretations is that offered by Stockwell (1970) who is, clearly, a supporter of the transformational approach. More significantly, he is not reserved in his critical remarks about other approaches. As such, he makes it obvious that proponents of communicative language teaching have no strong grounds for using communicative competence. I begin with the Stockwell claim that Chomskyan use of the term, 'generative,' has been subject to profound misunderstanding among linguists, on a worldwide basis. This is so, especially among American structuralists and notably those in Britain and the Netherlands. The origin of the misapprehension stems from lack of clarity between the manner in which a descriptive grammar provides a representation of an ideal speaker/hearer's unconscious knowledge of language and the form in which an actual speaker/hearer produces his everyday discourse. In an alternative sense, the generativists account for intrinsic competence which they assume, in principle, is available to an individual speaking a language, if an explanation is offered about ways in which the language user is capable of doing subtle and intricate things with language.

Stockwell adds that before Chomsky's work, no focus had been granted by American linguistics to one interesting question: What form of rule is required to satisfy the analytical objective that an explicitly scientific account of constraints on sentence formation should be employed by linguists?

Chomsky's answers to this question have in effect revolutionised the discipline of linguistics, at least the discipline as practised by the substantial segment of the academic community which has found itself persuaded by his arguments. Many assumptions and claims generally accepted before Chomsky's time have been challenged by the transformationalists, and as far as it is possible to judge in the almost total absence of serious replies to these challenges, have been successfully replaced by transformational views. (Stockwell, 1970: 296)

Stockwell broadens the scope of his charge by stating that the Chomskyan challenges have made far reaching inroads to foundational concepts of previous generations of structural linguistics exemplified by sacred theoretical constructs such as the phoneme, regularity and independence of sound change, sequentially grounded levels of linguistic description, as well as, the sanctity of textual citation used to support analysis. The transformational revolution has engendered application of investigative criteria which determine what counts as adequate justification for analysis. This is so, mainly because transformational grammar is integrated and interdependent to a far greater extent than what had been fractionally conceptualised, prior to Chomsky's work.

Critics in communicative language teaching can certainly ask about the methodological justification for Stockwell's backing of Chomsky. Stockwell' s reply would be contained in his view that Chomsky makes use of recursive rules to account for generative grammar. These are sets of rules which have the mathematical feature of indefinite reapplicability. Each succeeding application enumerates another member of the set. Further, enumeration is amenable to scientific testability of structural descriptions, as well as, to empirical verification. Chomskyan use of the term, 'generative,' means 'explicit.' The advantage of employing such a term is that it ought to distinguish between objects which are being investigated and those which are not: strings of noises which are sentences of a language and ill-formed strings of noises which do not belong to that language.

Let me initiate closure to my report of the Stockwell position by making direct reference to what he identifies as some implications of transformational grammatical theory for the study of human behaviour, across a broader spectrum.

If Chomsky and his colleagues are right, ordinary, everyday communication in language—virtually every such act of communication—is a creative performance governed by rules of such abstractness and complexity that there is no reasonable likelihood that they could be acquired by a child unless he were born into the world with highly specific innate gifts for this particular kind of learning. Thus the notion that human beings acquire language merely as a set of conditioned responses—the notion that the use of language is habitual behaviour in some meaningful sense of the term "habit"—is rendered quite improbable. On the contrary, the rationalist notion that this behaviour is dictated by a set of prior, and uniquely human, mental capacities achieved by a million or more years of evolution is strongly supported. (Stockwell, 1970: 300–301)

My rendering of Stockwell's stance sets Chomsky's linguistic competence very far apart from communicative competence. It shows, without a doubt that Chomsky's work is deeply grounded in a rigidly rationalist position, indelibly inked in the stamp of thinking from Bertrand Russell and René Descartes.

These are not the traditions from which communicative language teaching took roots. It is also instructive for all communicativists to note that Stockwell is not simply making a veiled attack on the rationalist nemesis, radical Skinnerian behaviourist, empiricist, psychology. He is, doubtless, raiding those pedagogical reaches of classroom practices connected to "ordinary, everyday communication in language" where "habit" has a very different meaning to that utilised by the behaviourists.

In so doing, he is expressing strong adherence to a position forcefully offered by Chomsky who says language is taught in only the most marginal sense. Teaching, he adds, is, by no means, necessary to language acquisition. It is both wrong to think that language is taught and learnt. Language is not learnt.

We begin our interchange with the world with our minds in a certain genetically determined state, and through interaction with an environment, with experience, this state changes until it reaches a fairly steady mature state, in which we possess what we call knowledge of language. The structure of the mind, in this mature state (and indeed in intermediate stages as well) incorporates a complex system of mental representations and principles of computation on these mental representations. This sequence of changes from the genetically-determined initial state to the final steady state seems to me in many respects analogous to the growth of our organs. (Chomsky, 1982: 176)

Chomsky asserts that it is in order to see the mind as a system of mental organs, each of which, including the language faculty, has a structure determined by persons' biological endowment. The form and direction of interactions between the mental organs and the environment are also governed by biological endowment. Growth of the organs emanates from the triggering impact of experience which structures and articulates them while they develop within persons.

I am also fully aware that the following argument can be made against me: though the communicative version of competence includes linguistic competence, that broad version of competence is not Chomskyan. If this is the case, communicativists need to show, very clearly, what type of grammar exemplifies their sense of competence. They should say, as well, how their view of grammar differs to the Chomskyan view of generative grammar and, as a result, can exemplify linguistic competence which they make part of their broad version of competence. If communicativists are to meet the requests I propose, they should offer very careful analyses of the bases to Chomsky's view of linguistic competence and show, explicitly, how those Chomskyan foundations are different to theirs.

To the extent that they have not, they cannot, legitimately employ communicative competence as a basis to fulfilling their aim. It is thus in order for producers of The Common European Framework to acknowledge that the grammar of any language is very complex and is not amenable to definitive or exhaustive analysis. It is, however, untenable for them to follow the acknowledgment by noting that competing theories of grammar exist but the Framework can neither judge among the theories nor advocate use of any particular one. To the extent that the Framework incorporates linguistic competence within communicative competence, its producers should specify the version of grammar associated with linguistic competence: linguistic competence via Chomsky does not emanate from grammar of any specific language. It is universal grammar. Producers of the Framework should show how they can or cannot reconcile their use of the term, linguistic competence, with the view about existence of competing grammatical theories.

Further, when they encourage users of their designation of grammatical competence to state the grammar theory followed and the impact of preference on practice, users run the risk of doing something which could strongly conflict with Chomskyan universal grammar. Thus, if a choice is made to use phrase structure grammar for exemplifying grammatical competence, that choice would wholly conflict with universal grammar. I notice that the producers have chosen to use phrase structure grammar as their means of exemplifying grammatical competence. This is hardly a legitimate move. Chomsky's linguistic competence is irreconcilable with phrase structure grammar.

Consider another argument against use of communicative competence as a basis to fulfilling the aim of helping learners produce target language. This is a cogent argument associated with Chomsky's view of communication. In so far as communicativists emphasise the purposeful nature of language as central and necessary to their aim of fostering target language use, they would have to be concerned with the matter of conveying information to, and inducing beliefs about language, in students.

Chomskyan Opposition to Communication

This is not a concern, though, which they can express, legitimately, by means of including linguistic competence in their broad version of competence. Chomsky's view of communication, which is linked, inextricably to, and derived logically from, his pronouncements about knowledge, creativity and freedom from repressive authority, contrasts sharply with views about the purposeful nature of language. In what he sees as the importance of avoiding a certain vulgarisation with respect to the use of language, he claims that if the term, 'communication,' means transmitting information or inducing belief, there is no reason to think that language—essentially—serves instrumental ends, or that the essential purpose of language is communication (1977).

He adds that someone who offers a view of the purposeful nature of language ought to explain what he/she means in expressing that view and why he/she believes such a function and no other function to be of unique significance.

> It is frequently alleged that the function of language is communication, that its "essential purpose" is to enable people to communicate with one another. It is further alleged that only by attending to the essential purpose can we make sense of the nature of language. It is not easy to evaluate this contention. What does it mean to say that language has an "essential purpose?" Suppose that in the quiet of my study I think about a problem, using language, and even write down what I think. Suppose that someone speaks honestly, merely out of a sense of integrity, fully aware that his audience will refuse to comprehend or even consider what he is saying. Consider informal conversation conducted for the sole purpose of maintaining casual friendly relations, with no particular concern as to its content. Are these examples of "communica-

tion?" If so, what do we mean by "communication" in the absence of an audience, or with an audience assumed to be completely unresponsive or with no intention to convey information or modify belief or attitude? (1980: 229–230)

His response is that we must deprive the idea, communication, of all importance or we must reject the view that the purpose of language is communication. He adds that no substantive proposals emanate from any formulation of the view that the purpose of language is communication or that it is pointless to study it apart from its communicative function.

Chomsky's views about communication might well be in error: communicativists have challenged and rejected them. Challenge and rejection do not, however, stem from examining how linguistic competence emanates from his interpretation of Descartes, Russell, Rousseau, and von Humboldt. But communicativists do include linguistic competence in their broad version of competence. And while they state that they have examined linguistic competence, found its scope to be too narrow and resorted to devising a broad version within which it is included, inclusion is not logically admissible. Communicativists have not examined the basis to Chomskyan linguistic competence.

Alternatively expressed, my argument is that the communicative emphasis within CLT on the purposeful nature of language does not emerge from a parallel or identical view about the purpose of language held by Chomsky. Therefore, communicativists should not use communicative competence as a central basis to fulfilling their aim of helping students. I wish to strengthen this inference by pointing to glaring contradictions within Bachman's extended linguistic competence. This expansion incorporates illocutionary and sociolinguistic competence in pragmatic competence, one subdivision of linguistic competence.

It is a focus on illocutionary competence which enables an observer to identify the inconsistency. Bachman does accept the Chomskyan notion of linguistic competence. This is not, however, acceptance which is synchronous with what should properly be called the illocutionary aspect of semantic competence conceptualised by John Searle whose ideas about language use are opposed to those of Chomsky's. My point here is that an analyst cannot logically fuse or incorporate elements of the Searlean and Chomskyan views of competence. This is the very argument I would advance against Blum-Kulka and Levenston who use semantic competence as a broad version of competence.

Searle (1974) says semantic competence is the ability to perform and understand speech acts or illocutionary acts. These acts are some of the many acts associated with a speaker's utterance in speech situations, speakers, hearers, and utterances (1971). Further, in these situations, the acts are concerned with performances such as making statements, asking questions, or issuing commands and are expressed in verb forms like state, assert, command, or order. He points out that if semantic competence is viewed from the standpoint of one's ability to use sentences in performing speech acts, the acts will be seen as rule-governed and intentional.

> The speaker who utters a sentence and means it literally utters it in accordance with certain semantic rules and with the intention of invoking those rules to render his utterance the performance of a certain speech act. (1974: 29)

To know semantic competence is to identify connections among semantic intentions, rules, and conditions specified by rules.

Searle's view of semantic competence is grounded in his quarrel with Chomsky's notion of linguistic competence. He argues that Chomsky's theory of language is that sentences are abstract objects produced independently of their role in communication. His position is that any attempt to account for the meaning of sentences independently of their role in communication is inadequate. Searle (1982) says Chomsky regards man as essentially a syntactical animal. He never asks what the syntactical forms are used for, and conceptualises syntactical theory in purely syntactical primitives. There is no allowance for what the syntactical forms mean or how persons are supposed to use them.

He adds that the most interesting questions about syntax are inquiries about how form and function interact. For him, the study of syntax will always be incomplete unless linguistic use is analysed. He states, pointedly, that Chomsky has denied what he regards as obviously true, that the purpose of language is communication. Searle's position on communication is given strong support in a claim:

> I regard the notion of speech acts as one of the most fruitful notions of contemporary linguistic theorising. It orients our scientific endeavours towards the function of language in human communication. In doing so, it allows for a combination of differential methods and fields of linguistic, as well as, of philosophical investigation such as, e.g., the theory of grammar, the theory of meaning and the theory of discourse. (Wunderlich, 1980: 291)

Wunderlich states that the language specific aspect of speech act theory is concerned with:

- The language specific devices utilised in speech acts;
- The phenomenology of language specific speech act patterns, complex speech units, and discourse types;
- The phenomenology of language specific institutional speech acts;
- The phenomenology of language specific indirect speech act routines and indirect speech act formulae;
- The language specific classification of speech acts grounded in the previous four aspects.

In what I deem a very strong reference to meaning in speech acts, Bierwisch (1980) observes that communicative sense and meaning in linguistic utterances have their foundation mainly in speech acts. He insists that the idea of communicative sense belongs to the domain of social interaction. Further, while it can be realised in various ways production of verbal utterances is the most elaborate and effective.

Searle's reference to semantic competence is part of a much bigger problem for proponents of communicative competence. Foundational to the Searlean explanation of semantic competence are profound analyses of speech acts. Having taken his cues for analysis from J.L. Austin, his teacher at Oxford, Searle emerged as the leading expert on speech act theory. Within the philosophy of language, neither he nor Austin is the sole analyst of speech acts. The fact that their work is central to the field means that applied linguists who make claims about connections between illocutions or illocutionary competence and communicative competence must meet a very important requirement. The requirement is that applied linguists must show how they use or do not use categories of the two speech act theorists to derive their views of communicative competence. The necessities should be met, in view of the fact that arguments for the presence of communicative competence in communicative language teaching are arguments which emanate from a tradition of empirical inquiry. Communicativists have not, however, met this goal. They offer no body of coherent research to show how their categories of communicative competence have, or have not, been derived either from Searle's or Austin's categories. The effort to provide such a body of research would, however, be logically inadmissible.

Anyone, other than Searle, who applies semantic and illocutionary competence to understand language use cannot, legitimately, accept and use Krashen's notion of language acquisition: the Krashen view is that, unlike what he calls learning, acquisition is subconscious. Linguistic proponents of semantic and illocutionary competence do accept the Krashen view of the subconscious. Searle's view of semantic competence, from which the idea of illocutionary competence is derived, is deeply grounded in, and inseparable from, application of consciousness. To the extent that such is the case, linguists who propose semantic and illocutionary competence are doing something which is not reconcilable with Searle's dependence on consciousness.

The issue of irreconcilability is part of a complex burden for communicativists. It is the complexity I shall explore now, after which, I shall look at consciousness as another way of furthering my case. If communicative competence exists via the route of illocutionary competence, communicativists must decide whether communicative competence is demonstrated, via Krashen's route of the subconscious in language acquisition or if it exists via the Searlean route of consciousness. This is not, however, a task which they have performed. More importantly, whatever communicative competence signifies, it is not something which is taught in the real world of natural language use. Any proponent of communicative competence who claims it can be evidenced in classrooms must, therefore, pose the question: is it re-presented or idealised in classrooms? The reasonable response is that it is not re-presented. Even in its idealised version, communicativists would still have to contend with the incompatibility between consciousness and the subconscious.

My arguments above are neither speculative, nor irrelevant. Let us recall the five year Bilingual Proficiency Project undertaken by the Ontario Institute for Studies in Education whose implementors state that they wanted to isolate specific aspects of communicative competence and test the proposition that they exist. I note, initially, that these aspects do not include illocutionary competence. How is it possible to establish compatibility between the Project's aspects of competence, which encompasses Chomskyan grammatical competence, and Searlean illocutionary competence? My response is that while possibility cannot be ruled out, such is not just a distant prospect among communicativists, distance cannot also be reduced or removed, in a climate of irreconcilability.

The significance of question and response is clearly exemplified in an inquiry about pragmatics:

Where does pragmatics fit into the Canale and Swain framework? Is it assumed not to exist? Or is it thought to be coextensive with discourse competence? On some readings of the content of the report one would be led to say that project members have chosen a very circumscribed characterisation of pragmatic knowledge and decided to label it "discourse competence," which they define as being composed of rules of coherence (speech acts) and cohesion (deixis)…On other readings, however, one suspects they have in mind some of the kinds of textual knowledge that are focused on in discourse analysis—that is certain aspects of discourse structure… (Schacter, 1990: 42)

What does Schacter mean, when she uses the term, pragmatics, though? In her own words, she claims that for those operating within the Chomskyan framework, pragmatics refers to recursive employment of conditions of appropriateness to infinite sets of well-constructed sentences. She adds that a phenomenon, pragmatic competence, which she characterises as a working hypothesis, is indicated by systems of constitutive rules represented in the mind that are foundational to applying grammatical knowledge.

Let me offer an assessment of the conceptual difficulty linked to formulations of communicative competence, thus highlighting the ambiguity that burdens presentation of the formulations.

Are they specifications that will enable us to retrospectively describe what people have done with language—in the past? Or are they actually prescriptions for the future in all but name? Are they the bases for pedagogic devices—instruments to be discarded as soon as the acquisition task has been completed, or are they necessary permanent elements in the equipment of the language user? (Brumfit, 2001: 51)

In what I consider to be his unmistakable identification of the illegitimacy in application of communicative competence to language teaching and learning, Brumfit observes that Chomsky's understanding of the human mind is that it is constructed in a manner which necessitates acquisition of specific grammars suitable to no particular natural language but the idea of communicative competence rests on the negotiability of socially constructed interaction.

This very sense of negotiability in social construction is patently exposed by Paulston (1980). As such, she points—albeit unintentionally—to illegitimacy. In offering the views of an academic colleague while making a plea for the application of communication competence, she issues the assertion that communication demands interpersonal responsiveness, the social purpose of language—not the simple presentation of language which is truthful, honest, accurate, or stylistically pleasant. Further, among the notable goals of communicative language use are getting things done, easing social tensions, and persuading others. In addition, the Wilkins claim about analytic approaches to teaching, which he states are indicative of notional syllabuses, stands firmly in the category of negotiability of socially constructed knowledge.

Let me say that implications of the Brumfit identification and Paulston exposure for the communicative movement are quite damaging. The notion of social construction—with its solid grounding in versions of Husserlian and Schutzian phenomenology which (today) are strongly instantiated by such movements as phenomenological, ethnomethodological, dramaturgical, and conversation analytic sociology, as well as, critical discourse analysis—can readily intersect with the Freireian approach but are irreconcilably antithetical to the Chomskyan and Cartesian senses of mind.

Let me initiate my reference to damage by dwelling on ideas of Schutz's about phenomenology, collaborative work between Harold Garfinkel, ethnomethodologist, and Harvey Sacks, conversation analyst. I shall then attend to actual work of conversation and critical discourse analysts.

Wagner (1970) offers a glimpse of social construction, when he states that Alfred Schutz—influenced by Edmund Husserl and Max Weber—posed a basic query: What is the social reality with which sociologists concern themselves? For Schutz, the appropriate reply resided in human consciousness, within mind. He did not regard the facts of social reality as deterministically based. They emerged from ways in which persons used their intersubjective experiences to construct it. No sociologist who claims to be interested in addressing her/himself to the social construction of reality can ignore the interrelated significance of negotiation, language use, interpretation, and culture.

Schutz was, of course, a leading phenomenological sociologist who referred to subjectively meaningful experiences arising from persons' lives as conduct, rather than behaviour, which (if devised in advance, and having a basis in a preconceived project) should be termed action. He further distinguished covert action, performance of mere thinking, from overt action which requires bodily movements. This second form of action he called working. He thus appropriately viewed working, action in the outer world, as based on a plan and characterised by an intention to achieve what is planned by means of bodily movements. He has also claimed that in persons' lives it is through acts of working that they communicate with each other.

> In order to communicate with others I have to perform overt acts in the
> outer world which are supposed to be interpreted by others as signs of
> what I mean to convey. Gestures, speech and writing are based on
> bodily movements. (Schutz, 1970: 205)

It is clear that Schutz made connections between language use and intersubjective
experiences. For him, the typifying medium through which knowledge is socially
transmitted is the vocabulary and syntax of everyday language. He, however, offered no proposals to study such language. Those proposals come from within
conversation analytic sociology, whose founder, Harvey Sacks, went beyond his
teacher, Erving Goffman, to study not just the ritual aspects of language.

A very strong foundation for Sacks's inquiry can be located in the collaborative work of Garfinkel and Sacks who employ the term, "members' practices," to
refer to mastery of natural language.

> We understand mastery of natural language to consist in this. In the
> particulars of his speech a speaker, in concert with others, is able to
> gloss those particulars and is thereby meaning something different than
> he can say in so many words… (Garfinkel and Sacks, 1970: 342)

In a comment on their use of the term, "meaning differently than he can say in so
many words," Garfinkel and Sacks state: "It is not so much 'differently than what
he says' as that whatever he says provides the very materials to be used in making
out what he says." Importantly, they also state:

> The fact that natural language serves persons doing sociology—
> whether they are laymen or professionals—as circumstances, as topics,
> and as resources of their inquiries furnishes to the technology of their
> inquiries and to their practical sociological reasoning its circumstances,
> its topics, and its resources. (1970: 338)

Given their comments on (1) "meaning differently than he can say in so many
words," (2) a claim about what mastery of natural language "consists in," and (3)
their view that natural language furnishes practical sociological reasoning with its
resources, I can offer an appropriate inference. Explicating members' practices is a
paramount task of conversation analytic sociology.

What is conversation analytic sociology? According to Montgommery
(1986) conversation analysis is not principally concerned with verbal action as
demonstration of linguistic order but verbal action as indicators of situated social
order. The reference to social order is captured by Hutchby and Woffit (2002).
They state that while talk is the verbal instantiation of language the focus of con-

versation analysis is interactional organisation of social action. Further, this emphasis takes the form of systematic examination of recorded, naturally occurring talk in conversation. The interest in systematic examination is conveyed by Thornborrow whose position is that utterances derive meaning via their sequential positioning in natural talk which unfolds as turn taking where utterances gain their contextual importance.

For Thornborrow and Hutchby and Woffit, one significant version conversation analysis takes is an examination of institutional talk which is described as:

> ...talk which sets up positions for people to talk from and restricts some speakers' access to certain kinds of discursive actions. For instance, in media settings, the role of a T.V. or radio news interviewer typically (although not exclusively) involves doing the questions, while the role of interviewee involves doing the answers... (Thornborrow, 2002: 4–5)

She would also argue that institutional talk takes place within classrooms. The notion of restriction is central to the Thornborrow view that institutional talk reflects interaction in which connections between a speaker's institutional role and her/his discursive role is a local occurrence which shapes the organisation and direction of conversation.

The vital point to be grasped here is that the advantage which a questioner/interviewer brings to a setting does not necessarily hold up while conversation is unfolding. Thornborrow offers appropriate conceptualisation of the matter, when she states that institutional talk is discourse in which the discursive resources and identities coconversants can use for performing particular actions are weakened or solidified as a partial, but crucial, feature of their institutional identities.

It is the weakening and solidification in the form of what Thornborrow sees as power that is central to critical discourse analysis (CDA). CDA practitioners examine ways in which persons who have power express, replicate, and strengthen it via their discourse practices. Thus, primary analytic attention is given to how speaker/hearers are able to speak in ways they do and what they actually say. Significantly, "power play" is a feature of negotiation and meaning or what Fairclough regards as power in discourse exemplified as social struggle among co-conversants (Fairclough, 2001: 57).

I shall offer three examples of "power play" exemplified as formulations and embedded questions. Let me start with formulations, the original conceptualisation of which, comes from positions enunciated by Heritage and Watson (1979) and Heritage (1985). Heritage states that interviewers reiterate interviewees' meaning by referring explicitly to what has been implied or presupposed by interviewees' prior responses.

In line with the views from Heritage and Watson, Thornborrow (2002) characterises formulating actions as conversational strategies produced by one speaker for another with the aim of establishing the gist, or sense of what has been uttered previously. She is referring to a strategy which can take the form of selectively re-presenting and assessing the substance or outcome of interviewees' utterances with the aim of exploring controversial elements of the utterances (Hutchby and Woffit, 2002).

Formulations, which are performed in third turns, are checks of speakers' prior unclear or opaque meaning designed to seek confirmation or disconfirmation of that meaning. Crucially, it is questioners whose discursive roles are those of formulators. Further, the preferred responses to formulations are confirmations. Hence, disconfirmations entail more conversational work from respondents and may be sources of trouble and struggle about meaning and sense. I would say struggle and trouble are integrally linked to what Heritage (1985) characterises as interviewers' use of formulations as weapons which bring them interactional advantage, at the same time as they perform their institutional tasks of clarifying issues for audiences.

Formulations constitute one type of control some co-conversants exercise as power in discourse.

> A formulation is either a rewording of what has been said, by oneself or others, in one turn or a series of turns or indeed a whole episode; or it is a rewording of what may be assumed to follow from what has been said, what is implied by what has been said. Formulations are used for such purposes as checking understanding, or reaching an agreed characterisation of what has transpired in an interaction. But they are also used for purposes of control, quite extensively for instance in radio interviews, as a way of leading participants into accepting one's own version of what has transpired, and so limiting their options for future consideration. (Fairclough, 2001: 113–114)

Fairclough adds that while formulations may be the institutional prerogative of the powerful there is no certainty that such persons always manage conversations.

Thornborrow's account of formulations emanates from the understanding that persons whose institutional roles are those of managers of talk pose questions, choose their respondents, and note when queries have been answered sufficiently. While performing their interactive roles as recipients of information they apply formulations cooperatively or uncooperatively as third turn recipients.

They are thus strongly positioned in those third turns to control what occurs in the very next co-conversant's turn. They can choose to focus on specific meanings from an initial response. The choices can be used for clarification or challenges. Co-conversants, on the other hand, can fight back or resist (Thornborrow, 2002).

Here are some interesting examples of challenge and fighting back, clarification, as well as, cooperation. Once I have examined them, I shall strengthen my arguments against the use of communicative competence.

Challenge and fighting back

An exchange between Toronto's ex-Mayor, Mel Lastman, and an interviewer in regard to the Mayor's apology for his racist remarks.

1. *Interviewer:* What damage do you think you did to the Olympic bid?
2. *Lastman:* I'm sorry I made the remarks. My comments were inappropriate.
3. *Interviewer:* That's not what I asked.
4. *Lastman:* That's my answer.

At turn 3, there is a formulation in the form of a challenge while the Mayor fights back at 4.

1. *Interviewer:* I think what a multicultural city like Toronto wants to know is why you made it [racist remark] in the first place?
2. *Lastman:* I'm sorry I made the remarks, Mr. Warren. Thanks.
3. *Interviewer:* What can you do to make amends, do you think?
4. *Lastman:* I'm sorry I made the remarks, Mr. Warren. Thanks, guys.

At turn 2, the Mayor fights back and tries to close the conversation by saying "Thanks." At turn 3, the interviewer seeks a clarification which is not forthcoming at turn 4, where the Mayor fights back, once more, by trying to bring closure in uttering "Thanks guys."

One of the most notable instances of "power play" occurred in an exchange between an attorney for O.J. Simpson, F. Lee Bailey, and prosecution witness, detective Mark Fuhrman.

1. *Bailey:* I will rephrase it. I want you to assume that perhaps at some time since 1985 or 6, you addressed a member of the African American community as a nigger. Is it possible that you have forgotten that action on your part?

2. *Fuhrman:* No. It is not possible.

3. *Bailey:* Are you therefore saying that you have not used that word in the past ten years, Detective Fuhrman?

4. *Fuhrman:* Yes. That is what I'm saying.

5. *Bailey:* And you say under oath that you have not addressed any black people as niggers in the past ten years, Detective Fuhrman.

6. *Fuhrman:* That's what I'm saying, sir.

7. *Bailey:* So that anyone who comes to this court and quotes you as using that word in dealing with African-Americans would be a liar, would they not, Detective Fuhrman?

8. *Fuhrman:* Yes, they would.

9. *Bailey:* All of them, correct.

10. *Fuhrman:* All of them.

Formulations from Mr. Bailey occur at turns 3, 7, and 9. They are all efforts at clarification. More importantly, what Matoesian (1993) terms an embedded question occurs at turn 7 within the formulation. That question, "would they not," exemplifies what Conley and O'Barr (1998) see as tactics of domination employed as hidden assessment of witness behaviour.

My example of cooperation occurs in the form of an excerpt from an exchange between a second language user of English and a Counsellor from Human Resources Development Canada (HRDC), a Federal Government Ministry in that country.

Cooperation

1. *Counsellor:* Yea. Can you read the form or…?

2. *Subject:* Uhu, I can read, bud I dun unde—I, samting I dun understu- stan.

3. *Counsellor:* Yea, somethings are fine, other things you don understand. Okay, we'll—I'll go over this with you then, just to make sure everything is okay.

4. *Subject:* Yiea.

Cooperation from the Counsellor, the first language user of English occurs at 3.

Following Brumfit, my accounts of phenomenological, conversation analytic sociology, and critical discourse analysis are meant to form a substantive basis to the claim that in so far as proponents of communicative language teaching embrace the relevance of conversation to classroom practice, they cannot legitimately incorporate linguistic competence in their broad version of competence. Chomsky is, doubtless, opposed to the communicative factor in sequentially organised talk. Hence, when leading proponents, Widdowson and Candlin, in particular, emphasise the significance of conversation to the communicative movement, they need to free themselves of linguistic competence.

In addition, while Goffman, Harvey Sacks's teacher, was very interested in Hymes's ethnography of communication, student Sacks was firmly focused on developing a field, conversation analysis, rooted in interpretive sociology, rather than anthropological linguistics. Conversation analytic sociology therefore does not bear the burden of weighty baggage from communicative competence.

My claim is firmly grounded in familiarity with work from critical discourse analysts and conversation analysts: (Atkinson and Drew, 1979), (Atkinson and Heritage, 1984), (Blommaert, 2005), (Drew and Heritage, 1992), (Garfinkel and Sacks, 1970), (Goodwin, 1981, 1990), (Hutchby, 1996), (Sacks and Schegloff, 1975), (Sacks, Schegloff, and Jefferson, 1977), (Thornborrow, 1991, 2001), (Turner, 1976), (Wootton, 1975). This is a suitable juncture at which I remind myself that there is a significant strand of communicative language teaching whose proponents strongly advocate the application of communicative strategies within interaction, rather than dependence on a psycholinguistic view of communication.

I continue my case against communicativists by exploring the Searlean dependence on consciousness to show how it is explicitly different to the subconscious. Searle is emphatic that consciousness is the most important feature of reality, for all other aspects of our being are valuable, worthy, significant and meritorious, only in connection with it. "If we value life, justice, beauty, survival, reproduction, it is only as conscious beings that we value them" (1999: 83). What is the meaning of consciousness? It means a state of awareness which starts when persons wake in the morning and extends during daytime, up to the point of falling asleep, again. He adds that three essential aspects of consciousness are its inner, qualitative, and subjective nature. They are internal, in the sense that they occur within the body. They are qualitative, because of the modes in which they feel; they are subjective, because they are experienced, in the first person. They are, thus, available to individuals in ways which are not available to second and third persons.

Subjectivity does not, however, preclude a scientific analysis of consciousness. From Searle's standpoint, to conclude that it does is fallacious. He makes his case by introducing a simple, but cogent, demonstration. Physical entities —mountains, glaciers—exist, because they have what he terms objective modes of existence. Their existence does not rest on being experienced by a subject. On the other hand, pains, tickles, itches, feelings, and thoughts have subjective modes of existence. They exist as being experienced by subjects. The fallacy is exposed by pointing out that a pain is ontologically subjective, a statement, "JRS [John Roger Searle] now has a pain in his toe," is not subjective. It is just objective facticity, rather than a subjective viewpoint.

It is to what Searle regards as the ten most salient aspects of consciousness that I direct my attention, now. The first and most significant attribute of consciousness is what Searle calls ontological subjectivity: all conscious states exist, as a consequence of being experienced by an agent. Secondly, consciousness is presented to people in unified forms, the combination of varying stimuli into a totality of coherent, unified, perceptual apprehension. Thirdly, consciousness provides people with entry to the world additional to our conscious states. Individuals employ cognition to indicate how the world actually is and they utilise conation to indicate how they want the world to be or the state in which they are trying to make it become. Searle says that this third feature is clearly bound up with intentionality, a matter which I shall elucidate, later to strengthen my case for irreconcilability.

The fourth feature of consciousness is that it appears as some type of mood, flavour, or colouration in experience. Fifthly, consciousness is structured as organised wholes in which our experience of intentional objects are figures against backgrounds. The sixth aspect of consciousness is that it comes as different degrees of attending. Attending, which is both central and marginal, can be altered and shifted. The seventh feature of consciousness is made up of what Searle calls its boundary conditions, awareness of our locations, spatiotemporally. Feature eight refers to the familiarity with which consciousness is expressed. Familiarity lies on a continuum from the most familiar to the strangest. Features nine and ten are the overflow and pleasantness features. The first is indicative of how we use our experiences to remind ourselves of other experiences, while the second is concerned with degrees of enjoyment, or their lack thereof, of experiences. Like feature eight, feature ten is scalar.

I build my case for irreconcilability by addressing myself to intentional states or intentionality, a matter which Searle claims is crucial to performance of speech acts, of which there are five types. What are intentional states? Searle (1979a) regards them as states directed at, or about, objects and states of affairs in the world. Examples of intentional states are beliefs, hopes, fears, and desires. All intentional states consist of representative contents in psychological modes. For instance, a person can (a) hope, (b) fear, (c) believe that X will leave. All of these three instances contain the same representative content expressed by (that X will leave) in different psychological modes: (a) hope, (b) fear, (c) belief (Searle, 1979b).

Perhaps, the most generalised presentation of consciousness takes the form of a claim from Searle (1999) that there are five different types of speech acts: commissives, assertives, directives, expressives, and declaratives. Commissives represent a language user's commitment to undertake action expressed in the propositional content of a speech act. Hence, promises, vows, pledges, contracts, and guarantees are commissives which have what are known as world-to-word direction of fit. They are not true or false but can be pursued, kept, or broken.

Assertives have the word-to-world direction of fit. They are aimed at committing hearers to the truths of propositions. Examples of assertives are statements, descriptions, classifications, and explorations. The basic criterion for locating assertives is determining whether they are, literally, true or false. Like commissives, directives have world-to-word directions of fit indicative of desires. Examples such as orders and requests are not true or false. They are to be obeyed, disobeyed, adhered to, granted, or denied. Expressives have no direction of fit. Truths of their propositional contents are taken for granted. Examples are apologies, thanks, congratulations, condolences, and greetings. Declarations are uttered with dual direction of fit, world-to-word and word-to-world. Examples are pronouncements about initiating wars, marriages, employment dismissals, resignations. Declarations either attain, or do not attain, changes as a consequence of their success or its absence.

Failure to Examine Communication Roots in Speech Acts

I note, with equal force, that communicativists have not shown whether their use of Hymesian categories of communicative competence bears any connection to Searle's or Austin's views about speech acts. Failure to meet this need is all the more glaring, because the Hymesian view of communicative competence embodies the performance of speech acts in speech events. It is not at all clear, though, that Hymesian views of speech acts are the same as those of Searle's or those of Austin's. Nor is it the case that Searle's views are identical to those of Austin's. I have already identified the Searlean classification of speech acts. Let me examine the position of teacher, Austin, on speech acts, and point to difference between their positions, hence the need of analysis from applied linguistic proponents of communicative competence to determine if their support of Hymesian communicative competence bears any relation to the two philosophers' views of speech acts.

In his efforts to classify illocutions, Austin (1962) identifies five "families" of related and overlapping speech or illocutionary acts: verdictives, exercitives, commissives, behabitives, expositives. The first are indicated by the rendering of verdicts from officials such as jurors, umpires, or arbitrators. Exercitives constitute the exercising of powers, rights or influence, and are exemplified by the performance of appointing, voting, ordering, urging, warning, advising. Commissives are typified by making promises or giving undertakings; they also include espousals or taking sides. Behabitives represent attitudes and behaviour. They are exemplified by performances such as cursing, challenging, commending, apologising or congratulating. Expositives clarify how utterances fit into the course of a conversation or argument. Appropriate indicators are replying, arguing, illustrating or postulating.

In Austin's view, verdictives have obvious connections with truth and falsehood, fairness and unfairness, soundness and unsoundness. Behabitives, which encompass expressing or venting feelings, include reactions to other persons' behaviour and fortunes, as well as, expressions of attitudes to the past or imminent conduct of others. These attitudes can be conveyed as resenting, paying tribute, criticising, grumbling, complaining, applauding, overlooking, commending, deprecating. There is no body of research from applied linguistic proponents of communicative competence which makes use of Austin's five families of speech acts, for the purpose of fusing linguistic and communicative competence. There is also no body of such research and purposes associated with Searle's categories of illocutionary force, illocutionary point, regulative and constitutive rules, background assumptions, intentional states, as well as, his later critique of Chomsky.

I shall offer my accounts of the categories by exemplifying what Searle terms direct speech acts, acts which are full blown and explicit or are literally uttered, understood, and performed. Searle's analysis of direct speech acts does not mean that speech acts should (necessarily or exclusively) be identified with a sentence, well-formed or otherwise. The word, sentence, token of the word or sentence is not the unit of communication. Rather, it is the production of the token in the performance of the speech act that constitutes the basic unit of communication (Searle, 1971: p. 39).

I begin my examination of Searle's work on direct speech acts by addressing myself to five matters: (a) proposition indicating elements and function indicating devices; (b)regulative and constitutive rules; (c) universality of constitutive rules; (d) formulation of necessary and sufficient conditions for performance of a specific illocutionary act, that of sincerely and insincerely promising; (e) illocutionary points of speech acts and the psychological modes in which illocutionary acts are performed.

In dealing with the distinction between proposition indicating elements and function indicating devices, Searle (1971) says that even though different illocutionary acts can be identified in a group of sentences, other acts are, however, common to those sentences. For instance, different illocutionary acts of (a) questioning, (b) asserting about the future (predicting), (c) requesting or ordering may be associated, respectively, with:

(1) Will John leave the room?

(2) John will leave the room.

(3) John, leave the room.

Searle views these sentences as possessing a common content which may be expressed by the clause, "That John will leave the room." He adds that, with little distortion, each of these sentences may be written so this common content is isolated, e.g., "I ask *'whether John will leave the room.'* I assert *'that John will leave the room'.*"

It is this common content that Searle calls a proposition, which could be distinguished from the acts of questioning, asserting about the future (predicting) or ordering. What is relevant here is seeing a distinction between a proposition, on the one hand, and the manner of expressing this proposition, on the other. Thus, in sentences, (1), (2), and (3) above, the clause, "that John will leave the room," may be seen as the proposition indicating element and questioning, predicting, requesting or ordering may be seen as representative of their function indicating devices. Searle points out that it is the function indicating devices in these sentences which show how propositions are to be viewed. They indicate, the illocutionary forces, the types of illocutionary acts speakers perform in uttering sentences.

While dealing with the distinction between regulative and constitutive rules, Searle (1971) claims that regulative rules regulate previously existing aspects of persons' behaviour, e.g., rules of etiquette regulate interpersonal relationships but such relations exist independently of rules of etiquette. On the other hand, constitutive rules do not just regulate, they also create or define new forms of behaviour.

> The rules of football, for example, do not merely regulate the game of football but as it were create the possibility of or define that activity. The activity of playing football is constituted by acting in accordance with these rules; football has no existence apart from these rules. (Searle, 1971: 41)

In an exemplification of constitutive rules of a game, Searle says that in football a touchdown is scored when a player crosses the opponents' goal line in possession of the ball while play is in progress. And in what I see as his attempt to point out similarities between the playing of games and language use, he says such things as posing questions or making statements are rule-governed in ways quite similar to those in which getting a base hit in baseball or moving a knight in chess are rule-governed forms of acts.

Now, if I were to ask when is a touchdown scored, Searle ought to reply by saying when a player crosses the opponents' goal line in possession of the ball while play is in progress. I would argue that to produce such an answer, Searle would be drawing on rules of football. Further, I could say those rules are the basis to—or underlie—his answer. I would also add that, regardless of wherever football is played as a rule-governed activity, when Searle says a touchdown is scored, he would be drawing on underlying rules. He would also be drawing on universal underlying rules. Therefore, when he claims that asking questions or making statements are rule-governed in ways similar to those in which getting a base hit or moving a knight are rule-governed acts, I think he is saying: such things as posing questions are governed by universal underlying constitutive rules.

I believe my conclusion makes sense and is supported by views from Searle on the universality of underlying constitutive rules of language. He says the semantic structure of a language may be viewed as a conventional realisation of a series of sets of underlying constitutive rules. And speech acts are acts performed by producing utterances in accordance with these sets of constitutive rules. To say that speaking a language is performing acts according to rules is not to be concerned, however, with specific conventions which a person invokes in speaking a particular language. It is to be concerned with the underlying rules which the conventions manifest or realise (Searle, 1969: 41).

What is important about this claim is that rules for performing speech acts are not merely constitutive rules. They are also constitutive rules of no particular language, and are underlying rules, as well. This is clear in:

> Different human languages, to the extent they are inter-translatable, could be regarded as different conventional realisations of the same underlying rules. The fact that in French one can make a promise by saying "Je promets" and in English one can make it by saying "I promise" is

a matter of convention. But the fact that the utterance of a promising device (under appropriate conditions) counts as the undertaking of an obligation is a matter of rules and not a matter of the conventions of French or English. (1969: 39–40)

Thus, given Searle's claim that there are five families of speech acts, any applied linguistic proponents of semantic and illocutionary competence are obliged to recognise these five families in all languages—not just English. Further, and more importantly, their exemplification of communicative competence in teaching programmes should be clearly reflective of how these five families are performed, universally, in all languages. None of these steps has, however, been taken by communicativists.

Searle's task of formulating underlying constitutive rules for the act of promising consists of setting up necessary and sufficient conditions for such performance with the aim of deriving rules for the function indicating device in this illocutionary act.

He states that given that a sentence, T, is uttered by a speaker, S, in the presence of a hearer, H, S sincerely promises that P to H, if and only if:

(1) Normal input and output conditions obtain. Output refers to conditions of intelligible speaking while input refers to conditions for understanding. Together, they cover such things as S and H's both knowing how to speak a particular language and their being aware of what they are doing.

(2) In uttering T, S expresses that P. This condition isolates the propositional content of the illocutionary act. Conditions (2) and (3) are the propositional content conditions.

(3) In expressing that P, S predicates a future act, A, of S. The act cannot be a past or previous act. Act as used here includes refraining from acting.

(4) H would prefer S's doing A to his not doing A, and S believes H would prefer his doing A to his not doing A.

(5) It is not obvious to both S and H that S will do A in the normal course of events. Conditions (4) and (5) are preparatory conditions.

(6) S intends to do A. Condition (6) is the sincerity condition.

(7) S intends that the utterance of T will place him under an obligation to do A. Condition (7) is the essential condition.

(8) S intends that the utterance of T will produce in H a belief that conditions (6) and (7) obtain by means of the recognition of the intention to produce that

belief, and he intends this recognition to be achieved by means of the recognition of the sentence as one conventionally used to produce such beliefs.

(9) The semantical rules of the dialect spoken by S and H are such that T is correctly and sincerely uttered if and only if conditions (1)-(8) obtain.

Semantical rules for employment of the functioning indicating device, P, for promising are:

(1) P is uttered only in the context of a sentence or longer stretch of conversation, the production of which, predicates a future act, A, of the speaker, S. This is the propositional-content rule derived from propositional-content conditions, (2) and (3).

(2) P is to be uttered, only if the hearer, H, would prefer S's doing A to his not doing A and S believes H would prefer S's doing A to his not doing A.

(3) P is to be uttered, only if it is not obvious to both S and H that S will do A in the normal course of events. Rules (2) and (3) preparatory rules, are derived from conditions, (4) and (5), preparatory conditions.

(4) P is to be done, only if S intends to do A. This is the sincerity rule derived from condition (6), the sincerity condition.

(5) The utterance of P counts as the undertaking of an obligation to do A. Rule (5) is the essential rule.

The rules are ordered: rules (2)-(5) apply, only if rule (1) is satisfied; rule (5) applies, only if rules (2) and (3) are satisfied.

Searle (1971) addresses himself to performance of other speech acts such as giving orders, greetings, and assertions. The preparatory conditions for orders include seeing the speaker in a position of authority over his hearer, the sincerity condition is that the speaker wants the order to be met while the essential condition is related to the fact that the utterance is an effort to get the hearer to perform the act ordered. Preparatory conditions for assertions include the hearer's basis for supposing that the asserted proposition is true. The sincerity condition is that the hearer has to believe the assertion to be true. The essential condition is linked to the fact that the utterance represents the speaker's attempt to inform the hearer and persuade him of the truth.

Searle (1979a) also employs concepts of illocutionary point and psychological mode to account for performance of speech acts. The illocutionary point of an illocutionary act is specified as the purpose in producing the utterance. For instance, the point or purpose of a promise is the undertaking of an obligation by a speaker to do something. The psychological mode or state in which a speech act is uttered refers to a speaker's expression of an attitude or state to the propositional content of that speech act. Thus, in saying something such as "Give me a hamburger, medium rare with ketchup and mustard, but easy on the relish," the speaker expresses a desire (want or wish) that his hearer does something.

I continue my analysis of speech acts by dealing with what Searle (1979b) says are sincerity conditions These conditions are also the intentional states of speech acts. If this is the case, I would say there is a performative relation between intentional states and speech acts. I shall explore this relationship to show that, not unlike Chomsky, Searle does seek to conceptualise links between language and the mind. These conceptions are very different, though. Hence, it makes no sense for proponents of communicative language teaching to make linguistic competence part of communicative competence.

The relationship between intentional states and speech acts may be attended to, initially, by looking at the example, "Give me a hamburger, medium rare, with ketchup and mustard, but easy on the relish." Searle (1979a) notes that literal meaning is generally viewed as the meaning a sentence has independently of any context. Further, it maintains that meaning in any context where it is uttered. In challenging this view, however, he states that to claim that a sentence has literal meaning is to say that its literal meaning is relative to a set of background assumptions and persons understand the literal meaning of sentences only against a set of background assumptions about contexts in which those sentences could be uttered.

Thus, a person may enter a restaurant determined to say literally what he means and utter: "Give me a hamburger, medium rare, with ketchup and mustard, but easy on the relish." Searle argues that in producing such an utterance, the person is drawing on a great deal of background information, among which, would be institutions of restaurants and money, and exchanging prepared food for money. In this instance, the person has said exactly and literally what he meant, but this literal meaning is relative to background assumptions that are not overtly, but implicitly, present in the semantic structure of the sentence.

Backgrounds are constituted by persons' capacities, abilities, inclinations, habits, taken-for-granted presuppositions, and expertise which allow them to operate in the world (1999). Backgrounds are both deep or universally cultural and local or specifically cultural. The deep background refers to matters such as all humans walking upright and eating by placing food in their mouths. Local background is indicative of variation in cultural practices such as persons consuming food at different times of day and not eating the same things. Searle, however, adds that there is no rigid distinction between the local and particularistic.

This is an appropriate juncture for me to note how the founder of ethnomethodology, Harold Garfinkel describes ways in which members of society use background expectancies, the seen but unnoticed background features of everyday scenes, as interpretive schemes. While members are responsive to background expectancies, they are simultaneously at a loss to be specific about their features:

> The seen but unnoticed backgrounds of everyday activities are made visible and described from a perspective in which persons live out the lives they do, have the children they do, feel the feelings, think the thoughts, enter the relationships they do, all in order to permit the sociologist to solve his theoretical problems. (Garfinkel, 1967: 37)

Garfinkel's reference to the everyday is deeply embedded in his profound respect for the work of Alfred Schutz whom he credits for having conducted a series of classic studies of the constitutive phenomenology of the world of everyday life. In such studies, so states Garfinkel, correctly, Schutz described seen but unnoticed background expectancies as the attitude of daily life. I add, imperatively, that Schutz's work on the everyday was grounded firmly in consciousness, the very matter to which Searlean backgrounds are linked, inextricably.

From Searle's standpoint, the utterance, "Give me a hamburger, medium rare, with ketchup and mustard, but easy on the relish," is also a speech act. As a speech act, it would still be an utterance, the performance or accomplishment of which, depends on information not overtly—but implicitly—present in its semantic structure. I can, therefore, say that as a speech act, this utterance would have background assumptions. And as a speech act, it would also have a sincerity condition, an intentional state. Now, according to Searle (1979a), intentional states have backgrounds or what he calls inexplicit assumptions. I could thus infer that in so far as the hamburger example is concerned, not just a speech act with background assumptions has been uttered, an intentional state with background assumptions has been expressed, as well.

There would seem to be a confusion in my inference. On the one hand, it could be taken to mean that I am saying speech acts are performed against two sets of background assumptions, those to speech acts and those to intentional states. On the other hand, I could be interpreted as saying that speech acts are performed against background assumptions, only to intentional states. I should make it clear that the deciding factor in this apparent confusion should be Searle's comments. When his comments on how language is derived from intentionality are examined, it is obvious that background assumptions against which speech acts are performed are assumptions to intentional states.

I begin to do this by looking at the effort from Searle to make explicit what he views as connections and similarities between speech acts and intentional states. He points out that in doing this, he is, in no sense, implying that intentionality is essentially linguistic. He is merely drawing analogies between speech acts and intentional states for the purpose of making intentionality clear. Once he has clearly pointed to intentionality, he would argue that language is derived from intentionality, rather than the reverse. He—in fact—says the task of analysis is to explain language in terms of intentionality.

He lists five similarities between speech acts and intentional states:

(a) *Similar distinctions between propositional content and illocutionary force in speech acts, and representative content and psychological mode in intentional states.* In the same way as X can order Y to leave the room, or suggest that he will leave the room, X can believe, fear, or hope that Y will leave the room. In the speech act cases, ordering and suggesting, there is a distinction to be made between the propositional content, "that Y will leave the room," and the illocutionary force with which the propositional content is presented in the speech act. Equally, in the case of the intentional states, belief, fear, hope, there is a distinction between representative content, "that Y will leave the room," and psychological mode, belief, fear, or hope.

(b) *Similarities in regard to direction of fit between speech acts and intentional states.* Whereas speech acts such as statements or assertions are supposed to match an independently existing world (mind-to-world direction of fit), those such as orders or promises are supposed to bring about changes in the world such as the world matches the speech act (world-to-mind direction of fit). There are also speech act cases in which there is no direction of fit, e.g., if X apologises for insulting Y, the point of his speech act is not to commit him to either a mind-to-world, or world-to-mind direction of fit. Rather, it is to express his sorrow about a state of affairs specified in the propositional content.

(c) *Distinctions similar to the aforementioned two may be seen in regard to intentional states,* e.g., if X believes that P, and his belief turns out to be wrong, it is his belief and not "the world which is at fault." Beliefs—not unlike speech acts, statements, which can be true or false—have a mind-to-world direction of fit. On the other hand, desires and intentions, which cannot be true or false but can be complied with or fulfilled, have a world-to-mind direction of fit. Some intentional states have no directions of fit, e.g., if X is sorry that he insulted Y, his sorrow cannot be true or false in the sense that his belief can be. His sorrow may be "appropriate or inappropriate," depending on whether or not the mind-to-world direction of fit of his belief is, or is not, satisfied. His sorrow would not, however, have a direction of fit.

(d) *What underlies similarities (a) and (b) is that in performing a speech act with a propositional content, a speaker expresses a particular intentional state with the propositional content and the intentional state is the sincerity condition of the speech act,* e.g., if X (i) makes a promise to do P, (ii) gives Y an order to do P, or (iii) apologises for doing P, then he expresses respectively (i) an intention to do P, (ii) a wish or desire that P be done, (iii) sorrow for having done P.

(e) *Where there is a direction of fit, the notion of conditions of success or satisfaction applies to speech acts, as well as, intentional states.* On the one hand, speech acts such as statements can be true or false. And if they are true and only true, they are satisfied. On the other hand, the intentional state, belief, can be satisfied if, and only if, things are as a person believes them to be. (Searle, 1979b: 75-79)

Not merely are the categories, (a)–(e), different to those used by Austin, they are clearly exemplified by Searle's use of phrase structure grammar which is not the same as Chomsky's transformational-generative grammar.

How does Searle derive language from intentionality? He states that while beliefs, fears, hopes, and desires are intrinsically intentional (they have directions of fit) there is nothing intrinsically intentional about the actual performance in which a speech act is made, noises coming from a speaker's mouth. Thus, in so far as speech acts can be regarded as meaningful, the issue for analysis, that of meaning, is how to get from what Searle calls physics to semantics. Specifically, what is the direction to be taken from sounds to illocutionary act? In responding to this question, Searle claims that there is a double level of intentionality involved in performing a speech act utterance.

First, there is an intentional state which is expressed. Then, there is the intention with which the utterance is made. This intention with which the utterance is made, what Searle designates as a second intentional state, bestows intentionality on the physical phenomena. Searle then considers how this intentionality is bestowed. He says the mind imposes intentionality on utterances not intrinsically intentional by intentionally transferring conditions of satisfaction of the expressed psychological state to the external physical entity.

He also offers what he calls a description of the two levels of intentionality involved in performing the speech act.

> The double level of intentionality in the speech act can be described by saying that by intentionally uttering something with a certain set of conditions of success those that are specified by the essential condition for that speech act, I have made the utterance intentional, and necessarily expressed the corresponding psychological state.
> (Searle, 1979a: 89)

A speaker thus imposes intentionality on his utterances by transferring to them certain conditions of satisfaction, which are the conditions of certain psychological states.

I shall now try to assess Searle's claims about intentionality. Searle identifies two levels of intentionality, the intentional state expressed, and the intention with which the speech act utterance is made or performed. I interpret the first level as the sincerity condition of the speech act while the second would correspond to the essential condition. In so far as the second level of intentionality bestows intentionality on physical phenomena and corresponds to the essential condition, it is this level of intentionality which makes the speech act purposeful. Specifically, it indicates what the speaker wants his utterances to do.

Further, I interpret Searle's comment that the mind imposes intentionality on utterances not intrinsically intentional by transferring satisfaction conditions of the expressed psychological state to the external entity to mean: the mind makes utterances purposeful by directing conditions of satisfaction expressed in the sincerity condition to sounds. It would seem as though this directing is done by way of the essential condition. Thus, not only can I say two levels of intentionality, the sincerity and essential conditions, are involved in the production of a speech act, I can also state that in the production of a speech act, there is a relation between sincerity and essential conditions. This is the relation to which Searle addresses himself, when he refers to describing the two levels of intentionality involved in producing a speech act. I interpret this description as: in directing what are specified in an essential condition on to sounds, a speech act is made purposeful or meaningful and its sincerity condition is necessarily expressed.

I see my interpretation as consistent with Searle's (1979b) view that a person could not make a statement without expressing a belief or make a promise without expressing an intention, because the essential condition on the speech act has, as conditions of satisfaction, the same conditions of satisfaction as the expressed intentional state. (The exploration I have just offered is boldly reiterated in Searle 1999: 99–106.)

Let me say that his exemplification of links between essential and sincerity conditions via use of phrase structure grammar is diametrically opposed to Chomsky's display of linguistic competence via routes of transformational-generative grammar. Proponents of communicative language teaching should be aware that this difference cannot serve to establish commonality between Searle's and Chomsky's interest in deriving language from the mind. Here is clear reference to incompatibility.

My pointing to incompatibility is not tangential to validity of the claim that communicativists have no basis to using communicative competence in their efforts to help target language learners. Cranston (1969) notes, quite correctly, that Austin advanced his ideas as a reaction against Bertrand Russell. Russell, communicativists should realise, is central to Chomsky's views on linguistic competence. It is to Cranston that I refer, once more, to solidify my case. Austin, he observes, saw philosophy as having been distorted, as a consequence of adherence to standards of formal logic. For Austin, economy and precision of formal logic served to remove differences in language, a system which is neither clear nor simple, but expansive and complicated, and, thus, amenable to informal logic. Chomskyan claims about linguistic competence are based on precision and formal logic. Results derived from these claims cannot be consistent with results drawn from claims advanced by Austin and student, Searle, who has offered rather meticulous analyses of speech acts.

Cranston's claims deserve further scrutiny which shows, without a doubt, that communicativists have no basis to using communicative competence. The point of the examination is to solidify the argument about inconsistency. Searle (1980) identifies three important intellectual traditions associated with the systematic study of language. He locates the first in work of the early Wittgenstein and Logical Positivists such as Rudolph Carnap, as well as, Bertrand Russell. The major purpose of this work has been making connections between meaning and truth. Proponents of this tradition focus on determining truth conditions of sentences. Chappell (1964) assesses the principal premise of this tradition as claiming that ordinary language is defective and problematic. The task for philosophers is, therefore, to eliminate the problematic by substituting "a logically perfect language" for it.

The second tradition, identifiable in work of thinkers such as the later Wittgenstein, Paul Grice, John Langshaw Austin, Searle's teacher, and Searle, himself, is primarily associated with the study of linguistic usage. The central issue for these thinkers is not the relation between meaning and truth but relations between meaning and use or meaning and speakers' intentions.

> Here, the conviction is that "ordinary language is all right," and that philosophical difficulties, which are indeed linguistic in origin, arise not because our language is faulty but because philosophers misdescribe and misconstrue it. It follows that the way to achieve success in philosophy—and this again means understanding and the solving of problems—is to determine how our language is in fact used, and thence show where and how philosophers have gone astray. (Chappell, 1964: 2)

The third tradition, is the science of linguistics where Chomsky, " the most prominent of the philosophically influential linguists," is located.

For Searle, proponents of the first tradition failed to grapple with complexities and subtleties of language. Such failure, he claims, led philosophers in the second tradition to explore diverse forms and varieties of language use and structures. The failure to which he refers, a position more strongly expressed than that taken by Cranston, is forcefully conveyed in an attack against the distinction between analytic and synthetic truths.

> Modern empiricism has been conditioned in large part by two dogmas. One is a belief in some fundamental cleavage between truths which are analytic, or grounded in meanings independently of fact. The other dogma is reductionism: the belief that each meaningful statement is equivalent to some logical construct upon terms which refer to immediate experience. Both dogmas, I shall argue, are ill-founded. One effect of abandoning them is, as we shall see, a blurring of the supposed boundary between speculative metaphysics and natural science, another is a shift toward pragmatism. (Quine, 1951: 20)

So, just what is the diversity and variety explored in the second tradition? The appropriate response comes from Searle (1982), a student of Austin's, who correctly conceptualises his teacher's work on speech acts, an invention, as a reaction to the positivist interest in truth conditions of sentences—work which "baptised" language use as speech acts (1999).

According to Searle, Austin's work on speech acts revealed that there were countless productions of sentences which did not conform to truth or falsehood.

The uttering of sentences ("I promise," "I bet," "I apologise," "I congratulate you," "Thanks") constituted actions named in verb forms of the sentences. Austin went on to make distinctions between acts of producing utterances, illocutionary acts, and perlocutionary acts, accomplishing various effects in making utterances.

One of the best examples of Austin's reaction to the Logical Positivists comes from his exploration of what he accepts as the method of linguistic phenomenology for studying speech acts (Austin, 1956). In speaking about this method, he makes it clear that a preferable investigative decision is to examine areas where ordinary language is rich and subtle. Adopting such a position means analysing language by dealing with the realities which persons use language to talk about: what should be said on particular occasions, what should be uttered in specific situations, what is meant in these situations and why such meaning is conveyed. The analyst who wants to know what constitutes a speech act must decide what is the correct name of the action, what are the rules for use of the action, is the action a part or stage of another action. In what is obviously his respect for richness and subtlety, he adds that actions which are categorised as the most simple are not. He wants to know whether matters such as intentions, conventions, planning, strategies of execution, understanding of settings, and motives are involved in determining what an action is.

In offering a simple conclusion, at this point, I submit that given the Searlean differentiation among traditions and Cranston's observations, the presentation of communicative competence as a broad version of competence by which Chomskyan linguistic competence is subsumed, is not legitimate. When, however, this inference is juxtaposed with what Searle (1982) deems the remarkably powerful nature of Chomsky's positive contribution, it gains even further strength. What is the positive contribution?

Searle regards it as universal grammar, the "common underlying or deep structure" programmed in children's minds. This is the very deep structure he has applied for the purpose of demonstrating ways in which different speech acts are produced in actual languages. According to Searle, universal grammar lies at the core of Chomsky's syntactical accounts, showing how finite sets of rules in languages can generate infinite sets of sentences in those languages. Searle takes the additional step of advancing the position that Chomsky's rules have had interesting consequences for philosophy: a new set of syntactical devices with which to work on actual languages, and extremely abstract syntax associated with questions such as how do children acquire language by using axiomatic set theory that is far more complicated than language.

Now, Searle uses the deep structure of universal grammar to reveal performance of certain speech acts, semantic competence. It is the case that he also uses phrase structure grammar to reveal performance of speech acts. In so doing he is revealing semantic competence, as well. Given the dual Searlean syntactical applications, communicativists who use speech acts to demonstrate communicative competence must show, conclusively, how it is revealed via two very different syntactical arrangements. Such a demonstration has never been remotely approached by them, however. If they do attempt such a demonstration, they will be confronted with a major insoluble contradiction. They must consider the unfeasibility of embracing semantic competence into which Searle incorporates universal generative grammar, as well as, communicative competence which its founder, Hymes, formulates, because he finds universal generative grammar questionable.

They can, however, seek to resolve that contradiction by using later ideas of Searle (1999) who has rejected universal grammar. He states that from the Chomskyan standpoint children are formulated to be learning natural human languages, as a consequence of applying unconscious rules of universal grammar. As a brain process, the child's rule adherence, though computational, is not brought to consciousness. Searle, however, rejects the Chomskyan position as incoherent.

Why? Its utilisation cannot provide responses to the question: "What's the difference between those nonconscious brain processes that are not mental at all and genuine unconscious mental states that, when conscious, are states of the brain?" He adds that an unconscious mental state must be consciously thinkable, if it is to be given any mental status and not deemed a nonconscious brain process.

Even if they follow Searle and reject universal grammar, they must show what version of grammar has been used as a replacement and how it exemplifies a significant part of that broad spectrum they characterise as communicative competence. This, I have already stated, they have not done. Nor have they explored the Searlean claim of incoherence as a basis to conceptualising communicative competence.

The case against the communicativists becomes even stronger, when I offer an examination of what I consider one of the most ambitious efforts to actualise communicative competence. The thrust comes from the work of Munby in communicative syllabus design. His principal goal is to focus on what he terms the communication needs of learners, particularly ways in which needs are derived from syllabus specification. Needs, for Munby, emerge from application of a sociocultural orientation in which there is concentration on the social functions of language. He adds that prior to the making of decisions about what the learner should be taught, decisions should be made about the communicative modes and activities, as well as, relationships in which they must engage with their co-conversants.

> ...the specification of communication requirements or needs is prior to the selection of speech functions or communicative acts to be taught. By drawing up a profile of communication needs one can more validly specify the particular skills and linguistic forms to be taught. (Munby, 1978: 24)

Munby makes it rather obvious that the direction of his interests has been guided at the macro level by ideas of Dell Hymes and Michael Halliday and at the micro level by the thinking of Widdowson, Wilkins, and Candlin.

What are Munby's directions? He rejects the view of competence offered by Habermas, and embraces versions of communicative competence offered by Halliday and Hymes. He regards the accounts of Habermas as of slight practical significance, because it pays no attention to actual speech situations. For Munby, such an approach is too decontextualised and too idealised. Munby accepts a sociolinguistic view of knowledge and communication in which contextual or environmental features, that are overwhelmingly sociocultural, condition competence or are involved in the genesis of communicative competence, and the accomplishment of meaning potential. He claims that the sociolinguistic view is advanced, both by Hymes and Halliday, who respectively, illuminate crucial factors of contextual/sociocultural suitability and the semantic basis to linguistic knowledge.

In putting the sociolinguistic view to work, Munby devises a model for indicating communicative competence. The model consists of a communicative needs processor (CNP) in which features affecting needs are categorised as two types of parameters in dynamic associations with each other, those which process nonlinguistic information (*a posteori*) and those that provide the information (*a priori*). The first group are made up of dialect, target level, communicative event, and communicative key. The second group is made up of purposive domain, setting, interaction, and instrumentality.

Purposive domain represents the type of language to be taught and learnt and the occupational or educational purpose for acquiring it. Setting entail physical and psycho-social elements. The physical refers to spatiotemporal areas where the target language is to be used. Once such areas have been determined, the psycho-social elements are located. These include matters such as environments where the target language is to be used, e.g., noisy, demanding, culturally different, unfamiliar, aesthetic. Interaction signifies individuals with whom learners communicate in the target language and is employed to predict the interactions expected to occur between learners and co-conversants. What are decisive in the field of interaction are the sets of roles performed by interlocutors. Instrumentality encompasses the conditions on input: the medium, mode, and channel of communication. Is the medium written or spoken? Is the mode a monologue, written to be read or monologue, written to be spoken? The channel of communication refers to whether communication is direct, face-to-face, or indirect.

Munby claims that once the *a priori* elements are taken care of, the *a posteori* elements are devised. Dialect could be either British, American, or regional varieties of both and also covers questions such as social class. Target level covers specifying the level of command in language use required. It consists of size, complexity, range, delicacy, speed, and flexibility. What, for instance, are the size and complexity of utterance or text, range and delicacy of language forms, micro-functions, micro-skills, speed, and flexibility of communication which learners can handle both productively and receptively? Communicative events refer to communicative activities and subject matter. Activities are determined from analysing events into parts which enable skill selection. Subject matter consists of topics or groups of vocabulary items used in communicative activities. The communicative key is a specification of likely attitudes which need to be produced or understood, in regard to particular communicative events. The key is formed, after psycho-social, interactive, and role sets have been located.

Munby derives three implications from his model:

(1) It is at the discoursal level that communicative units such as speech functions or rhetorical acts, rather than grammatical features occur.
(2) Rhetorical rules and contextual meaning should be compatible with the acts and functions, for they are of the same significance as grammatical rules and referential meaning.

(3) Interest in communicative competence signals a need to reshape the areas of syllabus construction, so that consideration might be given to the value of discourse. (1978: 26-27)

I am, by no means, enthused about Munby's scheme which I shall analyse as hugely problem bound. Let me begin by identifying a critical remark from Davies. He sates that Munby's communicative syllabus is indicative of a sterile reductionist direction within applied linguistics which advances a belief in blue-prints, simple and all encompassing solutions to "real and difficult and probably intractable problems of language learning and teaching" (Davies, 1981: 322). Davies cautions that such a movement should be discontinued. He adds that Munby misses the point of tension, fertile ground for analysis. The tension exists between language needs, which are private and language demands which are pub-lic. The Davies reference to reductionism is a pointer to how an analyst devises cat-egories which bear very little relevance to what and how persons in the real world of language use operate. I am fully justified in making this claim. Munby regards his great interest in locating communicative needs as a learner-centered interest. It is not learners who participate actively in deriving of needs, though. It is analyst Munby who devises needs. What would the Munby project look like, if he took account of the tension and created room for learner participation in the construc-tion of learner centered syllabuses?

The case against Munby does not end here. He rejects Habermas's view of communicative competence but accepts the Hymesian view. Central to the latter view is the great importance Hymes attaches to speech acts. Munby has not sought to offer any systematic investigation of how a speech act analysis can be integrated with his acceptance of communicative competence. Further, not only has Habermas accepted the analysis of speech acts offered by Searle, he also says:

A general theory of speech actions would thus describe exactly that fundamental system of rules that adult subjects master to the extent that can fulfil the conditions for a happy employment of sentences in utterances, no matter to which particular language the sentences may belong and in which accidental contexts the utterances may be embed-ded. (Habermas, 1979: 26)

More importantly, Habermas uses an analysis of Searlean speech acts as a starting point for his theory of communicative action which he says has a principal basis in interpersonal relations. Munby, however, grants no analytical attention to how Searle, in his criticism of Chomsky, uses speech acts to exemplify semantic competence. Nor, for that matter, does he provide any examination of how speech acts can be incorporated in his acceptance of communicative competence.

I submit that Munby has no legitimate grounds for rejecting Habermas's position. I shall outline that position as Munby expresses it and Habermas, himself, conveys it. Habermas is quoted:

> Above all communicative competence relates to an ideal speech situation in the same way that linguistic competence relates to the abstract system of linguistic rules. The dialogue-constitutive universals at the same time generate and describe the form of inter-subjectivity which makes mutuality of understanding possible. Communicative competence is defined by the ideal speaker's mastery of the dialogue-constitutive universals irrespective of the actual restrictions under empirical conditions. (Munby, 1978: 11)

Munby also claims that Habermas avoids real world constraints on language use, ignores actual speech situations, and does not shed much light on the elucidation of communicative competence, because he confines communicative competence to the ideal speaker.

For his part, Habermas (1979) sees communicative competence as indicative of a speaker disposed to mutual understanding who wishes to embed a well-formed sentence in real world relations exemplified in three ways: (a) choosing propositional sentences in a manner that either the truth conditions of the proposition expressed or the existential presuppositions of the propositional content mentioned are met, so that a hearer might share the knowledge of the speaker; (b) the expression of intentions, so that linguistic presentations indicate what is intended, and a hearer might trust the speaker; (3) speech act performance in a manner which satisfies recognised norms or accepted self images, so that a hearer might share the speaker's value orientations.

I fail to see how Habermas's approach can be anything other than idealised and decontextualised. The Habermas view of communicative competence is clearly infused with heavy doses of semantic competence, for he relies on a Searlean analysis of speech acts. In an equally significant sense, Searle (1982), not unlike Habermas, approaches the matter of competence as a philosopher, not a linguist. Searle could not be more explicit, when he says linguists, whose interests are factual and empirical, pose different questions to philosophers, whose concerns are conceptual. While philosophers want to know how meaning and communication are possible, linguists wish to determine the facts about actual natural languages. The linguists' interests are empirical but the philosophers' interests are not merely empirical, they are transcendental, as well. Searle's transcendentalism is not in any doubt when he emphasises that the rules for performing speech acts belong to no specific language but are universal.

It is also noteworthy for me to point out that when proponents of communicative language teaching embrace it, via their preferred Hymesian routes they have set up for themselves, they cannot be embracing communicative competence in any specific language. They must be addressing themselves to communicative competence independent of any particular language. Such would be the case, in so far as Hymesian work in the ethnography of speaking was not restricted to any specific language. Munby cannot, and does not (in fact) elude this requirement: his very categories of purposive domain, setting, interaction, instrumentality, dialect, target level, communicative event, and communicative key are decontextualised, idealised, and not specific to any language. This is necessarily the case, given his acceptance of the Hymesian position which has emerged from anthropological work in the ethnography of communication. I, therefore, conclude that if Munby is faithful to Hymesian roots, he cannot dismiss Habermas.

My criticism of Munby points to a much larger problem for the communicativists. Like him, some of them do not use Habermas's position, offer no basis to their absence of use, but at the same time, they do employ Searle's ideas in attempts to exemplify communicative competence. The picture of communicative competence they advertise cannot, therefore, be the same as that displayed and used by Munby. The two presentations are, thus, confusing.

I complete my case against the communicativists by looking at a very significant piece of work from three British linguists whose ideas have been extremely influential, not only on Munby, but also on Wilkins, Breen, Candlin, and Widdowson, all of whom have been standing at the forefront of the communicative movement. The influence comes from Halliday, McIntosh and Strevens (1964). I will address myself to other ideas of theirs, later. My immediate focus is geared to showing the trio's criticism of transformational theory and their view of its irrelevance to target language teaching.

Halliday *et al.*, correctly state that transformational theory, principally owed to Chomsky's analysis, is partially derived from the thinking of linguists, Robert Stockwell, Maurice Halle, Robert Lees, and Zellig Harris. Halliday *et al.*, do not regard it as an integrated theory encompassing all levels of language and do not see is as conveniently adapted to description of texts which are exemplified in the study of literature or comparison of different registers. In addition, it is not easily applicable to statistical statements about language in categories such as what is "more and less probable," rather than what is "possible and impossible."

Halliday *et al.*, are explicit in their view that transformational theory "is not comprehensive or adaptable enough" to suit the aims of linguistic theory. They identify what they term transformational uni-directionality from sentence to sound which makes it problematic to incorporate intonation systems within grammar. Significantly, the transformational sequence of rules in grammar cannot easily account for different degrees of descriptive delicacy which are often desirable for language teaching purposes.

It is, therefore, one thing for Munby and other communicativists to claim inadequacy of Chomskyan linguistic competence. It is an entirely different and very problematic issue to incorporate linguistic competence within communicative competence. Given what Chomsky states about communication, language learning, and his view of linguistics, the communicativists would have been better positioned, had they paid attention to this observation from Halliday *et al.*,: linguistics has different purposes and various types of statements are suitable to these purposes. A grammar written for language teaching does not look like a grammar written for linguists. Should I not repeat that when Chomsky used transformational theory to write universal generative grammar he had no interest in language teaching?

Chapter Three
Freireian Liberation Pedagogy

M y arguments against use of communicative competence as a central basis to communicative language teaching are complete. I propose, instead, that the ideas of Paulo Freire be used as a main thrust of communicative language teaching. Once I have explored the Freireian relevance, I shall bring closure to my work by outlining what communicative language teaching should look like.

Paulo Freire was a Brasilian educator who dedicated himself to abolishing cultural invasion, manipulation, rule by division, conquest, and domination among oppressed people. The core of his interest is expressed as strong preference for using *conscientizacao* to abolish illiteracy. With a deep-rooted commitment to humanistic values in education, Freire seeks to avoid mere transmission of knowledge. He wants to promote social transformation among the disenfranchised and marginalised through encouraging their curiosity and activism. Thus for him, reading is not a task to be understood as reading the written word without a reading of the world. This is a world which encompasses not merely lovable nature, it also includes the social structures, politics, culture, and history of which he is a part. Reading is also not the strolling over of words. It is involvement in discourse aimed at creating links between text and context. It means being aware that what is in texts is historically embedded.

Among the leading contemporary ideas about historical embeddedness those of Blommaert (2005) stand prominently. He offers explanation of the concepts, entextualisation and intertextuality which together enable analysts to locate language within larger historical settings. Consequently, microlevel events can be situated within macro patterns, thus facilitating appreciation of specific discourse occurrences as unmistakably social, cultural, and political. Intertextuality allows for an exploration outside limits of specific "communicative events" so that matters such as on whose behalf the events are used, and their traditions of use might be apprehended. Entextuality is signified by ways in which discourse is decontextualised and recontextualised to become new discourse within different contexts.

Let me emphasise that in assessing *conscientizacao* I am not proposing the replacement of communicative language teaching. I am advocating that communicative language teaching be modified substantially through an infusion of *conscientizacao*. I am not offering a set of methods or strategies for teaching language as communication. Nor, for that matter, am I interested in what Schutz (1970) deems recipe knowledge, ready made standardised schemes passed on by authorities as unquestioned and unquestionable guides in all settings normally occurring within users' social worlds. In the words of linguists, Halliday, McIntosh and Strevens, whose work I explore later, teaching is an art.

I provide *conscientizacao* as a version of understanding which can be used to demonstrate that persons are rooted in awareness of themselves in and through relationships with others. They relate to others and experience themselves as so relating (Laing, 1965). Their identities are established through the manner in which they relate to persons and nonpersons in their worlds (Esterson, 1972).

Conscientizacao is also offered as a way of showing that empowerment is vital to countless numbers of oppressed target language learners who are supposed to be beneficiaries of communicative language teaching. Here, my use of empowerment is borrowed from Lankshear (1994), who says it entails indicating the subjects to be empowered, the structures to which the subjects being empowered are in opposition, the qualities or processes by means of which empowerment occurs, as well as, the outcomes of empowerment. My project for *conscientizacao* does not include the last two. It is, however, firmly situated within Freire's critical pedagogy:

> Critical pedagogy argues that pedagogical sites, whether they are universities, public schools, museums, art galleries, or other spaces, must have a vision that is not content with adapting individuals to a world of oppressive social relations but is dedicated to transforming the very conditions that promote such conditions. This means more than simply reconfiguring or collectively refashioning subjectivities outside the compulsive ethics and consumerist ethos of flexible specialisation or the homogenising calculus of capitalist expansion. It means creating new forms of sociality, new idioms of transgression, and new instances of popular mobilisation that can connect the institutional memory of the academy to the tendential forces of historical struggle and the dreams of liberation that one day might be possible to guide them. This is a mission that is not simply Freirean but immanently human. (McLaraen, 1994: xxxii–xxxiii)

McLaren clearly credits Freire for embracing a view of far reaching educational change necessitated by the global burden of capitalism. He also identifies some of its notable instantiations as private enterprise, free trade, and wage labour which have entrapped individuals within an ideology of Eurocentrism.

Conscientizacao

What is *conscientizacao*. "The term '*conscientizacao*,' translated to mean, awareness or critical consciousness, refers to learning to perceive social, political, and economic contradictions, and to take action against the oppressive elements of reality" (Freire 1970: 19). *Conscientizacao* means identifying the learning of content with the process of learning. It will not emerge as a derivative of great economic change. It has to emanate from critical educational efforts that have a foundation in favourable historical circumstances. It is the development of an awakening of critical awareness. While replying to an important query about meaning of the idea, 'conscientization,' Freire chooses to be very explicit. He regards conscientization as a deepening of the coming of consciousness and adds it cannot be employed without the prior emergence of consciousness which is integrated with critical reflection and curiosity.

He emphasises that he never refuted the signification of the term, but warns about the need to avoid its idealistic interpretation:

> During the seventies, with exception, of course, people would speak or write about conscientization as if it were a magical pill to be applied in different doses with an eye toward changing the world. One thousand pills for a reactionary boss. Ten pills for an authoritarian union leader. Fifty pills for intellectuals whose practice contradicted their discourse.... (Freire, 1993: 111)

He acknowledges that in response to the interpretation he had stopped using the term but later chose to clarify it better in seminars, interviews, and writing. It is, thus, with acute awareness of the need to evade the trap of such interpretation that I proceed with my examination.

The interactive route to *conscientizacao* is a dialogical one which is traversed horizontally by reflective cosubjects who are, simultaneously, teachers and learners. In the words of Goulet (1998), the unifying theme in Freireian practice is critical consciousness, the engine of cultural emancipation.

Why was the Freireian concern a concern with eradicating illiteracy? I shall address myself to this query, after which attention will be given to operations of the engine. Paulo Freire was an unapologetic antiimperialist who observed, quite correctly, that a basic condition of colonial domination is linguistic imposition by colonisers on the colonised. It is, thus, not accidental that colonisers designate their own languages as languages and languages of the colonised as dialects. This is categorisation akin to inferiorisation and impoverishment, on the one hand, and richness and superiority, on the other (Freire, 1978).

He, therefore, insists that language is a major preoccupation of societies which seek their own recreation by liberating themselves from colonialism. In the struggle for recreation, the reclaiming by the people of their own word becomes a basic factor. This is, doubtless, the struggle for literacy education which Freire characterises as one dimension of cultural action for liberation which is linked, inextricably, to other aspects such as the social, economic, and cultural politics of dominated societies.

The connections are echoed powerfully in references to both John Dewey, the American educator, and Julius Nyerere, the Tanzanian leader and liberator, who are credited with advocating a version of education devoid of naive significance. Nyerere and Dewey are posited as emphasising education, not as education for life, but as critical education, critical understanding of life actually lived.

This vehicle of cultural emancipation is driven by a profound sense of radicalism the liberating educator must use to enter into dialogue with the oppressed whose struggle he is committed to advancing. In this partnership, the very causes of oppression are objects of joint reflection. Here is advocacy of versions of communication through which the oppressed locate themselves in the existence of educators who position themselves, reciprocally, in the lives of the oppressed. And in the act of placement, which is humanistic, there is every effort to apprehend historical reality (Freire, 1970: p. 52).

It is clearly the case that he sees no distinctions between learners and teachers. He makes this position quite evident in the statement:

If the dichotomy between teaching and learning results in the refusal of the one who teaches to learn from the one being taught, it grows out of an ideology of domination. Those who are called upon to teach must first learn how to continue learning when they begin to teach. (1978: 9)

The involvement of learners—he adds—in defining educational content is of indisputable importance. They have rights, as active participants, to define what they need to know. One of the most cogent conceptualisations of this stance emerges from the pronouncement that education must be initiated with efforts to solve the teacher-student contradiction, a reconciliation of difference, so that members of both groups are, simultaneously, teachers and students. In the collective, persons become teachers-students with students-teachers.

Goulet (1998) offers an appropriate assessment of conceptualisation by noting that Freire views the successful educator, not as a persuader, an insidious propagandist, but as a communicator who applies his ability to dialogue with educatees in modes of reciprocity. What does dialogue signify? It signifies collective action aimed at removing illiteracy along a plane of equality. Dialogue is not a relation between "I" and "it." Dialogue is, necessarily communion between "I" and "thou," two subjects, for whenever "thou" is altered to "it," "dialogue is subverted and education is changed to deformation" (Freire, 1998: 52).

The sense of communion implies reflection, as well as, knowing, which is very specific to Freire. Knowing necessitates the curious presence of subjects who interpret the world through the constancy of invention and reinvention. It claims from each person a critical reflection on the very act of knowing.

> It must be a reflection which recognises the knowing process, and in this
> recognition becomes aware of the "raison d'etre" behind the knowing and
> the conditioning to which that process is subject. (1998: 100)

Promoting dialogue is strongly suggestive of relegating—if not condemning—what is antidialogical. I must now direct my attention to explicit Freireian condemnation of the antidialogical, as a way of strengthening the relevance of liberation in educational practice. Freire (1970) identifies four features of the antidialogical, all of which, are indicative of imperialist domination. They are conquest, divide and rule, manipulation, and cultural invasion. I shall focus on conquest, manipulation, and cultural invasion.

In acts of conquest, the conqueror imposes his objectives on the vanquished and converts them to his possessions. He imposes his own patterns and structures on the conquered who internalise the forms and become ambiguous persons. Manipulation entails ways in which the dominators secure conformity of the oppressed to their objectives of inferiorisation. Cultural invasion involves a narrow interpretation of reality, a stagnant sense of the world, and the imposing of values from the invader who has a fear of abandoning those values. One of its principal signifiers is that decisive positions from which actions affecting the lives of the invaded are taken should be those occupied by the invaders. Invaders are actors who choose; the invaded are followers who have the illusion of acting via the experience of the invaders. Cultural invasion is particularly insidious. Freire regards it as violence, penetration of cultural contexts of the invaded whose prospects for development are demeaned and creativity impeded.

My reference to Freire clearly intersects with what has come to be known as the sociological imagination which I shall use to illuminate Freire's value. Mills (1959) applies the sociological imagination as a means of locating ways in which persons become falsely conscious of everyday life. The sociological imagination facilitates apprehending connections between history and biographies within societies. Its pursuit encompasses a tripartite inquiry: (1) What is the structure of a particular society? What are its essential components? How are the components related and how do they differ from other versions of social order? (2) What is the place of society in history? What are its mechanisms of change? Where is the society positioned within humanity and what meaning does it have for humanity? In what ways does the specific aspect of society under examination affect, and is affected by, the historical period where it moves? (3) What types of persons are dominant in that society, currently, and what kinds of individuals are emerging as dominant? How are both groups of humans chosen and shaped, freed and oppressed, made sensitive and blunted?

Mills notes that the most productive difference with which the sociological imagination operates is that which exists between personal troubles and public issues of social structure. Troubles take place within individuals and the range of their direct links to others. They are relevant to ourselves and the restricted contexts of social life of which we are personally familiar. Thus, articulation and solution of troubles reside within persons as biographical entities and their immediate settings. Troubles are private. They are indicative of values appreciated by individuals who sense threats to the values.

Issues, on the other hand, lie beyond the localities of settings within the inner lives of persons. Issues are public matters over which there is debate about what values really are and what pose threats to them. Issues—continues Mills—exemplify crises within institutional arrangements frequently articulated as Marxian "contradictions" or "antagonisms."

He adds that in order to conceptualise issues and troubles, specific queries must be posed. What values are appreciated but threatened? What values are appreciated and supported by defining trends of particular periods? Further, inquiries about threats and support should be framed in terms of salient contradictions of structure. When persons appreciate a group of values and do not experience threats, they enjoy well-being.

They face crises, however, when they appreciate values but sense threats. Persons also experience indifference, when they are, neither aware of any values, nor sense any threats. Anxiety, which can become a destructive unspecified malaise emerges under circumstances in which persons are not cognisant of values but sense threats.

He is also insistent that the queries to which he refers are the kinds of questions the best social analysts have posed. These are the types of investigations whose conduct cannot be avoided by any mind possessing the sociological imagination.

> For that imagination is the capacity to shift from one perspective to another—from the political to the psychological; from examination of a single family to comparative assessment of the national budgets of the world; from the theological school to the military establishment; from considerations of an oil industry to studies of contemporary poetry. (1959: 13–14)

It is representative of the analytical ability to move from the most impersonal and distant to the most intimate aspects of selfhood and to discern links between the two. Its foundation is made up of an intense desire to become aware of the social and historical significance of the self in society and the period within which this self gains its being and quality.

Let me apply the sociological imagination to the masses who are subject to communicative teaching practices. Several members of these masses come from societies deemed politically independent. Independence is, however, neither political, nor economic: what Mills would have deemed their national one or two crop economies are based upon agricultural and industrial products whose prices are determined in established centres of capitalist control. The masses suffer under the deadweight of racial and class divisions systematically instituted in the days of colonial and neocolonial oppression. These are also the very individuals who crave and use routes of emigration with the false expectation that movement to European metropolises shall bring them socioeconomic salvation.

At the political level, leaders of independent countries are incapable of using the multicultural experiences of the poor who suffered under colonialism as a basis to identifying the groundwork for national and regional progress, in educational and economic contexts. The point about incapability is especially meaningful. In the aftermath of brutal dehumanisation of nonwhite persons, economic and political strategies ostensibly geared to people emancipation have been premised upon reverence for, and movement between, two competing, but unfeasible, models of economic advancement: hypocrisy in ostensible free market capitalism of laissez-faire economics, and mixed economies whose cyclical crises are managed by paternalistic government intervention.

I want to dwell briefly on the hypocrisy of free market capitalism, for its existence does attest to promotion of what Mills characterises as false consciousness. Free market capitalism has always been touted by its leading advocates as far more advantageous to the poor than mixed economies. Some of its most vaunted presentations have, however, led to misery of the masses. In this regard, crippling consequences of discrepancies between free trade and fair trade of the North American Free Trade Agreement (NAFTA) and Association of South East Asian Nations (ASEAN) are reminders of lack of economic liberation for the masses.

My case can be solidified by referring to a report in the Canadian newspaper, the *Globe and Mail*. According to correspondent, Conway-Smith (2004), the rights of Mexican workers under NAFTA were being violated. She indicates that the workers labour in dirty, hazardous, conditions where they experience harassment, when they pursue their rights. In the words of one worker, "We were called bad names, and sometimes we were called 'bow-legged Indians.' I consider this racial discrimination." Mexican workers have also been intimidated by employers and government, when they attempted to form trade unions. Basic necessities in the workplace such as ventilation, emergency exits, drinking water, protective masks, and up to date first aid kits were also absent in Mexico.

The central point of the foregoing explanation is to highlight Western dominance which has a negative impact on lives of nonwhite persons, many of whom, have been attracted to capitalist European, North American, and Austral-Asian urban settings where their marginalisation is associated with second language education. This is the very marginalisation which can be framed in terms of contradictions between issues and troubles, as well as, values that are appreciated but threatened. Nonwhite second language learners in urbanised Western environments clearly want to improve their socioeconomic status. They value, very highly, the great significance of accumulating wealth. It is, however, within these urbanised settings that their goals of accumulation are continually thwarted.

I hasten to add that goals of accumulation for large numbers of new immigrants from former communist societies in Europe are also continually thwarted. Several of these individuals lured to the capitalist world where they are compelled to formally acquire a second language such as English and expect to fulfil dreams of great financial gain, quickly realise that they become part of the new underclass in Western global cities. Many of them, highly qualified intellectuals and professionals in their countries of birth, become all too uncomfortably attuned to the everyday drudgery of menial work they must do as nannies, porters, factory hands, waiters and waitresses, as well as, maids. The entrapment for them, at a personal level, is that they are acutely aware of the contradiction between official claims in their new societies about the wonder of socioeconomic advancement and their daily experience emanating from trivialising of their earlier academic achievements. Importantly, they are powerless to alter the inconsistency.

The first source of my claims comes from the work of Saskia Sassen on globalisation.

> In the last hundred years, the political interstate system came to provide dominant organisational form of cross-border flows, with national states as its key actors. It is this condition that has changed dramatically since the 1980s as a result of privatisation, deregulation, the opening up of national economies to foreign firms, and the growing participation of national economic actors in global markets. (Sassen, 2000: p. 1)

Sassen is quite clear that these are practices of globalisation which contribute to great expansion of the internationalised sectors of economies that have imposed new and heightened values on economic activities.

The devastating consequences of these practices, she adds, affect large areas of urban economic organisation. Thus, high prices and profits within international sectors and supportive areas such as top-of-the-line restaurants and hotels have led to great hardships for such entities as neighbourhood shops that serve local needs which are being replaced by the creations of upscale boutiques and restaurants geared to high income urban clientele.

In supporting Sassen's position, Graham (2000) points out that these large urban areas, global cities, grow by cumulative concentration of assets upon which corporate headquarters, high level service industries, world financial services, and the international cultural industries rely for their operation in a volatile globalising setting. According to Sassen, management of mutlinational production loci and capital movements, in these cities, has brought together new forms of communication and a supportive concentration of professional occupations such as law, accounting, and computer programming in the formation of new elite. This is the very elite whose members exist beside a class of poor, nonunionised and immigrant workers employed in small scale sweatshop operations providing luxuries for the elite.

This is the same elite whose presence is crucial to fuelling what Graham assesses as telereliance, something that is exceedingly high within international industries of products and services moved primarily by information and communication exchanges along the routes of electronic coordination.

Graham is dealing with networks supportive of very uneven construction of global connections which saturate high-level corporate, financial, as well as, media clusters managed by socioeconomic elites located in global cities. Here are some statistics about telereliance in global cities:

(1) More than 50% of long distance telephone calls within the USA are made or received by 5% of telephone customers, transnational corporations, whose control operations cluster in global metropolitan areas of America.

(2) New York's Silicon Alley emerges as the dominant global provider of Internet and multimedia skills, as well as, design.

(3) London has six overlaid fibre optic grids superimposed beneath Square Mile and other parts of the city (B.T., Mercury, City of London Telecommunications, World Com-MCI, Energis, Sohonet).

(4) London also has a comprehensive suite of microwave communication grids and numerous reselling service operators from all over the world.

(5) Sohonet has constructed a group of London film companies which links concentrations of film and media companies, television broadcasters, publishers, internet providers, graphic designers, and recording companies to Hollywood film studios via transatlantic fibre optic connections.

(6) Sohonet enables online film transmission, virtual studios, and intercontinental editing through broadband connections.

(7) MCI-World Com has been aggressively involved in fibre optic metropolitan links via Gemini which links London and New York, as well as, Ulysses which connects Paris, London, Amsterdam, and Brussels for major financial transactions.

(8) Fibre Optic Link Around the Globe (FLAG) provides ultra high capacity of 120,000 simultaneous calls via a 28,000 km grid from London to Tokyo.

(9) FLAG also links with a 12,000km Pacific Cable Network of Japan, South Korea, Taiwan, Hong Kong, Manila, Bangkok, Ho Chi Minh City, and Jakarta.

It is noteworthy that among the cities noted in telereliance, six are identified by Graham among the top twenty-five global cities ranked in 1998 as the most competitive in accordance with telecommunications infrastructure. The six are New York (ranked 1), London (ranked 6), Paris (ranked 9) Amsterdam (ranked 13), Tokyo (ranked 14), and Brussels (ranked 15). These are all cities where second language education is very popular and profitable. It is also very profitable and popular in other global cities such as Chicago (ranked 2), Los Angeles (ranked 3), Toronto (ranked 8), Mexico City (ranked 16), Milan (ranked 18), Kuala Lumpur (ranked 19), and Sao Paulo (ranked 23).

Later, for the purpose of highlighting the significance of Freire to second language education, I shall explore marginalisation as a very important feature of globalisation and solidify my examination of global cities. My goal now is to emphasise specific bases via examining the route of racism.

Antiracist Justification For Remediation

Why should Freire's work be foundational to remedying the communicative approach to target language teaching? There are historical, pedagogical, and sociological reasons for the modification. These are reasons, some of which, I frame in terms: (1) application of the power of colonialism, (2) internalisation of this power, (3) replacement or removal of achieved statuses of conquered people and assignment of ascribed statuses to them, (4) treatment of those persons as nonpersons or subpersons.

Let me expose these terms, initially, by indicating that systematic efforts to teach European languages such as French, English, Spanish, Dutch, German, and Italian in colonial possessions have been directly associated with what Freire assesses as conquest, divide and rule, manipulation, and cultural invasion. European teachers of these languages in conquered territories were the purveyors of cultural superiority. From a British imperialist standpoint, superiority came in the form of what Bhattacharyya, Gabriel and Small (2000) regard as the shifting terrain of white imagery. What was covered on this terrain? It was, among other features, the formation of fictional literary principles strongly linked to ideas of white masculinity and femininity within 19th century Britain.

Foundational to these formations about relations between Britain and overseas possessions were interactions between whites and nonwhites. Said argues that in the novel, *Mansfield Park*, stability and progress connected with Britain are owed to events abroad, specifically, what exists on Thomas Bertram's Antigua slave plantation. For Said, the plantation is "mysteriously necessary to the poise and beauty of *Mansfield Park*" (Said, 1993: 69). Bhattacharyya, Gabriel and Small also indicate that *Jane Eyre's* character was formulated on views about the plantocracy and racial theories which supported these views. The social standing of this character was largely bound up with death of Bertha, Rochester's Jamaican wife, who set fire to herself, so that Jane Eyre might become the feminist heroine of British fiction. Further, the Brontes were obvious reflections of imperial contexts. "Whilst they transgressed in terms of their feminine roles they did so, nevertheless, as white women" (Bhattacharyya, Gabriel and Small, 2002: 11).

The British example is instructive. Britain has been a preeminent imperial power, from which English teachers, sent overseas, promoted the ascendant significance of English literature. This is not a development lost to Halliday, *et al*. They observe that to numerous teachers of English in Britain and overseas, teaching English meant teaching English Literature.

> In countries such as India the pattern of education has been exported so successfully from British school and university practice that syllabuses exist which are nowadays *plus royaliste que le roi*. From such countries students come to Britain for training that will fit them to join the teaching profession in their home country and teach English literature (or rather a version of literary history and criticism; yet in many cases it is painfully clear that there are many among them whose command of English as a language is not sufficient to enable them to either discuss and teach great works of literature or to fully understand and or appreciate them. (Halliday, *et al.*, 1964: 184)

Given foregoing accounts of white imagery in literary principles, the reference from Halliday, *et al.*, to literary history and criticism, a reference that should be set against the foreground of British imperialism, does not elude me. These are the very principles inherent to the impact of what they term a weighty superstructure which cannot be supported by a foundation.

While they propose that the foundation be repaired and solidified, they state that because of prejudices their recommendation would be deemed a threat to the superstructure. Among the many reasons they offer for the negative assessment are: (a) responsibility for the teaching of English in its entirety within the hands of persons whose training is exclusively in literature and who see threats to their prestige and influence, (b) claims that the significance of literature is unquestionably transcendent to everyone who is associated with it. This is negativity from persons steeped in feelings of superiority which defined the ingloriousness of imperialist advancement.

More than two decades after Halliday *et al's.*, views appeared, Kachru (1986) wrote that the role of English within sociolinguistic contexts of Third World societies is either inappropriately grasped by experts from the rich First World or is ignored. Thus, within the Third Wold, there is a realisation that it would be difficult to expect the experts to provide insights and leadership within target language teaching which is contextually, attitudinally, and practically valuable, overseas.

There is no doubt that racism has been foundational to displays of superiority. It is to this basis that I turn my attention, as a very important way of highlighting the historical. One of my principal goals is to locate the flawed epistemological strictures which have overlain historical categorisations of race, a designation whose basis is, at best, highly questionable, because of its very racist underpinning. Effective performance of my task rests upon traversing that tortured trail whose contours of contradiction and paradoxes of pillaging have been employed in the service of erecting foundations of exile for nonwhite, as well as, white people, several of whom are not L1 users of European languages spoken in economically advanced Western societies. When I point to exile, I am using the conceptualisation of Freire (1998) who regards exile as a space/time dimension involuntarily occupied by the banished.

He says entry to this space is signified by rage, fear, suffering, early longing, love, fractured expectation, as well as, hidden hope that signals return. To suffer in exile means becoming aware that someone has departed from their context of origin, living bitterness, the clarity in blurring where appropriate moves are employed, for the purpose of liberation. Exile is, thus, not wholly defined by reason, pain and absence of optimism. Exile is suffering the total act of being.

I must make it clear that in addressing myself to this matter of race, I want to avoid the stricture of what Perea (2000) deems the binary paradigm, a formulation that race is constituted by two racial categories, black and white.

> There is no question…of defining race and racism (or, for that matter, ethnicity) and following them as unchanging entities through time. It is rather a question of seeing how historical forces shape and change the meanings of these terms over time and space. (Holt, 2000: 18)

Thus, in dealing with understanding race within the deindustrialised, globalised, service economies which dominate the world and do depend partially but significantly on the labour of Europe's working classes from former communist societies, Holt observes that race in the late 20th century and, in my view, the twenty-first, is not confined to a colour line. Racialised others might well be Caucasian. It is, however, obvious that the racist underpinning noted earlier has, nevertheless, meant great suffering of persons in the nonwhite world under the deadweight of institutional practices emergent from 17th, 18th and 19th century European capitalism now replaced by globalisation.

A significant aspect of the suffering cannot be divorced from the very designation of the term, race. Banton makes an important distinction between actors' and observers' models of the category, race. An actor's model is a device he employs to chart courses in daily life geared to locating "the shallow water, the best channels, and the likely reactions of other vessels" (Banton, 1996: 104). Observer models' consist of abstract concepts applied for the purpose of identifying regularities of which actors are not cognisant or of which they possess inadequate information. In adopting such a position, the observer derives mistaken conclusions which take a long time to clear up.

One such confusion exists in racial theories of the mid-nineteenth century adduced as observer models. Theorists claimed that there were zoological determinants which underpinned actors' models of their social interaction with which the actors needed to familiarise themselves and use as policy guides. Banton notes that accession to the plausibility of this requirement within Europe, North America, as well as, areas influenced by these continents, meant that observers' models became actors' models. The consequence of such acceptance, he adds, is that the theories were both ill founded and harmful.

Van den Berghe (1996) poses two questions about race. "Does Race Matter?" and "Do Social Races have any biological underpinning?" He responds to the latter, affirmatively, and defines a social race as a group sharing physical—as opposed to —cultural attributes. He adds that use of the category, social race, stigmatises subordinate groups and all efforts to offer alternative assessments are unfruitful. Further, from the standpoint of policy, the formalisation of race categorisation, despite any good organisational intentions of harmlessness, is often harmful in its impact.

Inglorious examples of harmfulness are recorded by Ross (1997). He locates reliance by U.S. courts on mixtures of science and common knowledge, for the purpose of assigning racial categories and designating persons as white and non-white. The groupings, based on anthropological considerations, was made up of Negro, Caucasian, Mongoloid, American (Indian), and Malay. By the 1920s, the U.S. Supreme Court had abandoned the scientific classifications and begun to depend on common sense and popular knowledge. One result of this modification was the case of the *United States vs. Thind*.

Bhagat Singh Thind, an Asian Indian, made a case for U.S. naturalisation on grounds of the Supreme Court's adjudicating equivalence of Caucasian and White. The Court's solution, since the launching of Thind's challenge, was to accept common sense knowledge as a reliable means of policing the boundaries of whiteness. Ross states that while scientific dependence by the U.S. courts on draw-

ing racial lines was relaxed between the 1920s and 70s, this dependence was re-
vived in the 80s and 90s. Biological definitions tied to new developments in
molecular genetics formed a strong basis to rendering judicial decisions in cases of
social benefits and entitlements. Use of the very definitions has also contributed to
formation of beliefs about race in the U.S.

Ross offers a clear marker of these harmful biological underpinnings, when
he observes that genetic differentiation among individuals is much less than that
among population groups. The slight individual distinctions have, however, been
granted enormous cultural importance, at a time when biological explanations of
social matters are strongly pursued. While alluding to the difference between individual and group variation, Eriksen (1996) places the category, 'race,' within in-
verted commas. The category is of questionable significance to him, for the
prevalence of "interbreeding" among human populations designifies rigid boundaries among races. Greater variation exists within one "race" than systematic
variability among groups. The category, 'race,' has no objective existence. It may,
however, assume sociological significance, for one suppositional foundation from
which racism is erected is the assumption that personality is associated with hereditary features which reflect systematic variances among "races." Eriksen has
established a connection between "race" and racism, the second of which Van den
Berghe (1996) analyses in terms of unmistakable links between genes and behaviour which did not evolve from natural selection.

He states that racism is an instance of culture "hijacking" genes selected for
purposes such as skin pigmentation regulating exposure to sunlight in different
latitudes, and giving the genes a notably divergent social agenda. The agenda is,
however, infused with a biological basis, maximisation of fitness via nepotism.
Just as importantly, the agenda has a major reciprocal impact on opportunities of
various groups, and ultimately, the direction of human evolution. Perhaps, the
most infamous modern commentary of the hijackers that soiled humanity of African heritage emanated from the lengthy period of oppression perpetrated in the
name of Afrikaner apartheid.

The keen observer might well inquire about the relevance of apartheid and
post-apartheid South Africa to the target language teaching enterprise. Let me deal
with this matter by noting that Roy-Campbell (2003) and Phaswana (2003) indicate quite progressive thinking on the part of postapartheid administrations
which designated eleven languages as official: Sepedi, Sesotho, Setswana, siSwati,
isiNdebele, isiXhosa, isiZulu, Tshivena, Xitsonga, English and Afrikaans. Of these
eleven, English and Afrikaans are not indigenous.

The point about indigenous languages needs to be made:

South Africa has a peculiar history with regard to African languages since use of indigenous languages as media of instruction was the norm under the policy of Bantu Education. This policy of racial separation sought to condemn Africans to a mediocre education as the development of these languages was circumscribed, therein providing only that level of knowledge that the Afrikaaner government wanted Africans to have access to. This has contributed to resistance by some South Africans to use of African languages as media of instruction, as they associate this practice with keeping them confined within a linguistic prison. (Roy-Campbell, 2003: 93)

I notice that neither is Hindi nor Urdu, which have been used by several Indian victims of apartheid, designated as an official language. While I shall not delve into the rationale for exclusion I must say that numerous users of these languages, in their state of victimisation, learnt English and Afrikaans as second languages.

Anyone who, therefore, searches for links between apartheid and its inevitable aftermath on the one hand and language teaching should be informed that for the vast majority of the black population, several of whom have been using Bantu languages, both Afrikaans and English inevitably assume the status of second languages. For some of them, through no fault of their own but owing to the machinations of racist separation, they did not embrace their own languages. Thus, in a climate of grossly blatant unfairness, these people, as well as, Indian citizens, have not, however, benefited from their language teaching programmes. Residents of the notorious Bantustans (homelands) under apartheid and South Western townships (Soweto) in a post-apartheid South Africa have been some of the worst sufferers of ineffective target language teaching practices inextricably linked to injustice.

It is to the analyses of Van den Berghe (1980) that I turn, for a rendering of Afrikaaner injustice. He uses the term, racial caste, to describe racist Afrikaner designations. Caste signifies an endogamous group whose hierarchically ranked membership in relation to other groups is determined by birth and for life. On the basis of the racial caste designation, apartheid South Africa was made up of four castes: Whites or Europeans who occupied the top of the hierarchy, Coloureds, Indians, and Africans, Bantus or "Kaffirs."

The Africans designated by Whites as Kaffirs (heathens), Natives or Bantus, were targets of the greatest discrimination, experienced the worst living standards, occupational status, and educational advantages. Use by whites of the term, South African, referred, almost invariably, to themselves. The consequences of South African racism emanated from official codification in apartheid, for which two principal spokespersons made bold assertions. According to Hendrik Verwoerd, keeping South Africa white meant fulfillment of a single goal—not guidance, leadership, but domination, control, and supremacy. B.J. Schoeman asserted that pick and shovel work is the natural work of the Native, who has special aptitude for repetitive activity. He was explicit in stating that the importance of apartheid lay in appreciating that non-Europeans will never have the same political rights as Europeans who will always be baas in a society where social equality will not take place.

Schoeman and Verwoerd were espousing the ideology of Afrikaanerdom which was encrusted in conceptions of rugged frontier individualism, distrust of authority, and self righteousness as God's chosen people. Afrikaaners yearned for a return to a past devoid of British capitalism and "cheeky Kaffirs." Further, Afrikaaner dominance aimed for Herrenvolk equality dispensing minimal supervision to maintain Africans and other non-whites in permanent states as Helots. Salvation for the white race lay in apartheid. Integration, which would end in African domination, miscegenation, and overwhelming of white civilisation, matters of horror and disgust to Afrikaaners, was inconceivable.

Why was this so? Afrikaaner intellectual apologists claimed:

> We Afrikaaners and White South Africans in general, have no homeland other than South Africa. The country is ours, and we have no intention to leave it. We have just as much right to be here as the "Bantu," and we have arrived in South Africa at about the same time as they. We want to preserve our superior "White civilisation" and maintain our racial identity, but we are surrounded by an overwhelming majority of non-Whites who threaten to swamp us culturally and racially. (Van den Berghe, 1980: 116)

Not surprisingly, the claim resided in what Smith (1996) regards as the myth of ethnic election which I explore in substantive and conceptual versions. The myth, spread by specialists, is promulgated as a belief in the status of "chosen people." This is a myth which is decisive to prolonged ethnic continuity, one of whose patterns Smith names the emigrant colonist. This version is exemplified among persons who have fled old homelands and are committed to building new communities in new homelands where they grant scant respect to the lives of indigenous people

That such a myth pervaded Afrikaanerdom is not lost to Van den Berghe. He formulates its proponents as having embraced the urge to search for an external sign of salvation. In their pursuit, what appeared as the most inevitable and obvious choice was their skin colour, very different to the heathen nature of dark skinned people traditionally associated with sin and evil. Biblical justification for claims to elevated status in white superiority was advanced in the perversity that Africans were descendants of Ham, cursed by Noah and destined by God to be servants of servants, hewers of wood and drawers of water. This myth is, by no means, restricted to South Africa. Smith associates it with the new American homeland of the Pilgrim Fathers who had fled religious oppression and sought to fulfil the promise of freedom in a new Jerusalem.

My focus on the expression of white superiority is, simultaneously, a focus on perverse logic which Williams Krenshaw (1997) states rests on claims within the USA about inherent inferiority of blacks and flawed assumptions of ascendancy. In the supremacist paradigm, blacks are portrayed as lascivious, emotional, and infantile, whereas whites are depicted as pious, hardworking, reasonable, and mature. These designations emanated from, and were sustained by, science, religion, and the humanities. Sustenance, in its most blatant and odious forms, occurred in a period when European brutality inferiorised Africa, Asia, the Americas, and the Caribbean for the greed of imperialism. Some of the strongest support was offered by European science.

Ross (1997) locates activities of the eugenics movement which gained prominence with Francis Galton, the founder of eugenics in the nineteenth century. Ross observes that the activities were designified after Nazism, only to re-emerge in different versions, mainly within Britain and the USA, via sociobiology and evolutionary psychology, during the last two decades of the twentieth century. I am compelled to say that Galton, cousin of Charles Darwin, would have been proud, both of his British relative, as well as, Joseph Chamberlain, who assumed the post of Secretary of State for the British colonies in 1895. According to Banton (1980), Darwin (in his publication *The Descent of Man*) emphasised the significance of natural selection as a development which affected civilised nations.

He also called for use of eugenic measures and claimed that the excellent progress of the United States, as well as the character of the people, resulted from natural selection: the more energetic, restless, and courageous men from all parts of Europe have emigrated and succeeded to the greatest extent. Darwin even advanced the claim that fertility among the "savage races" was dropping and could lead to their extinction, because of their smaller brains and incapability of altering their habits when they meet "civilised races." Banton adds that the transparency of Darwin's racism was evident in his acceptance of a blending view about races. Proponents of this view state that if a clever individual married a stupid person, abilities of the clever person would be nonexistent, in the next generation.

Galton's eugenics cannot be divorced from his invention of psychometry, which was laced with racist ideology. It is this ideology which paralleled the ideology of racist inferiorisation that was used to condemn the language use of colonised people. According to Daniels and Houghton (1972), Galton's use of psychometry moved psychology in British universities from threshold to respectability. How did he attain such a goal? After its invention, this discipline was used to demonstrate that it could penetrate mysteries of the human condition by applying complex multidimensional mathematical approaches to the "hard" data of psychology, in very much the same way as physicists conceptualised atoms subsequent to Newton.

Galton's psychometry was, however, antidemocratic. Its utilisation was committed to offering justification for preventing certain groups in society from participating in decision making. This was especially the case in the field of education, for psychometry endeavoured to demonstrate that only small fractions of society possessed adequate "g," general intelligence, which allowed them to take advantage of professional and higher learning. Thus, intelligence testing ascertained that "g" could be greatly found among upper and middle class white children. The views above about Galton are consistent with:

> It was, above all, Darwin's second cousin, explorer and scientist, Francis Galton (1822-1911), who sought to apply Darwinian principles to human society and to provide 'scientific' justification for a process of selective breeding designed to maintain and, where possible, improve the genetic condition of the human race. Galton was particularly concerned to ensure that 'racial purity' should not be undermined in increasingly democratic and egalitarian societies where the average level of ability and creativity might be in danger of declining as a result of those at the bottom end of the social scale 'over-breeding.' (Chitty, 2004: 80)

Galton's psychometry was grounded in explicitly racist claims he advanced in his publication *Hereditary Genius* (1869). He is quoted as having stated:

> The idea of investigating the subject of hereditary genius occurred to me during the course of a purely ethnological enquiry into the mental peculiarities of different races, when the fact that characteristics cling to families was so forced upon my notice. (Daniels and Houghton, 1972: 73)

The idea emerged from Galton's childhood aim to verify that cousin, Charles Darwin, had located clues to the origin of the species, and had, also, discovered varying social roles in commercial society. To fulfil his aim, he selected four hundred "illustrious men of history," his study of whom, established the theory that genius was hereditary. Galton later recorded the results of his study in *Hereditary Genius*.

According to Chitty, that is the very study in which he claimed to show that 'genius' was inborn and restricted almost exclusively to specific types of privileged families with innate qualities and abilities. He was also a staunch advocate of strict breeding policies and what he termed judicious marriage. In addition, he bemoaned the degradation of human nature by propogation of the unfit. In 1883, he introduced the term, eugenics, which he stated was derived from the Greek word, eugenes, a term applied to describe persons "heriditarily endowed with noble qualities." According to Brown (1998), twenty-six years later, he saw eugenics as the science encompassing those influences which serve to maintain inborn qualities of a race, as well as, those influences which develop the innateness to the greatest advantage.

Galton's theory was accepted by one of his most ardent admirers, Cyril Burt, the racist cheater, once regarded as the father of intelligence testing in Great Britain, but someone whom Daniels and Houghton deem the most brilliant social engineer of the 20th century.

By the term intelligence, the psychologist understands inborn, all-round intellectual ability. It is inherited, or at least innate, not due to teaching or training; it is intellectual, not emotional or moral, and remains uninfluenced by industry or zeal; it is general, not specific, that is to say it is not limited to any particular kind of work, but enters into all we do or say or think. Of all our mental qualities, it is the most far-reaching; fortunately, it can be measured with accuracy and ease. (Burt, 1933: 28-29)

Daniels and Houghton note that Burt's principal concern, how much of intelligence was owed to hereditary and environmental factors, could not be met with reason. If psychometry contends that persons' intellectual impediments are owed to poor genetic endowment, it produces the disease it is intended to cure. That disease, so state Daniels and Houghton, is a process of labelling individuals on the basis of recognising diagnosis as the initial phase of helping casualties of educational systems.

In 1969, Burt blamed the government of British Prime Minister, Harold Wilson, by issuing a diagnosis which wholly reflected Galton's view. He concluded that implementation of the government's progressive education reforms was responsible for basic education standards being lower than they had been fifty-five years previously (Chitty, 2004). I wonder how he would have responded, had he lived to become aware of a report about one of the strongest and most perverse of his legacies, Educationally Subnormal (ESN) schools in Britain. I am referring to a report titled "The Unequal Struggle" (1986) authored by Dr. Ashton Gibson under the auspices of The Centre for Caribbean Studies.

Most of Dr. Gibson's research was conducted within the Inner London Education Authority, some of the main findings of which, were: teachers make racist remarks to black students, deny opportunities to the students, and neglect West Indian culture. In addition, several young West Indians feel isolated, suffer from isolation and alienation, and experience great difficulty communicating with their teachers who are unaware of the students' problems. In specific terms, 70% experience difficulty understanding teachers, 50% reported that they spoke a different language at home to that used in school. While 91% believed that schools offered the best opportunities for vital education, only 2% attained any examination successes.

During the course of an interview with the BBC when the report was published Dr. Gibson stated his motivation for having embarked on the study: "I found it difficult to understand why ninety percent of all the children in Educationally Subnormal schools in London were West Indian children...And, therefore, I set out as a West Indian, to find some answers." Dr. Gibson did find answers which were disturbing. Also disturbed was Dr. Bernard Wiltshire, Deputy Director of The Inner London Education Authority who identified what he saw as the most telling statistic of the study.

He noted that there was no child in the study who could report that s/he completed school with any awareness about his/her history or background. He pointed out that such awareness is greatly related to self esteem and self confidence. For him it was thus not surprising that students lacked the motivation to experience what he deemed the drudgery of acquiring the type of school knowledge they needed. When asked by a BBC interviewer if the study pointed to British society being racist, he issued an emphatic response: "Oh! I think the report undoubtedly says that as far as West Indian children—the black children are concerned—the whole structure of the society operates as a huge stumbling block. British society is, really, very cruel to black children." The "Unequal Struggle" points, very significantly, to problems of language and culture for young people whose modes of communication are neither recognised as English nor a foreign language. I am talking about Caribbean youths whose strong and inevitable link to Creole language is trivialised, condemned in negative labelling, and stigmatised by educational authorities. This is not merely a British problem in the eighties, it is also a Canadian and American problem in the nineties and currently which is not apprehended with reason: there are no official efforts to appreciate Creoles as different languages to European languages, Creoles which should be taught and learnt as languages via second language teaching methodology.

I shall make the argument for appreciation and methodology in later sections. Here, I must maintain my focus on connections between psychometry and racism as part of the goal of locating anti-racist justification for remediation of communicative language teaching. My particular focus now is North America.

Within the USA, the specific advancement of psychometry in the guise of intelligence testing took the form of selecting officers of the military. The data from testing formed a basis to discussing racial variation in intelligence. It was in that context of discussion that racist propagandists within wider society sought to use the data for proving that white Anglo Saxon Protestants displayed intelligence superior to that of ex-slaves.

The Darwin/Galton/Burt legacy has been readily accepted by their racist admirers, both in Britain, the USA, and Canada. The most noteworthy of these North American admirers are Rushton in Canada, and Jensen, Herrenstein and Murray in the U.S. Some forerunners of such shameless academic posturing appeared in popular views of linguistic inferiority about blacks. In 1746, a British visitor to the American colonies offered this view of the colonists: "One thing they are very faulty in, with regard to their children…is that when young, they suffer them too much to prowl among young negroes, which insensibly causes them to imbibe their manners and broken speech" (Trudgill, 1979: 64–65).

From Trudgill's standpoint, black/white speech variation was generally assumed to emanate from inherent mental or physical differences between the groups. Black speech was interpreted as corrupt and debased. Thus, the differences noted above were typified, in fashionable beliefs, as verification of innate inferiority of blacks who could not speak English appropriately, quite plainly, because they lacked the ability to do so. What was, undoubtedly, a fashionable belief, but explicitly official within Southern states was the immense burden of disenfranchisement borne by black people in those states. Several of them were denied the right to vote because they failed literacy tests devised by racists.

The Trudgill accounts points to a broader problem of white unfairness neatly conceptualised by Kennedy (2000) who states that the most painful and searing of inferiorising comments about American blacks have emerged in the form of black inferiority to whites. In the period of slavery, the idea of black intellectual inferiority was embedded in the minds of pro-, as well, as anti-slavery whites and served as rationalisation for denying educational resources to blacks. In the century immediately following abolition, attempts by blacks to become equal participants within American intellectual culture was greeted with skepticism by whites who harboured low opinions of their intellectual capacity and, other whites who felt educated blacks were dangers to orderly society.

Throughout the 20th century, some white linguists studied black language use and did not attribute it to inferiority of users. They, however, refused to grant full language status to what has come to be known by leading black scholars as Ebonics that is rooted in the Niger-Congo branch of African language families. Not only is refusal implicitly racist, but the refusal is a veiled allusion to the linguistic ability of black people. I am referring to the fact that these linguists have consistently used different criteria for ascertaining language status of European languages and Ebonics. This is a point not lost to Crawford (2001). He correctly observes that the loci of analysis for European languages consist of grammar (morphology, semantics, syntax, phonetics, and phonology). Thus, English is categorised in the Germanic group of languages, because of its grammatical superstructure. This is so, despite the fact that the principal sources of English lexis are other languages. English is made up of a German grammar upon which vocabularies from languages such as French, Spanish, Latin, Italian, and Greek are overlain. Crawford is describing a situation which is consistent with that offered by Kurath (1970) who says the large scale adoption of foreign words by English users did not materially modify the structure of that language. Ebonics, on the other hand, categorised as an inferior appendage of English, is assessed by using lexis. This is so, despite the fact that the features of English hold true for Ebonics.

Ebonics users maintain grammatical structures of the African family of languages but display a lexicon derived from language varieties such as English, French, Dutch, Spanish, Portugese, as well as African influences. Crawford's position is consistent with that adopted by Burnett (1986) who states that vernaculars of the Anglo-Caribbean indicate strong African influence within their syntax and intonational systems, even though they are based on English vocabulary with some influence from Portugese, Spanish, French, and Dutch. Crawford thus regards analysis of Ebonics by some European scholars as one aspect of ongoing intellectual and cultural warfare against people of African ancestry.

The ramifications of Crawford's view become powerfully obvious when they are juxtaposed with those of Robins (1967), Breytenbach (1983) and Phaswana (2003) on Afrikaans, kitchen Dutch or Cape patois.

In a mild suggestion about linguistic divergences emanating from geographical separation, Robins states that the Dutch of early South African settlers developed differently from the Dutch of Holland. Moreover, Afrikaans, the so-called development of South African Dutch, has been deemed different to Netherlands Dutch. Not merely does Phaswana deem this South African Dutch slave/master and slave/slave communication, but he employs the ideas of Alexander (1989) and Brown (1992) to add that Afrikaans was used initially as a *lingua franca* by the majority of Cape residents. This "Cape patois," Afrikaans, which came from the Western Cape, started as the language of trade, education, and social interaction between whites and non-whites.

While pointing to social struggle that defined linguistic tension Phaswana notes that English first occupied the Cape in 1795. It was not, however, until the period of the second British occupation in 1806 that an official British strategy of Anglicisation was applied. English attained the status of commonly accepted language in the Cape Colony but indigenous languages and Afrikaans were demoted to inferior statuses. By 1882, Dutch and English (not Afrikaans) were recognised as the official languages of the Cape Parliament. At the conclusion of the first Boer war in 1902, when the British were victorious, Dutch lost its official status but was reinstated alongside English eight years later with the signing of the Act of the Union. Afrikaans speakers made vigorous challenges to reinstatement and in 1925 the Union Act was altered to include Afrikaans as an official language.

Breytenbach says, unequivocally, that Afrikaans is a Creole language. Conditions of its derivation are the same as that of other Creole languages such as the French used in the Caribbean or Indian ocean. He continues by asserting that the culture of tribal identity represented by historians and academics of the Afrikaaner establishment lives with the fiction that Afrikaans is the youngest member of the Germanic language families. This misrepresentation is necessitated by the need to heighten the dominance of European heritage whose implications of cultural-imperialist ascendancy have not been disowned.

The term, 'Afrikaans,' the Afrikaans word for "African," emerged mainly from the 17th century seafarers' Dutch and other dialects used in the lowlands. The birth of the language can, however, be located in the speech of imported slaves who did not speak European languages but needed to communicate in a *lingua franca* among themselves and to understand a Master. It is, thus, no accident that Afrikaans has been described as "kitchen Dutch," for a long time.

In its structural simplifications, it was influenced by language from Malays. Khoi-Khoi (people of the people) vocabulary also impacted its progress. Afrikaans Creole movement has been typified in sound and meaning shifts, repetition, and spread of diminutives. In a sociological context of Afrikaaner hegemony, the language bore the stigma of being identified with the policeman, the warder, the judge, and white politician. Afrikaans, language of the Boer, is the language of oppression and humiliation. It is the tool of the racist.

Racist tools were certainly in the possession of British imperial administrator, Chamberlain. Subsequent to his appointment (1895) ten years before the period of that infamous scramble for Africa, Chamberlain asserted his belief that the British race is the greatest governing race that the world has ever seen. Chamberlain was followed, soon after, by someone regarded as a classical scholar, humanitarian, and committed supporter of the League of Nations, Gilbert Murray. Commitment did not, however, prevent expression of views which conferred unquestioned racial superiority on Europeans.

> There is in the world a hierarchy of races...those nations which eat more, claim more, and get higher wages, will direct and rule others, and the lower work of the world will tend in the long-run to be done by the lower breeds of men. This much we of the ruling colour will no doubt accept as obvious. (Murray, 1900: 156)

Banton (1980) is quite clear that the central problem of racial thought, a problem which pervaded the 17th century, is not settled. Let me address myself to the matter of such thinking by starting with Linnaeus, the respected taxonomist. Linnaeus categorised homo-sapiens as: ferus (four-footed, mute, hairy), americanus (red, choleric, erect), europeanus (white, ruddy, muscular), asciaticus (yellow, melancholic, inflexible), afer (black, phlegmatic, indulgent, monstrous). West (1999) notes that when Linnaeus first acknowledged the hybridisation of species, he selected blacks and apes as probable exemplars.

Georges Cuvier divided homo sapiens into Caucasian, Mongolian, and Ethiopian. Each category was further divided in accordance with geographical, linguistic, and physical criteria. Cuvier had no room for Malays, Inuit, and American Indians. For Cuvier, the races were hierarchically divided. Whites were at the top; blacks were at the bottom. In addition, cultural and mental attributes were owed to differences in physique. Caucasians, who had made great progress in science, were supreme. Chinese, who were less advanced, had skulls shaped like those of animals. Although slavery was demeaning and Negroes were subjugated in it, they were immersed in pleasures of the senses. Cuvier's perversity is significant for the breadth of its influence. It is to this influence that I turn. Banton (1980) examines features of the impact as it was exemplified in Britain, France, and the USA. Here, views of Charles Hamilton Smith (Britain), Arthur de Gobineau (France), and Richard Colfax (USA) are recorded.

De Gobineau, dubbed the father of racist ideology, asserted that the great, noble and productive in humans emanated from Aryans who did not regard other races (with their evil hostility, their stark ugliness, and brutal intelligence) as equals. It was the Aryans who created the Hindu, Egyptian, Assyrian, Greek, Chinese, Roman, Teutonic, Mexican, and Peruvian civilisations. All civilisations, so claimed de Gobineau, emerged from the white race on whose existence others depended. No society could claim to be great and brilliant, if it did not preserve the blood of the noble group that created it.

Smith, the pioneer of racial typology, was a protege and colleague of Cuvier's. He designated three types: the Negro or wooly haired, the beardless Mongolian, and bearded Caucasian, the standard of supreme excellence. It was the Caucasian, sole creator of free and popular institutions, who had conquered powers of lightning, installed all the great religions, and was the rightful inheritor of what was glorious in revelation. Unlike him, the subordinate status of the Negro was derived from his small brain size. Negroes could make no contribution to the mixing of races which was vital to creation of civilisations. Whatever they received from the value of Nature's Bounty fitted them exclusively for slavery.

Colfax thrived in a context where American whites engaged blacks and aboriginals on unequal terms which were defined by white coercive and intellectual power. Banton theorises that in such a setting, the inferiorised are likely to be stereotyped. Such negativity can be enhanced through evaluative claims about external physical presence and heritability. Colfax, one evaluator, inferred that disadvantages associated with Negroes could not be modified. Although they were close to refined nations, they made no efforts to elevate themselves, beyond their doubtful status on the zoological hierarchy.

If white science exiled blacks from the realms of intellectual capability, blacks received no relief from leading thinkers within the Humanities where West (1999) regards them as constituting one segment of a major odoriferous bowel unleashed in the name of white supremacy. The impact of that launching, he adds, continues to pollute the air of post-modern times. West is addressing himself to what he regards as the structure of modern Western discourse made up of the controlling metaphors, notions, categories, and norms which shape predominant ideas of truth and knowledge in the modern Western world. All of these elements were determined and circumscribed by three principal historical processes: the classical revival, the scientific revolution, and the Cartesian transformation of philosophy. I shall focus on the classical revival.

West states that the modern West's recovery of classical antiquity produced a "normative gaze," a standard for ordering and comparing observations. The standard emanated largely from classical aesthetic values of beauty, proportion, human form, as well as, cultural standards of moderation, self control, and harmony. One of the strongest exponents of these values and standards was J.J. Wincklemann, who had never visited Greece and saw almost no original Greek art. He, however, regarded ancient Greece as a world of beautiful bodies. He saw Greek beauty and culture as the ideal measures against which other people's cultures should be gauged. In 1520 and 1591, Paracelsus and Bruno claimed that blacks had a separate origin from Europeans. Lucilio Vanini saw Ethiopian ancestry in apes and claimed that these Africans had once walked on all fours.

Among other servers of the stench released in the name of white supremacist scholarship, Montesquieu, Franklin, Jefferson, Hume, Voltaire, Kant, and Hegel stand prominently (West, 1999). One of Montesquieu's most infamous lines of logic was that whites should not even think about the possibility that blacks were people. Entertainment of this possibility would mean contemplating the position that whites were not Christians. Not only did Voltaire claim that blacks and aboriginals were distinct species from Europeans, he also exemplified the Black/European difference in highlighting the distinctions between Spaniels (Negroes) and Greyhounds (Europeans). Negroes were also incapable of using philosophy, and their intellectual capabilities were inferior to whites.

For Jefferson, Negro reasoning was inferior to that of whites, their imagination was dull, irregular, and without taste. Kant, who assessed Negroes as incapable of feeling beyond the trivial, claimed basic differences between the intellectual abilities of them and whites. Hegel saw Africa as devoid of history and proposed moral improvement of blacks, as a consequence of their enslavement. It is for Kant that Mills (1997) reserves some incisively critical remarks. Mills says the embarrassing fact for the white West is that Immanuel Kant, for whom complete personhood rested on race, the West's most important moral theorist for the past three centuries, is simultaneously, foundational in the modern period to divisions between persons and sub-persons upon which the Nazis drew. Thus, modern moral theory and modern racial theory emanate from the same source.

What is the explanation for this state of affairs? Kant's essay, "The Different Races of Mankind," is a classic pro-hereditarian, anti-environmentalist claim about the immutability and permanence of race. According to Mills, Kant's distinctions between black and white races were just as significant in regard to colour as they were in regard to mental ability. Hence, obvious proof that what Negroes said was stupid was that they were fully black, from head to foot. Not only did Kant hierarchise colour signifiers, for Europeans, Asians, Africans, and Native Americans, but he also correlated the gradations with differential degrees of innate talent (Mills, 1997). Europeans possessed all the requisite abilities to be morally self educating. There was hope for Asians, despite their inability to develop abstract concepts. Innately idle Africans could be educated as servants and slaves, via use of a split bamboo cane while the hopeless Native Americans could not be educated.

Kant was expressing heavy dependence on ideas of Hume who found no greatness in art or science among Negroes (free men and slaves). Members of neither category could match accomplishments of whites from the lowest plebeian ranks who use their advanced abilities to gain the world's respect. For his part, Hume restricted the status, civilised nation, to occupancy by whites who —alone—were ingenious manufacturers, artists, and scientists. In a reference to Jamaica, where he observed there was reference to a Negro person of learning, he scoffed at those who bestowed respect by saying that this person's intellectual abilities were minimal, parrot-like accomplishments from a plain user of words.

Mills (1998) does not spare John Locke whom Fisher (1949) assesses as the sober and humane Oxonian doctor who championed the theory that civil government is based on consent of the governed, the foundation of private property in labour, religious toleration, and rational education of the young. Mills says Locke is the pillar of constitutionalist liberal democracy, defender of natural equality, and opponent of patriarchalism to the West. This is the very Locke, he adds, who experienced no problems in reconciling his principles with investments in the Atlantic slave trade and assisting to write the Carolina slave constitution in the USA.

Fisher also designates him as the "oracle" of Whig philosophy. To me, his ideas on private property also make him an oracle of capitalism in the USA. Politically, this capitalism is, today, partially but significantly defined by neo liberalism of the Bush and other varieties. Economically, it is instantiated as aggressive moves, especially from U.S. corporate capitalists, to solidify *laissez-faire* on a global scale.

My references to racist thinking are clearly references to epistemological structures/strictures in a world of white supremacist logic whose purveyors had not equated non-whites with the status of persons. The intellectual grounding for such logic can be located in what Mills regards as the Racial Contract, bridging of two epistemological spaces which he says are separated. These spaces are the world of white mainstream philosophy engrossed with exchanges on justice and rights in the abstract and the world of African, Native American Third and Fourth world politically thinking centered upon questions of conquest, imperialism, colonialism, white settlement, race, and racism, slavery, reparations, as well as, apartheid. Issues of subordination are peripheral to mainstream philosophy.

They have, however, been central to political struggles of the majority of the world's populace. Their absence from what is considered serious philosophy is a reflection not of their lack of seriousness but of the colour of the vast majority of Western academic philosophers (and perhaps their lack of seriousness) (Mills, 1997).He points out that the general purpose of the Racial Contract, a contract among whites, is always to foster differential group privileges for them over non whites, the exploitation of non-white bodies, land and resources, as well as, denial of equal socioeconomic opportunities to them. Exploitation and denial contrast sharply with what Mills views as the colour coded morality of the Racial Contract which localises moral equality and natural freedom to white men. For instance, rights and freedoms boldly proclaimed in the American and French revolutions are not the same rights and freedoms enjoyed by non-Europeans.

I, therefore, note that when the rallying cries of the French Revolution, Fraternity, Liberty and Equality, were adopted by the black revolutionaries led by Toussaint L'Ouverture, in St. Domingue/Haiti, their European predecessors did not support them. Toussaint was, of course, tricked by Napoleon, the Corsican anti-semite, and eventually confined, until death, to a dungeon in France.

Mills observes that Benjamin Franklin, champion of the American War of Independence, worried about how the importation of slaves had blackened half of America. He wanted to know why the sons of Africa should be increased by locating them in America where excluding all blacks and tawneys augmented chances of adding to the lovely white race. He would not have received an appropriate response from some prominent persons who offered themselves as advocates of the anti-slavery movement. One such luminary was Samuel Stanhope Smith, a strident proponent of intermarriage, at the time of slavery, and leading opponent of hierarchic ranking of races. Smith, president of Princeton University, honorary member of the American Philosophical Society, stood at the pinnacle of American Academia in his time. He assumed that physical—particularly racial—variations were always degenerate from an ideal condition which was constituted by highly civilised white people. And it was intermarriage with whites which he proposed as guaranteeing fewer negroid features in future generations (West, 1999).

The Franklin position was clearly evidenced and embraced within colonial and post-colonial America. Bhattacharyya, Gabriel and Small (2002) state that a central feature under colonialism and slavery was the implementation of laws to prevent amalgamation and prosecute persons who practised it. Anti-miscegenation laws were also put in place, after the Civil War. Presidents did not condemn lynching and film producers did not screen scenes of intimacy across different racial groups. Academics in science and doctors of medicine claimed that race mixture constituted cultural and biological contamination of Europeans. One consequence of this undesirable state of affairs was a population of mixed heritage that was physically inferior and psychologically unstable. Paradoxically, however, the force with which whites had publicly expressed official aversion to miscegenation was much less intense than the strength with which it was accomplished, privately.

West and Mills are, doubtless, launching trenchant indictments against Western thinking of which Western philosophy constitutes a major locus. Mills (1997) observes that philosophy, "one of the whitest of the Humanities," has been conspicuously uninvolved with debates on multiculturalism, canon reform, and ethnic diversity. A standard undergraduate philosophy course, which covers more than two thousand years of Western political thought, will be initiated with reference to Plato, Aristotle, might deal with Augustine, Aquinas, Machiavelli, Hobbes, Locke, Mill, Marx, and end with Rawls and Nozik. Aspects of aristocracy, democracy, absolutism, liberalism, socialism, representative government, and welfare capitalism may feature in the first presentations, too.

Notably absent from the course, though, would be accounts of the basic political system which has shaped the world for the past several hundred years. That system, "the unnamed political system," which has made the world what it is, currently, is white supremacy. Mills offers compelling evidence of the shaping which he conceptualises as racial structure deemed unsuitable to Anglo-American political philosophy and adds that the lack of suitability portrays, at best, a disturbing provincialism and ahistoricity deeply inconsistent with the radically foundational inquiry of which philosophy is proud. At worst, it reveals complicity with the Racial Contract.

What is the evidence? It exists as European decision making accomplished in events such as: the Treaty of Tordesillas (1494), a division of the world between Spain and Portugal; the Vallodolid Conference (1500–1551) to determine whether Native Americans were human; debates over African slavery and abolitionism; the Berlin Conference (1884–1885) to partition Africa—all indicative of a world being governed by white people. Despite the evidence, absence is not one of chance.

> Rather, it reflects the fact that standard textbooks and courses have for the most part been written and designed by whites, who take their racial privilege so much for granted that they do not even see it as political, as a form of domination. (Mills, 1997: 1)

The Mills' position is quite transparent to Marcuse (1982), the distinguished German philosopher (critical theorist) notable for his Marxian Freudian synthesis. He accepts that philosophy, as it was generally being taught in colleges and universities, throughout the West, simply did not deal with such questions as racism. He also notes that he and fellow critical theorists could not comprehend any authentic philosophy which did not convey the human condition in concrete social and political settings, that exploded in the nineteen sixties and seventies as a frank contrast between the enormity of available social wealth and its miserable, destructive, wasteful applications.

Exclusion, according to Mills, is also featured in how space is depicted, in its domination by persons and sub-persons of different races. He is dealing with the racing of space, who or what people are, as a consequence of their derivation from certain types of loci which possess particular features, because of who or what inhabit them. Spaces occupied by Europeans were civilised spaces. Non-Europeans, on the other hand, who were savages, occupied spaces whose meaning was expressed in the etymology of the term, savage, a derivative of the Latin word, *silva* (wood). The savage is, therefore, the wild man of the wood, *silvaticus*, *homo sylvestris*, the man into whose wildness, wilderness has penetrated so intensely, that civilisation is not open to him.

The racing of space contains epistemological and moral aspects. A focus on the epistemological reveals that knowledge is confined to spaces occupied by European thinkers. Hence, knowledge of matters such as science is not possible among non Europeans.

Implications of this designifying are varied. Absence of cultural accomplishment means that Europeans, those who are capable of culture, are positioned to occupy spaces inhabited by non-Europeans. Since veridical apprehension was not associated with non-Europeans, court testimony was denied to persons such as slaves in America who were barred from giving evidence against their masters. In Australia, aborigines were forbidden to testify against white settlers.

> Significant cultural achievement, intellectual progress, is thus denied to those spaces [non-European] which are deemed (failing European intervention) to be permanently locked into cognitive states of superstition and ignorance. (Mills, 1997: 44)

Mills notes that when Joseph Conrad's Marlowe, in the *Heart of Darkness*, examines the Globe and concludes that numerous blank spaces exist, the blankness is reference to the inhabitants, themselves. Africa is, thus, designated the "Dark Continent," because so few Europeans have contact with it. In naming rituals, spaces occupied by Europeans are designated in acts of confiscation as "New England," "New Holland," and "New France."

If I draw from ideas of Kennedy (2002), I would have to conclude that naming rituals of a very different kind had very negative impact on the existence of blacks. Here are some of his examples from the United States. Landmarks on official maps carried names such as Nigger Lake, Niggerhead Hill, and Old Nigger Creek. These acts of naming, exclusively in the preserve of white males, had nothing to do with affection, but everything to do with insult and scorn of blacks. It was not until 1963 that the United States Secretary of the United States Interior insisted to the Board of Geographic names that references to Nigger be replaced by Negro.

I do know that in the British colony, British Guiana, and, also, independent Guyana, that numerous blacks used the term, Nigger Yard, to describe the inferior living conditions and the social accompaniments of other blacks whom they deemed to be of low socio-economic worth. To me, such use is clearly powerful evidence of internalisation.

The central theme in the foregoing exploration of European racism is white domination which existed in a variety of contexts. Those contexts do have a negative impact on the lives of non white persons who receive second language instruction within several urban locations of the contemporary Western world. I want to complete my analysis by addressing myself to the presence of racism in this contemporary world. This is a world Bhattacharyya, *et al.*, (2002) characterise as an expanse where racialisation is both adaptable and opportunistic. They add that while its applications have been modified to suit new settings, it is old myths that are produced, to satisfy the objective of creating new racialised significance.

One new setting which cannot be ignored is the setting of globalisation. They argue that the dominance of whiteness in globalisation has changed ideas of race and racism. In today's world, economies are racialised within production, distribution, as well as, consumption sectors, on an international scale. Whiteness is ascendant via the objectives of Western governments and agencies which create and respond to debt predicaments, manage food production, distribution, famine, and biotechnology. Racialisation is also evident in the impact multinationals exert on poorer regions. The dominance of whiteness resides in its capability to starve, murder, pollute, and impoverish.

Hill (2004) identifies what he deems five principal developments in contemporary global capitalism which I see as facilitating dominance of whiteness. They are: (1) sectoral and international spread of capitalism; (2) deepening of capitalist social relations with commodification of everyday life; (3) increasing employment of repressive economic, legal, military, state, and multistate mechanisms, globally and locally; (4) increasing use of ideological and state apparatuses within media and education systems; (5) increasing concentration of wealth and power in possession of capitalist classes.

The first encompasses privatisation, deregulation of controls on profit, and labour intensification. The second, aimed at reconstituting personhood, is implemented via the media and educational institutions. The third is attained locally via police action, imprisonment, surveillance, threats of, and actual job dismissals. Its main goal is to accomplish subordination to international capital and its state agents. The fourth is meant to advance capitalist social and economic links and justify punitive measures towards anti-capitalist actions and activists. The last is geared to enhancing hierarchical social relations via augmenting racialised and gendered class inequalities. It covers such strategies as stringent fiscal policy, reduced expenditure on welfare benefits, and unleashing market forces on pensions, healthcare, primary, secondary, and tertiary education.

It is not my intention to explore every facet of links between the new racialisation and international global capitalistic proliferation. I shall confine myself to cities, for they are directly involved in the lives of white and non-white persons who receive language instruction. Bhattacharyya, et al., (2002) apply the concept of global cities as one way of emphasising the destructive link noted above. They identify large urban settings such as London, New York, Los Angeles and Tokyo as intensely compressed areas for the forced reunion of rich and poor. These cities are homes to the head offices of transnationals, as well as, large scale financial and business organisations.

They serve as nuclei for massive movements of capital, which is interrelated. The presence of these business arrangements emerged from developments such as deregulation of markets, rapid changes to information and communication technologies, non-accountability to national governments, and the formation of institutions to facilitate enormous capital movement. One salient feature of this capitalist reorganisation is the emergence of a class of specialised and well paid professionals that coexist with groups of poorly paid service workers whose main role is to serve the varied needs of the new economic class.

There is, thus an obvious distinction between low income service employees, porters, cleaners, nannies, fast food and sex trade workers, on the one hand, and high income earners who conduct operations on behalf of the business and financial quarters. The racial feature of this distinction is quite profound. In Los Angeles, for instance, the death of the automobile and steel industries and destruction of traditional trade unions has had its worst impact on minorities. It is they who had to be content with non-unionised poorly paid employment in the service sector. These are the areas which have been largely open to new waves of Asian and Latin American immigrants. Thus, First and Third World exist side by side. The upshot of such juxtaposition is that marginalised groups are not included in the economic and financial largesse.

This coexistence, however, ceases when other physical faces of racialisation become visible. I wish to use the USA as an example, where the faces are revealed in what is the mundane manifestation of a racial divide, where West (1994) says 86% of white suburban Americans reside in locations which are fewer than 1% black. For him, significance of this phenomenon is that prospects for democracy rest principally on how cities fare in the hands of a suburban electorate. Thus, while interracial interdependence is inevitable, what he terms an enforced racial order signals the demise of the American nation to collective paranoia and hysteria, the unraveling of democracy. Trapped in this process are urban residents victimised by growing spiritual impoverishment, family and neighbourhood destruction, absence of love, the smothering of hope, all of which, are precursors to "social deracination and cultural denudement."

Like Winant (2004), I do not want to convey an impression that the USA is a society in which there is merely a rigid distinction between white and black. Today, Winant correctly identifies Asianness, Indianness, the revival of orientalism and, most dangerously in the aftermath of the World Trade Centre bombing, in 2001, the hideously significant resurgent Islamophobia, the ruse for which is war on terror. This is a war which President George W. Bush once described as the first war of the 21st century. One year after he had begun his battle, he sought to reassure corporate America—with its huge stake in globalisation and global cities—that he wanted the capitalist system to survive.

This is also the very President who could not see that he would fuel Islamophobia through his declaration that the war meant launching a crusade against terrorists. He did, of course, apologise for his use of the term, 'crusade.' He could hardly have learnt anything useful from his indiscretion, though. On the very day of the tragic London bombing, in July 2005, he validated the perversity of a sensibility about us and them when he condemned the bombing by speaking publicly about "our ideology" and "their ideology."

I know of, at least, two other notable figures who validated this very perversity, in the wake of the World Trade Centre bombing. In late September, 2001, staunch ally of President Bush's and ultra conservative, former Italian Prime Minister, Silvio Berlusconi, claimed that Western civilisation was superior to Islam. It is not accidental that the Berlusconi remark emanated from a society where some citizens were moved, in the nineteen nineties, to reject the appropriateness of a black woman of Somali heritage occupying the position of leading Italian beauty.

The Berlusconi pitch is a crass attempt to vitiate the validity of contributions to Western progress which depended on Islamic literary genius, humanistic tolerance, geographic insights, and scientific advancement, the last of which, set the stage for contemporary European medical practice. The Berlusconi rendition strongly echoes a position which emerged from an American conservative thinker in September, 2001. He is Robert Ledeen, who was at the time resident scholar, freedom chair, American Enterprise Institute, and consultant to the National Security Adviser and the Office of the Secretary of Defence. Mr. Ledeen was a participant in a television programme, "This is America." When asked by the moderator "Who is the enemy and why do they hate us so?" Ledeen stated:

> They hate us for what we are—not for what we do and what we are is
> something phenomenally successful. We are a Christian world which is
> phenomenally successful...we're so successful, we're so powerful and

they, who had a divine revelation, centuries ago, are living in misery.
They haven't produced a single thinker in centuries…they kick started
the renaissance and, since then, nothing, and they know that.

Prime Minister Berlusconi, Mr. Ledeen, and President Bush are very important figures who should all understand and appreciate the significance of inclusiveness.
Contrast their remarks with those of Ken Livingstone.

He is the London Mayor who clearly understands and appreciates the significance of inclusiveness. On the day of the London bombing, Mayor Livingstone
said publicly:

This was not a terrorist attack against the mighty and the powerful; it
is not aimed at presidents or prime ministers; it was aimed at ordinary
working class Londoners: Black and White, Muslim and Christians,
Hindu and Jew, young and old [an] indiscriminate attempt at slaughter
irrespective of any considerations of age, of class, religion, whatever.
That isn't an ideology. It isn't even a perverted faith, it's just an indiscriminate attempt at mass murder, and we know what the objective is:
they seek to divide London. They seek to turn Londoners against each
other and Londoners will not be divided by this cowardly attack.

I must note, with much more than passing interest, that Mayor Livingstone's talk
is indicative of the interactionally elegant and artfully impressive rhetorical devices, lists and contrasts. Atkinson (1984a and 1984b), as well as, Hutchby
(1997) analyse these devices whose use in the direct presence of large audiences
draws applause. Particularly noteworthy here is the Mayor's embedding of contrasts in lists which ends in the term, 'whatever.' The Mayor then uses contrast
which begins in "That isn't" and completes his remarks in a contrast, as well, "and
Londoners will not be divided by this cowardly attack."

Perversity in the indiscretion from the President, Mr. Ledeen, and Prime Minister Berlusconi has its roots in the rigidity of binary thinking that cannot be divorced from democratic racism. Here is a sense of this rigidity and its opposite:

Whenever we stand on the side of justice and love justice we refuse simplistic binaries. We refuse to allow either/or thinking to cloud our judgment. We embrace the logic of both/and. We acknowledge the limits of
what we know. (hooks, 2003: 10)

American feminist and media critic bell hooks (2003), captures the revulsive relevance of binary thinking and imagery to justice by addressing herself to racism in
televisual presentation. She states that in the wake of the tragic events of 11th

September, 2001, much television coverage focused on the New York Fire Department, well known for its notoriously racist employment practices. Several Americans, however, saw victims as primarily white, rather that persons from more than sixty countries of very different religions and colours. The cruelty in presentation relayed the binary us/them divide of Americans, chosen peoples opposed to the world of unchosen persons.

hooks adds that if the media had opted to concentrate upon the great diversity of victims who perished, there would have been no possibility of creating a "sentimental narrative" of us versus them. She is explicit in her assertion that although the tragedy was never uniquely American, it was distorted by the media to appear as specifically American. Consequently, numerous viewers who would not usually have been swayed, were, because of the manner in which a setting of rage and vulnerability was evoked in simplification where viewers saw a common enemy.

In their assessment of democratic racism, Henry, Tator, Mattis, and Rees, regard it as an ideology of inconsistent values which are made congruent. They argue that inconsistency exists as commitment to principles such as justice, equality, fairness, which conflicts with negative interpretations, and discriminatory treatment of minorities.

> The conflict between the ideology of democratic liberalism and the racist
> ideology present in the collective belief system of the dominant culture
> is reflected in the racist discourse that operates in the schools, the media,
> the courts, law enforcement agencies, arts organisations and cultural
> institutions, human services, government bureaucracies, and political
> authorities. The school, the university, the newspaper and the television
> station, the courtroom, police headquarters, the hospital, and the gov-
> ernment offices are discursive spaces. Within these spaces, controlled
> minimally by a dominant White culture, there exists a constant moral
> tension: the everyday experiences of people of colour, juxtaposed with
> the perceptions and responses of those who have the power to redefine
> that reality. (Henry, *et al.*, 2000: 24)

In support of their position on democratic racism, they list twelve versions of racist discourse which solidify attitudes and actions that are woven into value orientations of Western democracies.

The twelve discursive features of democratic racism are (1) the discourse of denial, (2) the discourse of colour blindness, (3) the discourse of equal opportunity

(4) the discourse of blaming the victim, (5) the discourse of white victimisation, (6) the discourse of reverse racism, (7) the discourse of binary polarisation, (8) the discourse of immigrants, balkanisation, and racism, (9) the discourse of moral panic, (10) the discourse of multiculturalism, (11) the discourse of liberal values, (12) the discourse of national identity (Henry, *et al.*, 2000: 384-385).

The discourse of binary polarisation is self evident. I want to explain denial, colour blindness, equal opportunity, and multiculturalism, for they serve to expose the duality with great clarity. The discourse of denial is offered as assumptions that racism is non-existent, although there is evidence of the inferiorising impact of prejudice and discrimination on persons of colour. Colour blindness is discursively presented as insistence that white people do not notice skin colours of racial minority people, while equal opportunity indicates that fairness is guaranteed via suppositions of treating persons equally. Multiculturalism discourse is offered as ideology which implies tolerance, cooperation, justice, reciprocation, mutuality, sensitivity, and diversity which are contradicted by the reality of white dominance..

What is the paradox of democratic discourse? Henry, *et al.*, note that the inconsistency is profoundly rooted in popular culture and discourse which I characterise as the taken-for-granted, seen but unnoticed, aspects within the world of everyday life. In offering my assessment, I am, of course, relying heavily upon phenomenological sociology in which consciousness in the everyday social reality of persons' social constructions is a seen but unnoticed resource.

> Democratic racism as racist discourse begins in the families that nurture us, the communities that socialise us, the schools and universities that educate us, the media that communicate ideas and images to us, and the popular culture that entertains us. (Henry, *et al.*, 2000: 24)

It is perpetuated in these very organisations, cultural territory managed by a white power structure where the daily experience of persons of colour is redefined by that structure. While Twine (2000) does not allude to democratic racism she does claim that there are efforts to conceal racism in discourse which she assesses as modes of speaking about race, definitions of racism, racial registers, and textual presentations. In referring to work done within "a race evasive culture" in New York, Kenny offers a position on the assumed merits of liberal democracy which is compatible with Henry, *et al.*,'s.

Kenny had returned to Long Island where she had done some ethnographic work that placed her firmly within the category of a potential "race traitor."

...if whiteness, or at least middle class whiteness, maintains its social hegemony through a kind of measured silence and anonymity, as numerous theorists of whiteness have suggested...an ethnographer of whiteness necessarily seeks to break this code and hence give the lie to white privilege. I had come to articulate that which normally cannot and should not be said... (Kenny, 2000: 113)

The flavour of Kenny's exposure is located in a view from Warren (2000). He claims that racism can become taboo for whites who have an emotional link to racial democracy and are defensive of the dominance of whiteness.

Warren conveys the denial by drawing approvingly from the work of Frankenberg (1993) who claims that North American whites distinguish between two sides of a discursive divide made up of the safe or pleasant and dangerous or nasty territories. Warren is reiterating the view that whites can and do, make explicit choices, demonstrate awareness of, and preference for, stances which bring them comfort exemplified by euphemism, incomplete description, and contradiction of self.

These are all features associated with avoidance of discomfort and avoidance of conflict. In the evasion, whites are separated from discomfort which they know is linked to their conveyance of inequality, power differentials, and dislike of fear. For Kenny, eluding conflict is an aspect of white discourse. Grillo and Wildman (2000) adopt a stance that is consistent with views about concealment of racism, defence of white dominance, and evasiveness in discourse about racism. They claim that racism/white supremacy is an illness which can be likened to cancer. Supremacy gives whiteness normative status from which whites are enabled to ignore race, except under circumstances where they think that someone else's race is intrusive of their existence. To victims of the ailment, race is a filter for exploring the world. On the other hand, whites, though they make up a race, do not view the world through such a filter. Whites associate persons of colour with obsession about race and experience difficulty in comprehending the emotional and analytical interest such persons grant to race. What is happening is a use of privilege which confers on whites a societal advantage different to any they gain from the reality of discriminatory racism.

I shall solidify the argument for democratic racism by dealing, once more, with the USA, Canada, and Great Britain, three societies where second language teaching is strongly established. I shall focus on the brutal killing by London policemen of a Brasilian immigrant in the aftermath of the horrible July, 2005 bombing in the city, strategic ploys by a Mayor of Toronto while apologising for racist remarks he had made about Mombassa, Kenya, and some analytical references to colourblindness in America as a society still operating with features of democratic racism. I begin with colour blindness in the USA.

Williams Krenshaw is scathing in her analysis of what she sees as gaps between the ideology of colourblindness and workings of racial power. She is questioning the adequacy of a view of reconstruction which does not grapple with the privileging of whiteness.

Colourblindness figures prominently within the liberal vision of race reform, a vision that framed the objectives of equality and the domains of racial power in narrow terms.

> Formal equality, constituted through the removal of racial barriers and animated by the normative objective of colourblindness, presented the objectives and practice of equality as one in which racial structures and racial identities have been "e-raced." (Willams Krenshaw, 1997: 103)

Colourblindness is not, however, the instrument for disrupting the historical profundity of injustice. She adds that colourblindness fails to identify race as an analytical issue and challenge instantiations of institutionalised racist dominance. Its major accomplishment is restricted to distancing itself from traditional signs of race and racism. This is distancing which is consistent with lack of implementation, at structural levels, of broad organisational changes geared to abolishing the superordination of whiteness.

Williams Krenshaw is issuing an indictment of a narrow conception of reform within a liberal paradigm. In this paradigm, chosen members of inferiorised groups receive what she terms the social capital of whiteness. Nevertheless, socioeconomic arrangements of values, ideas, and practices traditionally linked to white institutions are disproportionately weighed against the dominated. Transformation of whiteness signifies limited changes: in the USA, for instance, white schools change to schools, white firms change to become equal opportunity employers, and white society changes to just society.

The engine of equality is not driven and maintained by destroying formally white locales or basic rearranging of white social capital. Race equality in democratic USA signals that Afro-Americans "would have a shot—though not necessarily an equal shot—at getting some for themselves" (1997: 106). Despite the accessibility which eludes numerous American blacks, as a consequence of official abolition of inequality, a few are granted conditional permits to step beyond racial lines.

Nowhere was the logic more carefully orchestrated than in celebrity culture, where its ultimate expression was the very public e-racing of the few blacks who had "crossed over" with the standard blessing of "we don't think of them as black." (1997: 107)

Williams Krenshaw is pointing to the lack of a broad based appreciation of racial domination. Such appreciation is not guided, merely by an observation of racially-driven discrimination, its interpretive force is fuelled, also by traversing contours of cultural and organisational power imposed by dominant groups.

She adds that the mirror of post apartheid U.S. society should be faced as the foreground where subordination had become routinised and embedded. She is emphatic that the poverty plaguing advancement of the narrow sense of reform resides in its failure to re-evaluate the legitimacy of white domination within the American institutional fabric.

I turn to an actual example of discourse from a Mayor of Toronto, Mel Lastman, whose language is laced with the discourse of colourblindness and multiculturalism. His talk reflected clear persistence in structures of racism embedded within the very institutions such as schools, families, and the media from which the Mayor's primary and secondary socialisation emanates. Let me make my case for his discourse.

I have already shown (Walcott, 2003) that the Mayor was (ostensibly) one of the staunchest advocates of multiculturalism. Just prior to leaving for Mombassa, Kenya, to promote the Toronto bid for the 2008 Summer Olympic Games, he, however, spoke disparagingly to a national newspaper reporter about the Kenyan seaport location:

Why the hell do I want to go to a place like Mombassa…Snakes just scare the hell out of me. I'm sort of scared about going there, but the wife is really nervous. I just see myself in a pot of boiling water with all these natives dancing around me.

His utterances about Kenya were indicative of an ideology that supports contradictory values. He publicly proclaimed commitment to principles of democracy defined by equality, fairness, and justice. At the same time, he provided very negative assessment of people of colour. The inconsistency was merely part of a larger pattern of his failure to support initiatives and policies geared to improving conditions of oppressed persons. As Toronto Mayor, he never accepted any claims that systemic or institutional racism existed in the city.

He followed his Mombassa remarks with a public apology which appeared in the Canadian newspaper, the *Globe and Mail*. A cursory examination of the entire transcript reveals that the Mayor did apologise, profusely. He noted indiscretion, lack of appropriateness, and incorrectness. What he obviously did not do was either to accept that his remarks about Mombassa and natives were racist, or that in making those remarks he was racist. He was, in fact, very skillful in eluding efforts to get him to accept racism.

It is, thus, his skill that I wish to explore by showing: interviewer failure to manage topicality, the Mayor's control of the conversational agenda in his own management of topicality that took the form of repetitive apologising, the Mayor's interactive skill of evading the interviewers' interests in dealing with matters of race and the Olympic games. These are features which can be revealed by exploring power plays in the unfolding conversation.

The Transcript: Q represents a question and A a reply

1Q: Interviewer: Mayor, do you think your comments hurt Toronto's Olympic bid?

2A: *Lastman:* I am truly sorry, and I am going to say it again, I'm sorry that my comments were inappropriate. And I want to apologise to everyone for my remarks, particularly anyone who was offended by them.

3Q: *Interviewer:* Is sorry enough? Should you resign at this point?

4A: *Lastman:* I'm sorry I made the remarks

5Q: *Interviewer:* But is sorry enough?

6A: *Lastman:* I'm sorry I made the remarks

7Q: *Interviewer:* What damage do you think you did to the Olympic bid?

8A: *Lastman:* I'm sorry I made the remarks. My comments were inappropriate

9Q: *Interviewer:* That's not what I asked

10A: *Lastman:* That's my answer

11Q: *Interviewer:* How much damage have you done to a multicultural city as the Mayor?

12A: *Lastman:* I'm truly sorry

13Q: *Interviewer:* Are you considering resigning?

14A: *Lastman:* I am truly sorry that I made those remarks

15Q: *Interviewer:* Are you considering resigning as a result of making those remarks?

16A: *Lastman:* I am truly sorry I made those remarks

17Q: *Interviewer:* Are you considering resigning?

18A: *Lastman:* I am truly sorry

19Q: *Interviewer:* What else can you add in terms of damage control? Bob Richardson [Chief Operating Officer of the Toronto Bid Committee] said they are getting calls from around the world. What are you guys doing around damage control, about trying to correct?

20A: *Lastman:* I'm truly sorry I made the remarks. My comments were inappropriate

21Q: *Interviewer:* Are you going to continue to go to Europe and lobby for the bid and stuff within your schedule as planned?

22A: *Lastman:* I am very sorry about the remarks

23Q: *Interviewer:* Are you very sorry about the remarks you made? [laughter]

24A: *Jim Warren:* [Mr. Lastman's press spokesman] It's not funny.

25Q: *Interviewer:* In all due respect, there are people in the city who are from Kenya. There are people of African descent in the city. Just to be sorry does not explain why you did this. Why did you make this comment?

26A: *Lastman:* I am sorry I made the remarks and my comments were completely inappropriate. And I want to apologise to anybody who was offended by them

27Q: *Interviewer:* Mayor Lastman, did you have a head slapping moment when you thought you shouldn't have said that?

28A: *Lastman:* It was the wrong thing to say and I'm sorry I made them. I mean what do you want from me, except I'm sorry? I've apologised. I did the wrong thing

29Q: *Interviewer:* Did you goof? You made a mistake

30A: *Lastman:* Of course, I did. That's why I'm apologising

31Q: *Interviewer:* I think what a multicultural city like Toronto wants to know is why you made it, in the first place?

32A: *Lastman:* I'm sorry I made the remarks. Mr. Warren. Thanks

33Q: *Interviewer:* What can you do to make amends, do you think?

34A: *Lastman:* I'm sorry I made the remarks. Mr. Warren. Thanks guys

35Q: *Interviewer:* Mr. Mayor, do you think your comments were racist and are you a racist?

36A: *Lastman:* I'm sorry I made the remarks. And I am again sorry that my comments were inappropriate and I again apologise for anyone that was offended by my comments. Mr. Warren. Thank you very much.

I start my examination by looking at interviewer formulations and their failure. Formulations occur at five turns, 3, 5, 9, 19, 25, where interviewer utterances are placed: [Is sorry enough? Should you resign at this point?] [But is sorry enough?]

[That's not what I asked.] [What else can you add in terms of damage control?] [Just to be sorry does not explain this.] None of these utterances produced their intended result.

Mayor Lastman was not merely issuing a series of apparently scripted denials, he was also interpreting the intentions and conventions in his co-conversants' turns. This is no trivial accomplishment. Far more significantly, he did demonstrate, at crucial points in the exchange, that he was no passive respondent. He was actively involved in taking control. There are three junctures at which he did so.

7Q: *Interviewer:* What damage do you think you did to the Olympic bid?
8A: *Lastman:* I'm sorry I made the remarks. My comments were inappropriate.
9Q: *Interviewer:* That's not what I asked.
10A: *Lastman:* That's my answer.

My particular focus is on the exchange at turns 9 and 10. The interviewer formulation at 9, a challenge, is clearly followed by assertiveness or striking back from the Mayor. Thornborrow (2002) offers an account of striking back very similar to the one above. She refers to an exchange involving one of Britain's toughest and most respected interviewers, Sir Robin Day, and Prime Minister, Margaret Thatcher.

Thornborow quotes a report in the British daily, *The Independent* (8th August, 2000): "Once asked if she intended to sack certain ministers, she replied: 'You are going further than I wish to go.' Sir Robin countered that it was part of his job to push her but the Prime Minister retorted: 'Yes indeed. It's part of my job to stop you.' " Striking back from the Mayor can be seen in a two turn exchange at 29 and 30.

29Q: *Interviewer:* Did you goof?
30A: *Lastman:* Of course, I did. That's why I'm apologising.

In the sequence below, the Mayor attempts to close the conversation.

31Q: *Interviewer:* I think what a multicultural city like Toronto wants to know is why you made it in the first place?
32A: *Lastman:* I'm sorry I made the remarks. Mr. Warren. Thanks.
33Q: *Interviewer:* What can you do to make amends, do you think?
34A: *Lastman:* I'm sorry I made the remarks. Mr. Warren. Thanks guys.

My point about attempted closure is that prior to turn 36, the Mayor says thanks with the explicit aim of ending the talk. In a much broader sense, Mayor Lastman's victory in this battle is a very strong instance of the systematicity in conversation. Interviewers, within numerous settings are the co-conversants who usually initiate discourse. They do everything they can to determine the progress and outcome of the discourse they initiate. One of the ploys they use (and what was certainly applied in regard to the Mayor) is a technique which is integral to the production of what Sacks and Schegloff (1975) assess as adjacency pair production. Adjacency pairs are two utterances long, positioned adjacently, and produced by different speakers. Thus, greetings followed by return greetings and questions followed by answers are adjacency pairs. These are instances of use which exhibit obligatory relationship that all interviewers seek to attain.

This obligatory relationship, is captured, very well, in the observation:

> Adjacency pairs are located as contiguous utterances that stand to one another in a relationship describable by reference to their respective types, i.e., in that the occurrence of an instance of a first utterance type (e.g., question) provides for the expectable occurrence of its responsive-type (e.g., answer). The production of a recognisable utterance-type by one speaker, then, provides the conditions under which the first utterance produced by a next speaker will be attended to not merely as possibly an instance of an utterance type, but expectably an instance of the utterance-type (or one of the alternative utterance types) made relevant by the first utterance type. Thus a pair of adjacent utterances are analysable as instances of two utterance-type classes, where these two instances constitute a pair of actions as Question-Answer, Invitation-Acceptance/Rejection, Greeting-Greeting, etc. (Turner, 1976: 237)

From my standpoint, what governs the obligatory relationship that interviewers seek to attain is a device I describe as forms of speech whose use sets constraints on how hearers should speak and are not intended to allow them the freedom to construct their own meaning. I call them type 1 forms of speech. Questions clearly are of this type.

On the other hand, there are forms of speech whose use does not set constraints on how hearers should speak and are intended to allow them the freedom to construct their own meaning. I call these type 2 forms. Questioners' repetitions (partially or wholly) of replies given to prior questions are type 2 examples (Walcott, 1991). When Mayor Lastman's replies to questions (type 1) are examined, it is obvious that his co-conversant questioner is not given the replies desired. Instead of following the undesirable answers with a mixture of type 1 and type 2 forms, the interviewer opts for a series of further type 1 replies which, of course, do not sway the Mayor.

What is interesting conversationally is that interviewers are not constrained to follow replies to questions solely with type 1 forms. They have the advantage of choosing to use type 2 versions, immediately after replies to questions are offered. Turner observes that once adjacency pair production is complete, the production of the second part of a pair serves to return the floor to the producer of the first part. Importantly, though, the floor is returned, no next action in selected. It is precisely because no next action is selected, upon return of the floor to the questioner/interviewer, that I find it equally relevant to state the questioner/interviewer has the advantage of choosing to elicit other utterances from the respondent. In the case of the Mayor, the advantage was used but, crucially, I think was not successful, on account of choice to use only type 1 forms of speech, rather than a judicious mixture of type 1 and type 2 forms. Thus, via the route of conversational display cleverly accomplished, Mayor Lastman (albeit perversely) demonstrated democratic racism.

One of the most tragic consequences of democratic racism emerged in the aftermath of a second July bombing in London where a young Brasilian immigrant electrician, Jean Charles Menezes, was brutally shot by British undercover police, presumably because his physical appearance did not fit the profile of white-skinned Europeans. Mr. Menezes had come to London, a European hub of globalisation, to escape the poverty of his home state, Minhas Gerais. He was a law-abiding resident of a global city, officially adverstised for its fairness, diversity, justice, and tolerance. He was an ESL student in the British city. Yet, several people like him who come from underdeveloped societies, constitute the multicultural mix of London and other European global cities such as Paris, Frankfurt, and Berlin, but belong to the European underclass, have been all to familiar with the ugliness of unfairness, isolation, injustice, and intolerance.

In the autumn of 2005, some youthful members of this very underclass whose sociocultural roots are traceable to North Africa, took to the Paris streets, quite violently, in their words, to protest decades of exclusion, and marginalisation in the racism which defines the promotion of white superiority in France. Their anger was exacerbated by a remark from the Gaullist Interior Minister of the conservative Chirac government. He dubbed the youth scum. Thousands of miles on the other side of the Atlantic, Afro-Canadian youth in an ostensibly multicultural society, Canada, were telling ex-Prime Minister Paul Martin, the fiscally conservative leader of a liberal government that the apparently inexplicable spate of deadly gun violence since summer of 2005 which had been gripping marginalised areas of Toronto largely occupied by descendants of non- white immigrants was clearly owed to exclusion.

European global cities, and certainly their North American counterparts, exist in contexts of what Lasch and Urry (1987) view as disorganised capitalism exemplified by racialised globalisation: roles of transnationals as stateless corporate entities, the continual dependence of more than half the world's national economies on export of one or two raw materials, accumulation of wealth in just over a dozen nations and over two hundred transnationals, movement of manufacturing from the developed West to recently industrialised economies, demise of smoke stack industries, downsizing in place of mass production. Bhattacharyya, *et al.*, indicate that in conditions of mass production, migrant workers were attracted to highly industrialised operations associated with processing iron and steel, production of machinery and tools, construction, shipbuilding, automobiles, and garments.

Down fall of these operations and progress of high technology ventures in regions such as Silicon Valley (USA) and stretches along British motorways like the M4, noteworthy for their research and development emphasis on computer technology, have had deep-rooted effects on non–white labour. This is so, particularly in Britain among refugee groups whose members settle within inner city areas.

> In contrast, the demand for labour in the high-technology industries was met by a predominantly indigenous white workforce and, particularly in the U.S., by a cadre of highly skilled professionals primarily from South East Asia. Older immigrants and those of older immigrant origin were thus further marginalised in the workforce as industries moved out of the inner cities and located overseas or in the case of new information/communications industries in the new suburbs.
> (Bhattacharyya, *et al.*, 2002: 31)

Kundnani (1999) also identifies the increasing importance of possession of intellectual property and information, within the global setting. The Third World own one percent of world patents, a condition which conceals the scope with which Western corporations claim, via biopiracy, traditional Third World knowledge of medicines and agricultural products, then patent and sell the products as if the knowledge appropriated emerged from the West.

I would be negligent if my indictment of globalisation and global cities was not linked to an assessment of dramaturgical stress and its dangers for target language learners within those locations. Let me begin by stating that many nannies, porters, fast food workers, and cleaners who span the colour lines of diversity in global cities are second language learners who must live with dramaturgical stress, a powerful feature of their subordinate statuses. What is dramaturgical stress?

It is stress associated with persons self presentation and the dramaturgical strategies they use for monitoring the actions of others (Freund, 1998). It emerges as a consequence of managing impressions persons make on others, especially through working to maintain appearances which are incompatible with deep rooted feelings (Freund, 2003). Freund is drawing very heavily on Goffman's work of impression management and Hochschild's on emotion work. When the two are connected and applied to the colour lines, they point to emotional and physiological damage to subordinated language learners. Importantly, the root of such damage is gross inequality of social relations.

A proper apprehension of damage comes from examining the meaning of impression management, emotion and emotion work. According to Goffman (1959), who regards social life as theatre, persons act as if on stage by expressing themselves to leave impressions on others. They perform impression management. Hochschild (2003) defines emotion as bodily cooperation with an image, thought or memory. This is cooperation of which individuals are usually cognisant. Emotion work refers to management of persons' emotions and those of others. For Hochschild, stress arises in efforts to manage estrangement between self and feeling and between self and action displayed. The point to be grasped about estrangement is it exemplifies externality or separation from self (1983).

It is separation which provides an important clue to dramaturgical stress. Language learners in the persons of global city subordinate wage earners cannot be regarded as individuals who are in control of their own impression management while making a living. They cannot be seen as owners of the products and services associated with their occupations. They have to use impression management which their employers impose on them. As such, they would have to suppress authentic feelings of resentment, anger, fear, or frustration.

I am pointing to disjunctures between the authenticity of deeply harboured emotional discomfort and the inauthenticity of external comfort. According to Griffith and Griffith (1994), Engebretson and Stoney (1995), and Lynch (1995), these are not disjunctures which just damage emotional health, they also harm physical health. Freund (1990) categorises them as emotional false consciousness, a state in which there are splits between body equilibrium and ability to interpret embodied feelings. The danger here is separation between cognisance of inner psychosomatic sensation, and bodily expressions, and enhanced physiological reaction to distress.

Ideas about dramaturgical stress resonate with communicative language teaching in other ways. More than twenty-five years ago, Schumann (1975) was remarkably insightful in claiming that if language learners are socially, economically, politically, culturally, and technologically subordinate to members of target language communities, learning would be impeded. My observation today is not only does subordination exist within the contemporary world of global cities where Poles, Russians, Czechs, Slovaks, Hungarians, Kenyans, Sri Lankans, Algerians, Turks, Indians, Senegalese, Peruvians, Colombians, Brasilians, and Mexicans learn second languages, several learners in subordination must also contend with dramaturgical stress.

Worse still, some of them must endure stress at another level. In Toronto, Los Angeles, London, New York, Berlin, Paris, Chicago, Frankfurt, global cities in their new societies, they must live with status reduction which is linked to low waging earning capacity. They discover that their high level academic and professional attainments as doctors, mathematicians, engineers, architects, and university teachers are not recognised. It is with discovery that they begin to endure stress. Condemned to ply such peripheral routes as those of taxi driver, security guard, porter, cleaner, waitress, or nanny, they bear the burdens of dramaturgical stress. I also did not lose sight of the superficially light-hearted, but profoundly serious, public commentary in the autumn of 2005 from a Minister of Health at the provincial level in Canada. He said that if someone in a Canadian city were to have a heart attack, a taxi would be a very appropriate place; it is highly likely that the chauffeur would be a foreign-trained doctor.

Capitalist Roots And Cultural Imperialism

The groundwork for inequality, as well as, exclusion in global cities had been laid by advanced capitalism which took some of its strongest and most destructive roots in the 1970s and eighties, periods when communicative language teaching was being actively promoted, theoretically, and pedagogically within classrooms. I want to examine these capitalist developments as one way of highlighting the oppressiveness of a context in which second language users existed. I shall also show that an important feature of the oppression is cultural and linguistic imperialism which are rooted in racism. Once I have completed these tasks, I shall address myself to pedagogical reasons for employing a Freireian approach to second language education.

Advanced capitalism is indicative of a rise in national and transnational corporations, as well as, the organisation of markets for commodities, capital, and labour. Advanced capitalism also represents state intervention in markets, as functional gaps emerge (Habermas, 1975). Three significant features of advanced capitalism are its economic, administrative, and legitimation systems. Within the economic sphere, private production is partially market-oriented to competition and partly determined by the market strategies of oligopolies that tolerate a competitive fringe. Market considerations, however, are not significant to the public sector where industries such as armaments and space travel operate on the basis of huge investment decisions. Further, within the public sector, capital intensive industries are pre-eminent while labour intensive industries are the leaders, within the competitive sector.

From an administrative standpoint, the state is actively involved in global planning, by means of which, it regulates economic cycles, and alters conditions for using surplus accumulated capital. The task of alteration is not to be seen as mere facilitation. It is one of replacing market mechanisms through a variety of means: solidifying the competitive ability of the nation by instituting and sustaining supranational economic locations, as well as, securing international stratification via imperialist practices; fostering unproductive government consumption in the form of space exploration and arms production; improving the material infrastructure in the forms of transportation, education, health, urban, and regional planning, as well as, housing construction; developing the immaterial infrastructure via routes such as advancing science, investing in research, and providing patents; enhancing labour productivity in arrangements such as retraining schemes and vocational education; reducing the material derived from private production in the form of employment compensation, welfare, and repairing environmental destruction.

When market mechanisms become weak and state manipulation of capital formation appears as dysfunctional, official assumptions of fair exchange under capitalism break down, economic arrangements become recoupled with political arrangements, politicisation of relations of production intensifies, and an increased need for legitimation emerges.

Habermas wrote long before globalisation became a reality. His work was, however, remarkably prescient, in its foreshadowing the legitimation imperatives now pervading economic formations evident in the globalisation strategies of the Asia-Pacific and North American Free Trade Regions under the World Trade Organisation and Group of Eight, The International Monetary Fund, and The World Bank.

Habermas even took the emphatic position that advanced capitalist societies were in danger of at least four crisis tendencies: the economic system fails to produce the requisite quantity of consumer valuables; the administrative system does not implement the requisite quantity of rational decisions; the legitimation system does not offer the requisite quantity of generalised motivations; the sociocultural system does not generate the requisite quantity of action-motivating meaning (Habermas, 1975).

Despite the existence of these crisis tendencies, cultural imperialism has been vibrant. What is cultural imperialism? Bhattacharyya, *et al.*, (2002) see cultural imperialism as the imposition of dominant Western cultural values and products on the rest of the world. They note that as a concept, cultural imperialism, McDonaldisation of the world, encompasses the dominance of Western cultures, particularly U.S. culture, its harmful consequences on local cultures, its advancement of capitalist consumerist values, and its contribution to ways in which global culture revolves around the primacy of U.S. norms, rather than the advancement of respect for diversity.

Reference to the USA is, by no means, out of place. In remarkably prescient analyses, Chomsky (1967) addresses himself to the creation of a new worldwide superculture powerfully influenced by American life made up of its own universal electronic computer language accompanied by a massive psycho cultural divide between America and the developing world. The leading lights of the superculture, a class of politicians-intellectuals, illuminate America as the creative society which others emulate consciously and unconsciously. Chomsky identifies a proponent of the idea of the superculture as none other than Zbigniew Brzezinski, National Security Adviser in the Carter administration.

For Chomsky, the driving force behind views espoused by the Security Adviser is represented by a convergence of three factors—access to power, shared ideology, and professionalisation which subvert scholarship and threaten wider society. Subversion and threat constitute a particularly significant danger within a society which promotes specialisation and worships technical expertise. In such situations, so claims Chomsky, chances for the abuse of knowledge and technique are increased.

Chomsky is not merely correct about the creation of American superculture, American superculture is also being boldly proclaimed by leading politicians of the USA, and ex-colonial powers, as Western superculture which will bring salvation via the route of free market capitalism, to the impoverished non-White developing world. It was thus no surprise to me, when I heard the comments of Mr. Donald Evans, Commerce Secretary to President Bush in August, 2002. Secretary Evans was a major participant in "The President's Forum," an event in Waco, Texas, where leading American economic and financial minds gathered against a deeply troubling foreground of corporate irresponsibility. In a forceful reaffirmation of corporate capitalism, the Secretary saw the U.S. economy as "fundamentally strong." Very importantly, he characterised capitalism as a system which is the hope for the world, a planet of more than six billion, the vast majority of whom earn lower than $2.00 daily.

The dominant and preferred linguistic routes for spreading the proclamation of superculture are European languages. Among the recipients of the Western message are low paid service workers in large urban sectors of the Western world (Battacharyya, *et al.*, 2002). Their occupancy of these positions is organised around principles of efficiency, control, predictability, calculability, and economy. More importantly, several of these workers, non-white and white, I must point out, are second language learners.

The foregoing positions about superculture/cultural imperialism are consistent with that adopted by Galtung (1980) who sees cultural imperialism as a relationship in which some societies dominate others. Domination is forged, principally, by devices such as penetration, fragmentation, marginalisation, and exploitation. The last involves asymmetric interaction between groups exchanging commodities on terms of disparity. The exchange is facilitated by existence of a dominant Centre, typically made up of Western capitalist societies, and dominated Peripheries, usually underdeveloped countries. Connections between power at the Centre and Perpheries are exemplified by shared interests in language. These shared interests in language exemplify what Phillipson (1992) regards as linguistic imperialism.

For Phillipson, linguistic imperialism is powerfully present in its English form. He says the dominance of English imperialism is asserted and maintained by establishment and continuous reconstitution of structural inequalities between English and other languages. The term, structural, accounts for material possessions such as organisations and monetary provisions. The cultural represents ideological features such as attitudes and teaching principles. English imperialism is also indicative of lingiuicism which entails the presence of ideologies, structures, and methodologies applied for the purpose of validating the perpetuation of unequal division of power and resources among groups defined on the basis of language. In addition, disparity guarantees the provision of greater resources to English than other languages and is advantageous to groups that are proficient in this language.

Linguistic imperialism is strongly condemned by Ansre (1979) who defines it as a state in which the experiences of users of a language are oppressed by another language, to the extent that they internalise the view that only the dominant language should be employed for dealing with advanced versions of life such as education, philosophy, literature, and the administration of justice. Linguistic imperialism alters, in subtle fashion, the expectations and attitudes of persons who are impeded from appreciating and actualising the full potential of indigenous languages.

Ansre speaks unapologetically about the unsavoury nature of linguistic subordination. So does Ngugi wa Thiong' o (2003) who notes that what he calls "Black languages," known variously as Ebonics, African-American Language, Patwa, Creole, Kreyol, Haitian, Nation Languages, all of which, are rooted in the syntax and rhythm of speech of continental African languages, have not survived without the pain in schism. He is referring to division between the masses of black people who use them to express their everyday needs and world views and an educated black elite whose members separate themselves from the languages to express their progress in the modern world. Black languages, he contends, have been weakened as routes for knowledge in the arts, sciences, and technology. This is a situation he assesses as one of forming societies and nations of bodiless heads and headless bodies, features all structures of domination hope to generate among the dominated.

Ngugi wa Thiong' o, a Kenyan, was reiterating part of a distaste he had conveyed in (1986) when he also addressed himself to the impact of the "cultural bomb" of British imperialism. He noted that it barred learning in the oral tradition of Gikuyu and promoted to Kenyans alien versions of their society through the eyes of English notables such as John Buchan and Rider Haggard. The bomb had destroyed belief in their names, languages, environment, heritage of struggle, unity, ability, and finally, themselves. Their past had been transformed into a wasteland of no accomplishments from which they were inclined to distance themselves.

Ngugi wa Thiong' o's position is consistent with that expressed by Roy-Campell (2003) who notes that the colonial imposition of European languages such as Portugese, French, and English as valued modes of communication and knowing in Africa has led to their "naturalisation" as essential aspects of being educated in numerous African societies. Thus, knowledgeable and superior persons are Portugese, French or English, users of languages of power, while the knowledge of non-users who communicate in indigenous forms is denigrated for they do not produce languages of power.

In showing how language was used as a strong foundation of cultural imperialism, Rodney (1973) identifies the views of Eugenne Etienne, a Minister of the French Government at the beginning of the colonial era. Minister Etienne asserted that the French language in colonies was required as a form of national defence. In 1884, so notes Rodney, the French Government recognised and aided the Alliance Française as a tool of educational and cultural imperialism. Rodney is explicit in his view that Alliance Française documents indicate the organisation saw itself as an arm of French imperialism striving for entrenchment in Africa. In the late 19th century, for instance, Alliance Française wrote about Upper Guinea schools:

> They have to combat the redoubtable influence of the English schools of
> Sierra Leone in this region. The struggle between the two languages becomes more intense as one moves to the south, invaded by English natives and their Methodist pastors.

Rodney also notes that French colonialists viewed Africans who attained a French education as having the opportunity of becoming incorporated or assimilated into superior French culture.

The Belgians and Portugese operated in similar fashion. It was the Belgians who assessed educated Bantus in the Congo as those who had evolved from savagery to civilisation. Portugese colonials made rigid distinctions between natives and *assimilados*, the assimilated, or *civilisados* or the civilised, the last two of whom were regarded as capable of reading and writing Portugese. For Rodney colonial schooling in Africa meant education for subordination, exploitation, the creation of mental confusion, as well as, underdevelopment. Education of Africans was not geared to develop their pride and confidence in their own societies. It was aimed at establishing African deference to everything European.

Other analysts, notably Calvet (1987), have conceptualised linguistic imperialism as linguistic racism. I am fully persuaded by the claim of linguistic racism, for its ugly presence was quite transparent in the latter half of the 20th century within the USA and Britain. Let me begin with Britain, where I lived during the nineteen sixties and seventies, a period when reggae music was making its presence felt there. I know that one-well known disc jockey, at the time, Tony Blackburn of the BBC, was openly averse to reggae music. It was also on the BBC airwaves (World Service) that I heard an interview in which Tom Paulin, editor of the *Faber Book Of Political Verse*, featured. At the time, spring 1986, he was speaking to Christopher Hope, host of the arts programme, "Meridian," about howls of protest from self appointed guardians of the purity of upper class English who could not understand why he had published a poem of "Jamaican patois" in so prestigious and sophisticated a volume.

Here is the relevant excerpt from that exchange:

Christopher Hope: You have remained true to your stated intention in your introduction to that anthology and that is to be polemical. I mean it is a deliberately partisan or personal selection.

Tom Paulin: Well. It is in a certain sense in that what I am trying to do is to relandscape English literary history singlehanded. So, I say that the book is not just an idiosyncratic book—which all personal anthologies are but an attempt to put history back into the reading of poetry. And that necessarily involves a lot of shifting about of foregrounds in certain authors who have been forgotten about—foregrounding certain types of language which have been forgotten about. I think it is extremely significant, that the various Tory critics have looked at it, have squealed when they saw that I had a black poet right near the end. That is Linton Kwesi Johnson—and complained about him writing in what they call Caribbean patois, a very dismissive term used by one critic. They just can't bear the idea of these other forms of the English language muscling in on the great Anglican tradition which they believe in.

Linton Kwesi Johnson, a dub poet, is someone who sets Creole to the beat of reggae music, for the purpose of exposing injustice. Johnson's poem, "Di Great Insohrechshan" was written to deal with the Brixton riots in which antagonism between black Britons and a white police force was clearly evident. Here are three verses from his 1986 work.

it woz in April nineteen eighty-wan
doun inna di ghetto af Brixtan
dat di babylan dem cause such a frickshan
an it bring about a great insohreckshan

an it spread all ovah di naeshan
it woz a truly an histarical okayjan

it woz event af di year
an I wish I ad been dere
wen wi run riot all ovah Brixtan
wen wi mash-up plenty police van
wen wi mash-up di wicked wan plan
wen wi mash-up di Swamp Eighty-wan
fi wa?
Fi mek di rulah dem andahstan
dat wi naw tek noh more a dem oppreshan

an wen mi check out
di ghetto grapevine
fi fine out all I coulda fine
every rebel jussa revel in dem story
dem a taak bout di powah an di glory
dem a taak bout di burnin an di lootin
dem a taak bout smashin an di grabbin
dem a tell mi bout di vanquish an di victri

Paulin (1986) locates Johnson's work within the popular tradition of political verse. It is Paulin's view that Johnson work, which demands social justice, is imbued with profound "libertarian instincts." Reading such work is akin to locating a concealed, living tap root which nurtures a vibrancy in eloquence, permanently. In March, 2002, I heard Julian Keane, BBC World Service presenter of the programme, "The World Today," tell a representative of Penguin Books that readers would "get a fit" upon reading Johnson's dub poetry in one of Penguin's latest publications.

I turn to the Caribbean and USA where linguistic racism has been applied to denude blacks of their African linguistic expressiveness in settings where the monoculture of English unilingualism is well entrenched. I point initially to the Ebonics controversy, how white America rejected Afro-American proposals to reclaim an important aspect of their heritage and scoffed at the scholarship behind the proposals.

Let me state, from the outset, that current use of English language by several Afro-Americans is the consequence of one feature of oppression, brutalisation of their ancestry in slavery. This did, of course, mean that use of African languages was destroyed by the imperialists. Such is an indubitable reality powerfully offered in another region of inferiorisation, the Caribbean, by Brathwaite. He notes that English in the Caribbean, not unlike French, Dutch, and Spanish, is an imposed language. In dealing with historical background to imposition, he points out that the arrival of Columbus signalled the intrusion of European cultures and people and a corresponding fragmentation of aboriginal culture. The linguistic discrepancies signified a Caribbean thinking in, and speaking, four European languages, rather than one native language. Further, thirty years after the arrival of Columbus, countless aboriginals were destroyed. Trexler (1995) notes that two Columbus priorities, when he arrived in the Caribbean, was praise God and ask for gold. These actions were soon followed by requests for women who were sexually abused. Let me say that what I consider European genocide was responsible for what Brathwaite estimates as an annual aboriginal death rate of one million.

This cruelty was followed by the importation of people from regions such as the Ashanti, Congo, and Yoruba, in Africa. Thus, a new language structure appeared in the Caribbean.

> It consisted of many languages but basically they had a common semantic and stylistic form. What these languages had to do, however, was to submerge themselves, because officially the conquering peoples —the Spaniards, the English, the French, and the Dutch—insisted that the language of public discourse and conversation, of obedience, command and conception should be English, French, Spanish or Dutch. They did not wish to hear people speaking Ashanti or any of the Congolese languages. So there was a submergence of this imported language. Its status became one of inferiority. Similarly, its speakers were slaves. They were conceived of as inferiors—non-human, in fact. (Brathwaite, 1984: 7)

Brathwaite is clear that in the Caribbean region of cultural imperialism, "cultural disaster," the education system, European colonialist, dismissed the presence of African languages and preserved the language of the conquistador, the plantation owner, the administrator, the Anglican cleric. In the area controlled by the British, there was insistence that education should be the vehicle from which "the contours of an English heritage" would be drawn.

The people in colonial times most amenable to this heritage would be the Caribbean middle classes, individuals who (in training and outlook) are European:

They retain little or no trace of their African origin except the colour of their skin. Some have been educated at Oxford, the Sorbonne, Madrid. They are coloured Europeans, in dress (carried to such absurd lengths as wearing the dark colours and heavy-weight suits of the colder mother countries), in tastes, in opinions and in aspirations. They often marry white women, English, French, Spanish, Canadian, and American. When they go "home" every four years to enjoy a well earned holiday they imply by "home" not Africa, but England, France, even Spain. In the British islands they save or borrow to see the pageantry of England at the time of a Coronation or jubilee. The visit of a Prince of Wales, the honeymoon of a royal couple find them ready to display to the throne, their affection for the mother country. (Williams, 1942: 60)

In contrast to profound involvement with matters European, the middle classes are, however, deeply unaware of territories within the West Indies. These persons would grant the same significance to spending holidays in Timbuctoo as they would to Haiti.

Williams invites his readers to consider some subject areas in which the Trinidad open scholarship to university education in Britain is awarded by noting disciplines such as English political History, European History, Greek History, English Colonial History, English Economic History, Latin Textbooks, translation, composition and Roman History, French Textbooks, and Spanish Textbooks. For Brathwaite (1984) Shakespeare, George Elliot, Jane Austen, exemplars irrelevant to a non-European reality, loomed large in Caribbean educational practice. Afro-Caribbean persons, thus, became more knowledgeable about English Royalty than their own heroes, slave revolutionaries, such as the Maroons.

I must not forget the freedom fighters of Haiti, Dessalines, and Toussaint L'Overture, the second of whom Harry Belafonte, wanted to celebrate in film. The fruition of his effort, depended, however, on financial involvement from Hollywood, a contemporary bastion of European cultural imperialism conveyed by the massive presence of an English medium. No Hollywood film of Toussaint L'Overture has yet been screened by Hollywood.

This absence is merely a single instance of the hegemonic presence English and its cultural dominance enjoy in a society, the USA, where it is designated as the sole national language. The status is clearly evidenced as the sole medium of public discourse, conversation, obedience, command, and conception. After centuries of brutalisation, in the name of compulsion, Afro-American heirs to this perversity who continue to suffer have no choice but to regard English as their language. Anyone who has doubts about this forcible confinement should consider the Ebonics issue about which a debate over language education of children in the Oakland School District of California raged, towards the end of the 20th century.

It is to Rickford and Rickford (2000) that I turn, for the purpose of making a case for confinement. They indicate that on 18th December, 1996, the Oakland Unified School District approved a resolution on Ebonics, one response to nine recommendations offered by a Task Force on the Education of African-American students. The principal recommendation was: "African-American students shall develop English Language proficiency as the foundation of their achievements in all core contemporary areas." The Task Force had been set up to address itself to a problem evidenced in a District where more than half the student body was constituted by blacks, and where their academic performance was worse than that of any other ethnic group.

In 1996, for instance, two thirds of African-American children in the Oakland School District had been kept back a grade. Seventy-one percent were in special education classes and their average grade was D+. The response of the School Board to the plight was to help children make a transition to Standard English by respecting Ebonics as their "primary language" and using it as a bridge to English. In the words of one Afro-American teacher (T) who saw herself as a teacher of Ebonics, she values the language children bring from home and adds Standard English, a new language some of the children never had before, to the language from home.

Importantly, according to Toni Cook, an Oakland School District official who headed a Task Force on Ebonics, teachers should aim to capture students' attention, recognise their language style, when displayed, use displays as bases for correcting the students and guiding them to Standard English. Her major goal is affirming excellence which she states could be accomplished by the Board:

> Our children already come to us speaking—whatever you want to call it. Some call it Ebonics, some call it African language system. Some may even say it is bad English. But what we are doing is taking our children where they are. We're not devaluing them—using the Standard English Proficiency Teaching Strategy to bridge them where we want them to be. And that is: masters of the language of commerce, in this country, which is Standard American English.

From the standpoint of another Afro-American teacher in the Oakland School District, the need to understand the structure of Ebonics is an important basis for aiding students via transition into Standard English. She adds that the strategies for movement are second language learner strategies which I assess as grounded in teachers' use of contrastive analysis (Sridhar, 1980) and the grammar-translation method (Brown, 1980 and Ingram, 1978).

Here are examples of the strategy: (S1) and (S2) are students while (T) is the teacher.

S2: Why do we gaw dah have ah—bones?
T: Why do we gaw dah have bones?
S2: Why do we have bones?
T: Why do we have bones—is that Ebawnics or Standard English?
Student Chorous: Ebawnics.
T: So we have two ways of saying why we have bones in Ebawnics?
T: Who can tell me in Standard English?
S2: Why do some people have bones?

In another instance of strategy, teacher, T2, is in conversation with students, S3 and S4.

S3: Why people be so tall?
T2: How can you translate that into Standard English?
S4: Why are people so tall?

Those who believe that the idea of second language teaching in the context of Ebonics is far-fetched should attend to the views of Halliday, *et al.*, (1964) on what they term Jamaican Creole. They note that within the Anglo-Caribbean it is commonly claimed that almost everybody uses some version of English as his/her primary language. It is, however, their view that for users of Jamaican Creole, the status of which is not a matter for discussion, educated West Indian English would be better approached as an L2 teaching issue. Long after 1964, there have been Caribbean persons advocating for Creole in the Anglo-Caribbean to be recognised as a language. I certainly see the good sense of approaching the teaching of English as an L2 matter in most elementary and secondary schools.

There is little chance of achieving such goals: moves towards recognition are not matters of systematic or repeated consideration by Caribbean educational authorities, are either poorly supported by the general public or met with strong objections by self appointed guardians of English whose preferences are devoid of linguistic criteria. Here, I remind observers of the power of cultural and linguistic imperialism which is still evident in a post-independent Anglo-Caribbean some analysts see as burdened by neo-colonialist thinking.

It is this very power to which Rickford (2001) directs his attention, when he deals with strong objections to Caribbean Creole, during the 1950s and 1970s. He observes that respected British linguist, Robert Le Page, concerned about high failure rates of Jamaican children in the 1950s whom education authorities had hoped would produce Standard English, proposed that the children be taught in Jamaican Creole for the first two years of schooling. Rickford draws on the work of Cassidy (1970) to highlight public negativity to the Le Page proposal.

According to Cassidy, the proposal was deemed shocking. A newspaper columnist, Vera Johns of the *Kingston Star* dubbed it pernicious and insulting. "Good English" she claimed was not a foreign language to Jamaicans. Creole, though used by the majority of inhabitants, was intensely degraded by high status persons who linked it with poverty and ignorance. On 15th February, 1981, a statement about language appeared in the Sunday edition of the *Chronicle* in Guyana, a former British colony, where several urban inhabitants prided themselves on their use of more appropriate English than their Caribbean neighbours.

> Home Affairs Minister Stanley Moore said that too many Guyanese used Creole so as to escape proper English. He dubbed Creole as a vulgar, rough and ready mode of expression, and said sometimes it is simply bad English.

Moore, a British educated Barrister, and notable member in a government led by another British trained Lawyer, L.F.S. Burnham, was a Minister of an independent territory where the Burnham administration spared no effort domestically and internationally to criticise the evils of a colonial past. This was also the very administration that boldly saw its mission as making "the small [poor] man a real man" within the comfort of cooperative socialism. Several small women and men in Guyana, at the time, I hasten to add, were users of Caribbean Creole, the only mode of communication in which they could display linguistic accuracy and fluency.

Johns and Moore were making pleas for Standard English, a term, the meaning of which, is traceable to the rise and domination of the powerful. Halliday, *et al.*, (1964) observe that Standard English emerged in England as the London form of the South East Midland dialect. This emergence, they add, was a feature of the rise of urbanism and the modern state. No serious analyst of sociological matters should fail to recognise that such growth was inseparable from the development of industrial capitalism in England, a link which nurtured advancement in the power of the merchant class (Fairclough, 2001).

For Fairclough the progression of standardisation, a lengthy form of successful colonisation, was evidenced as control over major powerful societal organisations such as religion, literature, law, education and government. Standard English became the language of cultural dominance and the language of culturally dominant people who were central to transition from feudalism to capitalism. This is, doubtless, transition associated with British imperialism within Jamaica, other regions of the Caribbean, as well as, territories once part of a huge Empire where the sun never set and the British both literally and figuratively were never, never slaves. Vera Johns was therefore making a case for perpetuating domination.

I can speak about my own experience as a high school teacher of English in a post-independent Guyana of the 1970s when I was responsible for preparing students to sit for an overseas examination in English, The General Certificate Examination (London University). In my preparation I was using second language strategies, was eager to have the ideas of Halliday, *et al.*, applied at lower levels, and strongly proposed to my colleagues, all of whom were holders of credentials in literature, that English be taught as a second language. While I was fully supported by the Headmaster my proposal was roundly rejected by others who mounted a coordinated strategy of non-cooperation with me. Not unlike the matter of Caribbean Creole, it was strong objections which formed part of the debate about Ebonics.

What then sparked the raging debate over Ebonics? According to Rickford and Rickford (2000), it was the preamble to the nine recommendations by the School District on this mode of communication. In that preamble, there was a statement about African-American students being assisted to make the transition "from their home language, Ebonics, to achieve greater proficiency in Standard English." The School District had been challenged to adopt bold measures.

The action was to be two-fold. One important aspect of it was that African-American Language/Ebonics should be recognised as the primary language of many African-American students. African-American Language/Ebonics should be added to all District documents providing optional student placements within classes or programmes serving the needs of learners of limited English language proficiency.

Only days subsequent to passage of the resolution, which became a national media story, by that time, the bulk of reaction was made up of laughing, howling, complaining, and venting about Ebonics. Rickford and Rickford add that the resolution was amended in January, 1997. The alteration would not, however, have prevented Kwaesi Mfume, Maya Angelou, Jessie Jackson, apparently leading spokespersons for African-American causes, from criticising Ebonics. (I shall address myself to comments of Jackson's and Mfume's, after I have recorded some of the major modifications to the resolution.)

The Schools Superintendent was directed to devise a programme for improving the English language acquisition and application skills of African-American students. Other significant elements of the amendment were:

(a) Whereas, numerous validated scholarly studies demonstrate that African American students, as part of their culture and history as African people, possess and utilise a language described in various scholarly approaches as "Ebonics" (literally "black sounds") or "Pan-African Communication Behaviours" or "African Language Systems";

(b) Whereas, these studies have also demonstrated that African language systems are genetically based [have origins in West and Niger-Congo languages] and not a dialect of English [are not merely dialects of English];

(c) Whereas, these studies demonstrate that such West and Niger-Congo African languages have been officially recognised and addressed in the mainstream public educational community as worthy of study, understanding or [and] application of their principles, laws and structures for the benefit of African-American students both in terms of positive appreciation of the language and these students' acquisition and mastery of English language skills;

(d) Whereas, such recognition by scholars has given rise over the past fifteen years to legislation passed by the state of California recognising the unique language stature of descendants of slaves, with such legislation being prejudicially and unconstitutionally vetoed repeatedly by various California state governors;

(e) Whereas, standardised tests and grade scores will be remedied by application of a programme that teachers and aides [instructional assistants], who are certified in the methodology of featuring African language systems principles in instructing African-American children both in their primary language and in English [used to transition students from the language patterns they bring to school to English]. The certified teachers of these students will be provided with incentives including, but not limited to, salary differentials;

(f) Now, therefore, be it resolved that the Board of Education officially recognises the existence and the cultural and historical bases of West and Niger-Congo African language systems, and each language as the predominantly primary language of [many] African-American students;

(g) Be it further resolved that the Board of Education hereby adopts the report, recommendations and attached Policy Statement of the District's African-American Task Force on language stature of African-Americans;

(h) Be it further resolved that the Superintendent in conjunction with her staff shall immediately devise and implement the best possible academic programme for imparting instruction to African-American students in their primary language for the combined purposes of maintaining the legitimacy and richness of such language [facilitating the acquisition and mastery of English language skills, while respecting and embracing the legitimacy and richness of language patterns] whether it is [they are] known as "Ebonics," "African Language Systems," "Pan-African Communication Behaviours" or other description, and to facilitate their acquisition and mastery of English language skills.

I want to note three significant things about the resolution. First, America was being requested to recognise the impact of scholarly work conducted by African-American intellectuals. Second, a request was also made to recognise the legitimacy of efforts from African-Americans to reclaim remnants of voices in cultures destroyed, as a consequence of cultural genocide. And third, America was being asked to understand that the Oakland proposals did not stem from any revolt to repudiate English language. Despite the logic inherent to the work of the Oakland educators, this logic was clearly spurned (and no more shamefully) than by people who claim to be spokespersons for African-Americans—Jesse Jackson, Kwaesi Mfume, Maya Angelou.

The travesty of this repudiation becomes initially evident, when a reference is made to ideas of Professor Ernie Smith, Professor of Medicine, Ethnology, and Gerontology (Charles Drew University, Los Angeles). It is Professor Smith whose work Rickford and Rickford cite as having the greatest influence on the wording and philosophy of the Oakland resolution. Professor Smith, they state, is one of the strongest advocates of the view that "Ebonics was a separate, Niger-Congo based language rather than a dialect of English" (2000).

A partial glimpse of this view can be gained from an excerpt Rickford and Rickford take from a 1995 paper of the Professor's, "Bilingualism and the African-American Child."

> Afro-American and Euro-American speech emanate from a separate linguistic base...African-Americans have, in fact, retained a West and Niger-Congo African thought process. It is this thought process that is dominant in the substratum phonology and morphosyntax of African-American speech but stigmatised as being Black English. According to Africanists the native language of African-Americans is Ebonics—the linguistic continuation of Africa in black America...The Africanists posit that Ebonics is not genetically related to English. Therefore the term Ebonics is not a mere synonym for the more commonly used Black English...In fact, they argue that the term Black English is an oxymoron. (Smith as quoted in Rickford and Rickford, 2000: 170)

In dealing with the shame, I focus on Jackson and Mfume, whom I shall formulate as carriers of confinement. During the course of a conversation, in December 1996, at the height of the Ebonics controversy, Mfume appeared on the ABC programme, Nightline. In his discourse with Toni Cook of the Oakland School Board, the programme moderator, and another participant, Mfume was trying to regain the floor. His efforts consisted of these versions of talk: (a) "Buh now—le me finish my point." (b) "Le me finish Toni." (c) Toni—yuh have to let me finish like I let you finish your point."

While I do not want to embark on an intense analysis of Mfume's usage, the head of the NAACP was clearly not a user of Standard English. And in a rhetorical account which clearly served to dismiss the significance of Ebonics, Mfume asked: "...but could you imagine Malcolm X's by-any-means-necessary speech in Ebonics or Dr. King's I-have-a-dream speech in Ebonics?" I can certainly imagine the Malcolm X speech in Ebonics. A simple reference to notable facts about him will suffice, here. He was the son of an Afro-American father and an Afro-Caribbean mother from Grenada. Both parents were strongly influenced, and so was he, by the ideas of Marcus Garvey, the Jamaican, who promoted a back-to-Africa campaign for black Americans. It was Garvey's ideas which had a very powerful impact on the thinking of Bob Marley, reggae artist and Rastafarian who was deeply immersed in his African roots. Not only did Malcolm X adopt the African name, "Omowale," (the sun returns) but he stated publicly, also, that "I never acknowledged it [the slave surname, Little] whatsoever." I do not know what Mr.

Mfume acknowledged. Both of his names are unmistakably African. In them, a bold effort to reclaim what had been lost is evident.

Further, Malcolm X was a member of the Black Muslim organisation, the Nation of Islam, which gave him racial pride and dignity. In a clear demonstration of such pride and dignity, after a police raid on one of the organisation's religious centres, he used the vibrant orality which characterised his charismatic presence to state: "Let us realise that we are brutalised, not because we are Baptist. We are brutalised, not because we are Methodist. We are brutalised, not because we are Muslims. We are brutalised because we are black people in America."

I hope that Mr. Mfume would do more than expect mere imagination from observers who ask him to become familiar with statements in 1997 from the Linguistic Society of America about Ebonics: The variety known as "Ebonics," "African-American Vernacular English" (AAVE), and "Vernacular Black English" and by other names is systematic and rule-governed like all natural speech varieties. In fact, all human linguistic systems, spoken, signed, and written, are fundamentally regular. The systematic and expressive nature of the grammar and pronunciation patterns of the African-American vernacular has been established by numerous scientific studies over the past thirty years. Characterisations of Ebonics as "slang," "mutant," "lazy," "defective," "ungrammatical," or "broken English" are incorrect and demeaning.

Two more statements would be worthy of profound consideration from Mr. Mfume, as well as, the Reverend Jesse Jackson, who appeared for a television interview about Ebonics. Here is the first: The distinction between languages and dialects is usually made more on social and political grounds than purely linguistic ones. For example, different varieties of Chinese are popularly regarded as dialects, though their speakers cannot understand each other, but speakers of Swedish and Norwegian, which are regarded as separate languages, generally understand each other. What is important from a linguistic and educational point of view is not whether AAVE is called a language or a dialect but rather that its systematicy be recognised.

The foregoing expert reference to a distinction is fully consistent with the position of Halliday, *et al.*, (1964) who use institutional linguistics to assess criteria of deciding what count as languages. These three linguists would certainly find favour with the final pronouncement of the Linguistic Society of America that there is evidence from Sweden, the U.S., and other countries that speakers of other varieties can be aided in their learning of the standard variety by pedagogical approaches which recognise the legitimacy of the other varieties of a language. From this perspective, the Oakland School Board's decision to recognise the vernacular of African-American students in teaching them Standard English is linguistically and pedagogically sound.

Rickford and Rickford (2000) refer to an interview conducted by NBC correspondent, Tim Russert, who questioned guest, Jesse Jackson, on the programme, "Meet the Press." Jackson was asked to offer his thoughts about the proposal that "Black English," Ebonics, should be taught as an official language. The Reverend replied by stating that the proposal was "an unacceptable surrender bordering on disgrace." I ask about a surrender to what, and where was the disgrace? I watched the Reverend participate as a featured speaker in Louis Farrakhan's Million Man March on Washington DC. There he announced figuratively to the world that he could still feel the brutality of the lash and shackles from the days of slavery. I assume that in speaking he had to be referring to a deprivation of freedom clearly connected to painful wrenching from his African roots.

I would also find it difficult to conclude that the Reverend would reasonably associate a sense of disgrace with efforts to reclaim a very significant part of those roots, linguistic heritage. I ask, rhetorically, whether he has not been taking any pride in, but expressing shame over, his sustenance by those roots and their inescapable linguistic features? Are these not the very roots and features with which he is familiar, as a result of influences from jazz musicians such as Eric Dolphy, Charles Mingus, Edward Kennedy Ellington, John Birks Gillispie, Louis Armstrong, Thelonius Monk, Billie Holliday, Billy Strayhorn, John Coltrane, and Charlie Parker. If he is keenly observant, he would notice that the speech of these individuals has been laced with several notable features of Ebonics.

Interviewer, Russert was, of course, the purveyor of prejudice against African-American scholars, as well as, Oakland education officials. The implicature in his question was that a proposal had been made to teach Ebonics as an official language. No such suggestion emerged from the officials. Jackson's glossing Russert's damaging implicature and, thereby, legitimising its perverse meaning also amount to spurning of the logic in an important Afro-American scholarly effort. The powerful presence of an official culture of English unilingualism is thus the milieu where African-Americans are compelled to operate. The milieu is not one in which intense racial burdens they bear can be divorced from activities of a white power structure.

Some of those burdens appear in the form of an apparent contradiction captured by McLaughlin (2001). She notes that Ebonics supports an intensely prosperous music industry where large scale international consumption of hip hop, literature, jazz, rhetoric, and gospel music exist. The ugly side of Ebonics is, however, revealed in discrimination against its speakers in schools where millions of persons of African identity are shunted continuously within the circles of poor intellectual attainment, unemployment, homelessness, imprisonment, and nihilism.

No less ugly is what is assessed as linguistic profiling:

> Whereas "racial profiling" is based upon auditory cues that result in the confirmation or speculation of the racial background of an individual, or individuals, "linguistic profiling" is based upon auditory cues that may include racial identification, but which can also be used to identify other linguistic subgroups within a given speech community. (Baugh, 2003: 158)

From my standpoint, black language is enormously profitable to the recording industry. It is, however, the object of a derogatory, illogical, and unfair juxtaposition with white talk.

Baugh (2003) offers two interesting examples of linguistic profiling in U.S. courtrooms. The first is related to a case in which a white police officer's testimony, on cross examination, against a black male in Kentucky was upheld by a white judge.

Defence Counsel: Okay. Well, how does a Black man sound?

Police Officer: Uh, some male Blacks have a, a different sound of, of their voice. Just as if I have a different sound to my voice as Detective Birkenhauer does. I sound different than you.

Defence Counsel: Okay, can you demonstrate that for the jury?

Police Officer: I don't think that would be a fair and accurate description of the, you know, of the way the man sounds.

Defence Counsel: So not all male Blacks sound alike?

Police Officer: That's correct, yes.

Defence Counsel: Okay. In fact, some of them sound like whites, don't they?

Police Officer: Yes.

Defence Counsel: Do all whites sound alike?

Police Officer: No, sir.

Defence Counsel: Okay. Do some white people sound like Blacks when they're talking?

Police Officer: Possibly, yes.

The second instance, part of an exchange in the O.J. Simpson criminal trial, involved a judge, and two attorneys-at-law, all three of whom are named:

Darden: When you heard that voice, you thought that that was the voice of a young white male, didn't you?

Cochran: Object to the form of that question, your Honor.

Judge Ito: Overruled.

Cochran: Speculation, conclusion.

Judge Ito: Overruled.

Cochran: How can he tell if it was a white man, your Honor?

Judge Ito: Counsel, overruled.

Prosecutor Darden is, of course, African-American. His utterance is remarkable. Given what is being stated and what has been stated about the generalisations, black American speech and white American speech, his ambiguous initial utterance conveys a damaging implication. It points to the elevated and preferential status of white Americans while it signals the subordinate and undesirable position of American blacks. Bhattacharyya, *et al.*, offer an even cruder—if not, painful instance of juxtaposition. They note that curry, adopted as the national dish in Britain, is more popular than potato chips which can be consumed with curry sauce. Asian restaurants are, however, locations of racist violence and attacks. "Despite various attempts by informal bodies and local governments, the undoubted desirability of ethnicisied consumption does not take the violent sting out of other forms of social interaction" (Bhattacharyya, *et al.*, 2002: 159).

The Firthian Influence

British Asians have been regularly resident in territories ruled by imperial powers from which teachers emerged to promote and impose European language/European literature among non-white persons. Non-white individuals still reside in these territories, the majority of which (African and Asian countries), attained political independence. Many of their European teachers have long since returned to their own societies. A very significant change which occurred in the European locations was the emergence of the communicative approach to second- and foreign-language teaching. Not only did this development take very strong roots in Great Britain, but its growth also emerged from direct influences of J.R. Firth, a British linguist, who, in the words of notable followers, Halliday, *et al.*, (1964) rejected extremes of mentalism, as well as, mechanism and viewed linguistics as the study of how persons use language to live.

And according to Catford (1970), another linguist greatly influenced by Firth, who concluded that a major purpose of linguistics is the study of meaning, the British have distinct preferences for practical matters, applications, rather than theoretical considerations. In keeping with this choice, Firth emphasised "the sociological component" in linguistic studies, the examination of language as part of a social process, an aspect of human living, rather than just a set of arbitrary signs and signals. The emphasis is evident—so states Catford—in the Firthian view about contexts of situation or fields of relations, among persons playing roles in societies and what they utter.

So significant was the idea of role-taking to Firth that he found it necessary to emphasise that persons do not mix their various roles and language connected to the roles in something like a mixed stew. They use language appropriate to its situational context. Language users are social in the sense that they organise a varied repertory of interlocking roles without conflict or major disharmony. Linguistically speaking, such persons should be designated as commanding restricted languages, the description of which is justified as language via studying the social roles performed.

Catford's position is consistent with that offered by Stern (1981) who notes that British and continental European linguists have shifted, with greater ease than their American counterparts, from a structural view of language. This modification he attributes to Firth and Halliday, whom he states had always adopted a definite social and semantic view of language. It is, thus, no surprise to him that since 1979 British applied linguists have been at the forefront of efforts to foster, not just a social and semantic view of language, but have also applied it to target language teaching.

Catford also points out that Firth was enormously influenced by the anthropologist, Malinowski, who sought to establish meaning by locating words in contexts of situation, the actual physical environment of utterances. According to Malinowski, words derive meaning not just from utterances in which they appear, but also, from situations in which they are produced. Catford notes, however, that Firth modified Malinowski's view. For Firth, the context was a field of relations, internal or formal, and situational. Formal connections are manifested by links among items such as lexical, phonological, or syntactical components. Situational relations, on the other hand are evidenced as links among language items and constituents of the situation. Thus, language items are associated with elements outside its use within situations where it features in the various ways humans participate in situations.

Robins (1967) offers an appropriate conceptualisation of the Firthian view when he provides an example of how formal meaning (utterances and their parts) are brought into relations with situational meaning (situations outside language). The link is indicated as the relevant features of participants (persons, personalities):

(a) The verbal action of participants;
(b) The non-verbal action of participants:
    1. The relevant objects,
    2. The effect of verbal action.

Robins adds that meaning, which constitutes part of the more extensive system of interpersonal relations featured in human existence, is not a single relation or particular type of relation. It entails multiple and diverse relations which exist among utterances, their parts, as well as, relevant features and components of cultural environments.

Firth's impact on communicative language teaching clearly exists. This is not, however, the type of influence evidenced in efforts to help language learners deal with problems of colonial oppression and its continuing impact. I begin to make my case by showing that early developments in communicative language teaching were given the Firthian stamp. Further, the rejection of mentalism, as well as, mechanism were evident in these initial developments. I shall then explain why the influence does not exist in moves to deal with colonial and neo-colonial oppression.

Let me deal first with the rejection of mentalism. Early European proponents of communicative language teaching, Allen and Widdowson, (1994), Van Ek (1977), Breen and Candlin (1979a, 1980), Wilkins (1976), Widdowson (1979a, 1979b) were expressing their criticism of two language teaching methods, mechanism of situational methods and mentalism of the cognitive code learning approach.

Proponents of the first sought to prevent the learner from attending directly to forms of language by placing those forms in sentences which described situations. Here is an expert description of the first method.

> Language items are presented in situations in the classroom to ensure that their meaning is clear, and then practised as formal structures by means of exercises of sufficient variety to sustain the interest of the learner and in sufficient numbers to establish the structures in the learner's memory. The principal aim is to promote a knowledge of the

language system, to develop the learner's competence (to use Chomsky's terms) by means of controlled performance. The assumption behind this approach seems to be that learning a language is a matter of associating the formal elements of the language system with their physical realisation, either as sounds in the air or as marks on paper. Essentially what is taught by this approach is the ability to compose correct sentences. (Widdowson, 1979b: 117–118)

The cognitive code learning method (mentalism) also aimed to get the learner to compose sentences. According to Rivers (1983), proponents of this method recommended explaining grammar rules, practising their use through exercises and then seeing them in action in the context of reading (or listening) materials. What this method advocates is a deductive approach to learning by means of which rules of language are to be learnt before being applied.

The Firthian influence can be seen in efforts to use the language of everyday life and needs analyses as strong bases to actualising communicative language teaching. These emphases can be traced to Firth, via the pioneering efforts of Halliday, et al., (1964) who employ "methodics," for the important purposes of limiting, grading, presenting, and testing language items. They describe methodics as a framework of organisation for language teaching which relates linguistic theory to pedagogical principles and techniques. I deal with the everyday and needs analyses by focusing on the works of Wilkins, Widdowson, and the early work of the Council of Europe.

Wilkins (1978) claims that to view language as a feature of social life requires seeing that persons use it to conduct their everyday affairs. And in so conducting those affairs, they draw on, and make use of, the conventions of language. He states, also, that it is when persons' language use is seen as expressive of conventions and is a feature of the conduct of their everyday affairs that it may be seen in terms of communication. Widdowson claims that in order to ensure that language is taught as communication the selection, grading and presentation of language should be based on consideration of areas of language use. To understand what is conveyed in this claim, it is necessary to know what is meant, when he talks about language usage and language use, as well as, teaching language as communication. Reference to a distinction between signification and value may be initially helpful in understanding the significance of differentiating usage and use (Widdowson, 1978). Sentence meaning, he states, can be conceptualised in two ways: signification and value. In the first, the meaning of sentences is instanced as language usage: propositions are expressed in sentences by means of the combination of words into syntactic structures according to rules of grammar.

An instance of usage can be seen in B's sentence:

A: Could you tell me the way to the railway station?

B: The rain destroyed the crops.

Widdowson says that though a grammatically well-formed sentence, B's utterance has no communicative use as a reply to A's question. B's utterance would thus be an instance of language usage. In the second case, value, sentences and their parts become meaningful when they are applied for communicative purposes. An example of use would be B's utterance(s) in the exchange:

A: What destroyed the crops?

B: The rain/the rain did.

According to Widdowson, either of B's utterances could be seen as meaningful, in relation to A's question. Further, each could be interpreted as expressing the proposition, 'The rain destroyed the crops.'

From my observation of this example, I infer that language use involves employment of sentences and sentence parts in discourse to express communicative purpose. Widdowson (1979b) also says an approach to teaching whose principal interest is communication must be concerned with discourse. Communication occurs as discourse in which meaning is negotiated through interaction. In a relation of interaction, a sentence represents clues provided by a writer or speaker, clues to which a reader or listener refers, in order to promote propositional and illocutionary meaning. He adds that interaction creates hierarchical structures in which propositions and illocutions combine to form larger units of communication.

In an exemplification of propositional and illocutionary meaning, Widdowson points to the expressions: "One of the important mechanisms by which the individual takes on the value of others is identification. The term is loosely used to sum up a number of different ways in which one person puts himself in the place of another" (1979b: 254-255). Widdowson sees the second utterance as expressing a proposition which is connected to the first by means of the anaphoric link between 'the term' and 'identification.' This, he calls a relationship of cohesion. There is another relationship between utterances. The second proposition could be seen as a paraphrase of the first. The expressions, "the individual takes on the value of the other," and "one person puts himself in the place of another," Widdowson claims are conceptually alike. The function of the second proposition in relation to the first is what he calls a clarifying restatement. This relationship is one of coherence. It expresses the manner in which the illocutionary functions that propositions count as combine into larger units to form discourse.

Widdowson (1978) claims that though use and usage coincide, in normal language behaviour, these aspects of performance are treated separately by those concerned with the description and teaching of languages. Language teachers engaged in designing materials have generally tended to be concerned with usage. They select and organise language items, in order to demonstrate how sentences manifest the rules of language systems. In so doing, they indicate less interest in showing how rules may be realised for communicative purpose as use. Where does Widdowson locate areas in which use and usage coincide? These are areas in which persons produce language as a feature of their everyday existence

The Council of Europe is an organisation on whose behalf applied linguists have also made strong pleas for everyday language, as well as, needs analyses. The Council is a sociopolitical institution whose general aim is working towards accomplishing greater unity among its members, the majority of West European states. One of its specific goals is achieving this general aim through promoting foreign language study (Van Ek, 1977). Perhaps, a convenient starting point for looking at the Council's early work would be to note: (a) that one of its principal concerns is with teaching foreign language to adults; (b) an important basis to this concern is the identifying of their language needs; (c) what, in the first place, is the rationale for basing a concern for teaching adults on identifying their language needs?

I offer an appropriate response, by referring, initially, to Wilkins (1978). He argues that persons who—at some point in their school careers—were taught at least one foreign language, are unable as adults, to retain active command of the languages they were taught. He further argues that even if these persons did remember what they were taught, they would discover that it would not be of use to them, if serious demands were made on it. Wilkins is alluding here to persons' inability to use language as communication. In an explicit reference to this same inability, Trim (1973) argues that even if these persons are to be regarded as having acquired any effective knowledge of language, it would be that of their first language. Trim thus infers that it is to be expected that large numbers of them would be unable to communicate with other persons who use a language different to theirs. As such, they would be placed at a disadvantage, some aspects of which, may be exemplified via routes of inabilities: to summon help in a sudden emergency; to retrieve an important aspect of information from a publication; to greet a visitor; to ask the time of a passerby; and/or to understand an entertainment film.

One reason for the inabilities to communicate may be found in a comment from Wilkins (1978) that use of the content of what those persons were taught failed to provide them with practical mastery of language. Wilkins' point, here, is that when individuals learn foreign languages, they have different needs for so learning. For example, some persons may need foreign language for travel, others for occupational purposes, while others still, may require it as a matter of cultural interests. Despite this variability in needs, persons—who, at some point in their school careers, learned foreign languages—were presented with the same content, regardless of who those learners were or where they came from. Alternatively expressed, Wilkins' argument is that the disadvantage to which he and Trim refer is attributable to the fact that the various needs of persons who learned foreign languages in school settings were not taken into account, when they were taught in those settings.

If these persons, when they were young, did not all have identical needs for learning foreign languages, it seems reasonable to ask whether as adults they have various needs for learning foreign languages. Both Wilkins and Trim would respond positively. To Wilkins, most adults learn foreign languages for specialised and limited purposes. Trim (1973) says that the adult language learner is typically faced with a specific need for a particular language to be used for specific purposes in certain relatively predictable situations. The following example of his seems to clearly point to specificity of need. A BBC television cameraman may know, only at a month's notice, that he has to make a series of programmes in a West German city. He is to use, for this task, German studio facilities. According to Trim, what he would need to learn (both urgently and rapidly) is to produce and understand, in German, the restricted language of the studio floor.

An important point to be noted at this juncture is this: though not explicitly stated by Trim and Wilkins, the message they seem to convey is that teaching learners to use foreign languages as communication would be to teach language which is a feature of persons' everyday existence. This is, at least, the sense obtained from looking at Wilkins' examples of neglect of persons' varied needs for learning foreign languages, the instance Trim cites of persons' inability to communicate, as well as, his example of the adult learner's specific need for learning a foreign language. The Council has offered a systematic way of identifying needs of adults from which it derives functional language acts. I now look at how functional acts are derived from needs. It is to Richterich that I turn, for the purpose of performing this task.

Richterich (1973) claims that an adult learner should be able to learn a target language by means of a system of learning units progressively grouped such that they meet the main requirements of different categories of adults who want to use a language other than their native language. He adds that a unit is made up of a coherent set of functional acts. How are learning and language acts to be derived? How do learning acts lead to mastery of functional language acts? Language acts are derived from defining the needs of adult learners. The language needs of adults learning a target language are requirements arising from use of that language in the different situations which occur within the social lives of persons' and groups. Needs, he says, are imposed by realities of language situations. Thus, knowing a language means being able to respond to those realities.

Richterich also points to a distinction between subjective and objective needs and what he sees as a fundamental contradiction. Objective needs can be assumed to be general, from an analysis of typical everyday situations. These are needs which can be foreseen, analysed and defined. On the other hand, subjective needs cannot be regarded as general: they depend on events, unforeseen settings and persons. It is obvious that for Richterich there is some difficulty in defining subjective needs. There is a basic contradiction between the interest to define precise needs and aims and the reality that use of language as a means of communication and action in managing social situations demands ability to react appropriately to circumstances which cannot be accurately foreseen or defined.

Richterich opts to define objective needs via content analyses, opinion polls, and surveys. The first entails observing and analysing oral, as well as, written use of language by a given group of persons. Objective needs, which are foreseeable and generalisable, are then deduced from analyses. Opinion polls and surveys provide facts required for clarification of learners' motives. He recommends three ordered steps to deriving full definitions of predetermined groups of adults: (a) analysis of the oral and written use made of language by the category of adults concerned; (b) survey among persons already using the language in the same field as the category concerned; (c) survey among persons learning, or on the point of learning the language in the same field as the category concerned, in order to discover their motivations and their opinions for their needs.

The interests in use and usage, teaching language as communication via selection, grading and presentation, and needs analyses are embedded in pioneering work done by Halliday, *et al.*, on methodics. These linguists are explicit in their rejection of the mechanism of behaviourism which is foundational to situational teaching, and mentalism of transformational theory basic to cognitive code learning approaches. Let me say that the work of Halliday *et al.*, on limitation, grading, presentation, and testing in methodics rests on their wholehearted acceptance of Firth's views. I want to address myself to such acceptance which I shall follow with an exploration of methodics.

Halliday, *et al.*, (1964) state openly that their groundbreaking work is owed to two traditions in linguistic scholarship. One of those traditions is associated with work of J.R. Firth, Professor of General Linguistics, School of Oriental and African Studies, University of London (1942–1956). Firth rejected extremes of mentalism and mechanism. He stressed that meaning was a quality found in all types of patterning in language. Further, meticulous linguistic description depended on recognition that various levels of language (grammar, phonology) represented different modes of meaning.

In dealing with methodics, Halliday, *et al.*, say that what is paramount to teaching a language course must revolve around, limitation, an inventory of teaching items and devising the inventory entails delimiting the items and sequencing them. Such a consideration is logically followed by an examination of questions: What kind of language is to be taught? To what purposes will language learnt be directed? How much English do they require, so that they might be able to fulfil their purposes? What is the length of the course? What methods are used in teaching the course? They consider it both useless and unrealistic to deal with the first query by reasoning that the whole of English should be taught. It is impractical, they argue, to teach English as written and spoken at all times, in all locations, and about all topics. One realistic reply to the inquiry, 'what kind of language should be taught,' would be English that is needed for purposes of airline pilots. A list of items which meet these needs would include technical terms, 'runway,' 'degrees,' 'undercarriage,' 'boost,' 'emergency.' Further, ability to speak and understand spoken English via noisy channels is more significant than the ability to write acceptable English. The present tenses and imperative are likely to occur, very often. Limitation must occur at all levels of language and should rest on criteria, of frequency of occurrence, availability, teachability, and classroom needs.

Limitation of items in methodics is followed by grading, the most appropriate ordering of items for practical teaching purposes. Grading is subdivided into staging and sequencing. Staging represents course division into time slots, the number of lessons which comprise the course, decisions about skills students are to acquire and display, and teaching intensity, which is measured in classes per unit time. Sequencing is based on decisions about the order in which items are to be introduced. It means both the listing and teaching of items and is governed by criteria of frequency, availability, teachability, and classroom needs. In expressing a preference for an intelligent approach to sequencing, Halliday, *et al.*, say it must rest on possession of practical teaching experience with students. Use of practical experience enables the teacher to familiarise himself/herself with: (1) language sequences that contribute to speedy and effective teaching; (2) practical difficulties linked to introducing items; (3) aspects of language which are logically connected to others; (4) avoiding the introduction of items that lead directly to the edge of methodological precipices. Their insistence is based on reasoning that a teaching programme must be sensitive to precise needs of students.

Presentation is the next step in methodics. It covers more than methodology and is instanced as initial and repeated presentation. The latter version comes as reinforcement and remedial teaching. Central to the view about presentation is thinking that the stronger the integration of items to be presented as total language behaviour within real situations, at all language levels, the more effective teaching becomes.

The final step to accomplishing methodics is testing which comes in formal, and informal versions. Formal tests are used, for the purpose of devising instruments to assess attainment, progress, and ability. Ability tests are predictive. Their users attempt to assess aspects of performance closely connected with effective and rapid teaching. Attainment tests are employed to assess practical performance while tests of progress are measures of attainment, at different times. Informal tests are administered as strategies emergent from a teacher's direct and intimate knowledge of his students' linguistic abilities. The teacher develops techniques for observing, probing, and questioning his students. The teacher uses these approaches for determining matters such as when he should alter the pace of his teaching, repeat presentation of items, and specify particular students for special attention.

Despite solid Firthian residues in the European approach to communicative language teaching, what is notably absent from it is any effort to grapple with the enormous questions of domination or oppression. In European, as well as other approaches, there is no identifiable basis in *conscientizacao* premised on efforts to abolish colonial domination and its existing residues. There are no programmatic statements which exemplify commitments to struggle against social, economic, and cultural oppression. Nor, for that matter, is there reflection on causes of oppression or accounts about how teachers can learn in acts of critical self reflection.

Why is there noticeable absence? A simple and immediate response is that Firth was clearly not an applied linguist engaged in the field of foreign and second language teaching. A profound response can be found by using his very notion of the context of situation as the groundwork for analysis. The European context was obviously one whose relevant features were used for perpetuating European cultural dominance and superiority over non-white people who expressed an interest in acquiring target languages. This was also the very context in which great fear was expressed, both officially at the highest political levels and popularly, about new forms of non-white immigration.

Official creation of conditions for promoting the dominance of Western European cultural values also became paramount in a cold war foreground consisting of perceived threats from a communist menace. It is, thus, very noteworthy that the Council of Europe, a sociopolitical organisation, whose activities could not be divorced from the perceived threats took the initiative to be involved in a continental project geared to advancing the cause of target language teaching. My point here is that politics (not pedagogy) drove the interest in language learning. These were European politics actualised in conflict with the danger of communism. Hence, when Stern, whose work is influenced, also, by J.R. Firth, requested that greater attention be paid to how a socio-cultural element can be incorporated into communicative language teaching, there was little chance that proponents of this version of teaching would focus on matters of colonial and neo-colonial oppression.

Political considerations of dominance were also paramount in efforts to strengthen the hold of European culture among persons resident in ex-colonial territories. I offer strong exemplification of my case by looking at views, in 1983- 84, from the chairperson, British Council for Relations with other Countries. He said:

> Of course we do not have the power we once had to impose our will but Britain's influence endures, out of all proportion to her economic and military resources. This is partly because the English language is the *lingua franca* of science, technology and commerce; the demand for it is in-

satiable and we respond either through the education systems of 'host' countries or, when the market can stand it, on a commercial basis. Our language is our greatest asset, greater than North Sea Oil, and the supply is inexhaustible; furthermore, while we do not have a monopoly, our particular brand remains highly sought after. I am glad to say that those who guide the fortunes of this country share my conviction in the need to invest in, and exploit to the full, this invisible, God-given asset.[1]

Not merely did the preceding remarks emerge at the height of the communicative movement, they emanated, also, from a country standing at the forefront in a battle against communism, a country dedicated to British dominance over ex-colonial possessions, many of which were deeply opposed to its imperialist stand on racist South Africa.

It is with equal importance that I point out that the British Prime Minister at the time, Margaret Thatcher—along with U.S. President, Ronald Reagan—was very emphatic in believing that UNESCO, a United Nations agency largely funded with American dollars, was being politicised by Third World agendas. Their understanding of culture was diametrically opposed to that held by numerous ex-colonial possessions, many of whose leaders could not accept the Thatcher/Reagan intransigence over economic sanctions against South Africa. Thatcher and Reagan, therefore, felt it was imperative for Britain and the USA to withdraw temporarily from the agency. Not merely did withdrawal become a reality, both countries also returned, at a time when communism had been defeated and a "new world order" was being put in place.

The British Council began its initial operations in 1934, under Foreign Office auspices (long before 1984) a time preceding the heyday of the communicative movement. The pronouncement in 1984 cannot be separated from its evolving interests which are, doubtless, those of British dominance. In 1934, the Council was composed of businessmen and educational experts who explored an arrangement for advancing English language teaching, internationally, and further wider knowledge and understanding of British culture (Phillipson, 1992). Phillipson adds that in one of its official ceremonies in 1935, King Edward VII proclaimed:

The basis of our work must be the English language...(and) we are aiming at something more profound than just a smattering of our tongue. Our object is assist the largest number possible to appreciate fully the glories of our literature, our contribution to the arts and sciences, and our pre-eminent contribution to political practice. This can be best achieved by promoting the study of our language abroad... (1992: 138)

Four years later, when the Council was granted a Royal Charter, its purpose was sated as promoting a wider knowledge of the United Kingdom of Great Britain and Northern Ireland and the English language abroad, and developing closer cultural relations between the United Kingdom and other countries, for the purpose of benefiting the British Commonwealth of Nations. The Commonwealth then was made up of Britain and the dominion territories of Canada, Australia, New Zealand, and South Africa.

At about the same time, the Council's Annual Report indicated its aim as creating a basis of friendly knowledge and understanding of the people of Britain, their philosophy and way of life, which will contribute to a sympathetic appreciation of prevailing British foreign policy and the political conviction from which it emanates.

Both foreign policy and political conviction have been inseparable from the enormously significant operations of an Empire on which the sun never set, an Empire whose imperialist influence ensured the pre-eminence of English language in societies inhabited by non-white people. The imperialist imperatives of Empire are appropriately captured by Binns (2002) who places its carriers in two camps. The first was made up of abrasive and domineering colonialists such as servicemen and district administrators who designated the colonised as inferior and dealt with them as such. These colonials were well exemplified in what has come to be known as the scramble for Africa where Kipling saw the "white man's burden" as directing the continent away from savagery towards routes of civilisation.

The white man's burden was, however, associated with much more than steering Africa; it was unmistakably linked to conquest. Binns estimates that at the turn of the 20th century, Britain had seized large regions of Eastern and Southern Africa and secured, from France, all of West Africa, from the Sahara Desert to the Congo River. He adds that in 1897, the year of Queen Victoria's Diamond Jubilee, the *Times* newspaper saw a procession to St. Paul's Cathedral in the name of the celebration as a "wonderful exhibition of allegiance and brotherhood amongst so many myriads of men...the mightiest and most beneficial Empire ever known in the annals of mankind" (Binns, 2002: p. 23). Conquest was hardly a regional matter. It was a monumental move.

Binns notes that more than 20,000,000 people departed from the British Isles between 1815 and 1914, the start of World War I. When the war was over, another 13,000,000 subjects and almost 1,000,000 square miles were added to Empire. Journeys within Empire could be made from Cape Town, South Africa, to Rangoon, Burma, under British dominance.

> From the frozen waters of Northern Canada to the snow-capped peaks of New Zealand's Southern Alps; from the jungles of British Guiana in South America, across the Earth's widest girth, to the remote Pitcairn Island in the Southern Pacific, the world really was coloured red. Every British child knew what was literally true—that the sun never set on the British Empire. (Binns, 2002: 42)

The second group of colonials was comprised of expatriates such as missionaries and educators. Their view was that Empire could serve as the standard of culture and improvement for which non-whites could strive, as a means of amelioration. It was the missionaries who conveyed the imperial message with the most vibrancy and zeal. They transmitted the "muscular Christianity" of Victorian Britain and thrust it around the world. They also transported English sports, notions of English fair play, and the stiff upper lip of fine English Christian gentlemen resolutely poised to combat savagery and adversity.

Given the roles of the British Council, and dominance of Empire, it would not be reasonable to make any connections between their interests in the spread of English language and culture and the removal of oppression. Hence, no programmatic statements exemplifying commitments to struggle against social, economic, and cultural domination can be connected with either the Council or Empire.

The inference above is applicable, even to strong claims about learner centred infusions to communicative language teaching. The appropriate reference points here are ideas of Tudor (1996). He says the basic assumption behind learner centeredness is that language acquisition will be more meaningful, if students, rather than the teacher, make decisions about the conceptual, methodological, and linguistic content of the acquisition. What is being promoted is a 'partnership model' geared to attaining transference of responsibility.

At the classroom level, it is consultation between teachers and learners defined by negotiation which leads to curriculum design. Contributions from learners are integrated, at every stage of acquisition. Students become active participants in collaborative processes aimed at accomplishing outcomes such as syllabus negotiation and learner independence. Tudor acknowledges that target language teaching is a multi-faceted social and cultural activity which obliges practitioners to be cognisant, not merely of learners' psychological profiles, but also, their sociocultural settings. One of the relevant factors which must be considered is learners' cultural attitudes to language study and the roles of teachers and learners. Collaborative activities will not be successful if teachers are regarded as authority figures. Despite the acknowledgment, Tudor is explicit in declaring that it is the teacher's ultimate responsibility for ensuring that effective learning occurs.

The Freireian absence from communicative language teaching is particularly noteworthy, in post-independence periods. These have been characterised by significant flows of immigrants whose first languages are non-European, to European locations. Many of the immigrants are, indeed, descendants of the masses who have been exploited, as a consequence of colonial oppression.

Further, in a contemporary setting where the stranglehold of globalisation and monopoly capitalism which nurtures it bodes ill for many inhabitants of ex colonial possessions, there is no version of communicative language teaching whose proponents address themselves systematically to the destructive impact of a matter such as cultural invasion. Perhaps, one of the most harmful consequences can be seen in the activities of Rupert Murdoch, the Australian who became an American citizen for the purpose of expanding his News Corp media empire. In early 1993, Murdoch, owner of Sky Television in Europe, Fox Network in the USA, and several newspapers worldwide—including the *Times*, *Sun*, and *News of the World* in Great Britain—issued what he considered to be a far reaching announcement about international satellite telecasting. Murdoch has been pursuing his goal of creating a global village where all citizens of the world could be entertained or watch news programming without inhibition.

Facilitators of this modern version of instantaneous information transfer are metallic dishes. Murdoch's technological arrangement is a billion dollar business of privately owned satellite telecasting. Programming via the medium would be consistent with the owner's political philosophies: Murdoch, a staunch supporter of Margaret Thatcher's "free market "capitalism, has long since made it clear to editors of his British newspapers that they should not be politically independent. Their editorial inclinations ought to reflect views of the Conservative Party in Britain. The Australian/American is not a public servant to the world. He is a media baron motivated by prospects of super normal profits.

I think that if the world is to be a true global village, then satellite telecasting should originate, not just from rich developed countries. Programming about developing societies devised by residents from these locations should also be telecast in the developed world. This type of exchange is, however, unfeasible, because of prohibitive costs to the developing world.

The burden of cultural invasion can also be revealed by looking at the statuses of what have come to be known as vernaculars in ex-colonial possessions. Vernaculars, many of which do not have official language designation, are used by the oppressed. According to Phillipson (1992), use of the term, vernacular, is not accidental. He notes that the term is a loaded term. It refers to what is homebred, homemade, homegrown, rather than what emanates from formal exchange. In popular and technical usage, it connotes localised, substandard, nonstandard language which is very different to literary, cultured or foreign languages. The term can be traced all the way to the Latin *vernaculus* which means belonging to a household slave. For Phillipson, vernaculars are stigmatised in relation to languages elevated as the norms. Catford is, thus, correct when he states that the development of any discipline is influenced by the cultural and political setting in which it occurs. Such is, doubtless, true of linguistics which exists in a setting where linguistic and cultural imperialism predominate.

I think some of the most cogent evidence for the great strength of linguistic and cultural imperialism can be located by looking at the status of vernaculars. While extensive research and promotion, which require huge financial resources, are associated with Western languages, this is not the case in regard to vernaculars. Here is an appropriate example. The work conducted by the International Group for the Study of Language Standardisation and the Vernacularisation of Literarcy (IGLSVL) which resulted in publication of a document, "Vernacular Literacy: A Re-Evaluation" (Clarendon Press/Oxford, 1997), is a rather insignificant production when compared to the massive output of Western linguistic material.

In an equally significant sense, I note that despite the bold reaffirmation from the Council of Europe about plurilingualism and multiculturalism, there is no commitment on the part of the organisation to grant national language status to vernacular languages by Europeans. My reference here is to white residents born in Europe, as well as, non-whites who have migrated from various parts of the developing world to Europe. In Britain, France, and Holland, for instance, there are no official commitments by political and educational authorities to grant such status to Dutch, English, and French based Creoles.

Within Canada, there is a well established official movement to facilitate the teaching and learning of Heritage languages. Under the umbrella of multiculturalism, government funding is available for persons to be taught languages other than Canada's two official languages, English and French. Thus, persons can learn Spanish, Hindi, Italian, German, Ukranian, and Russian among other languages. Canada, a country that prides itself on implementation of multiculturalism, however, grants no national language status to any of its aboriginal languages.

Nor for that matter, is there any effort from educational or political authorities to recognise and promote Creole languages spoken by the vast cross section of non-white Canadians who originate from the developing world. Thus, no official talk about recognition and promotion of English, French, and Spanish based Caribbean, African and Asian Creoles exists within Canada. In 1990, the U.S. Federal Government instituted the Native American Languages Act to serve as a foundation for promotion, protection, and preservation of aboriginal languages (Singh, 2004). Singh adds that this was pioneering legislation in an effort to recognise rights of Americans who use mother tongue languages other than English. Promotion, I emphasise, does not take the form of official recognition to vernaculars or aboriginal languages as national languages for use within the USA. Further south, Mexico is in the same position as the U.S. in regard to aboriginal languages.

A Practical Case For The Freireian Presence—LINC

The juncture of promotion is, thus, an appropriate point at which I can solidify my argument for a Freireian presence in communicative language teaching. My focus is on one of the richest societies, Canada. Canada, once a dominion possession of Great Britain's, though dominated by two European groups, Francophones and Anglophones, has been accepting large numbers of immigrants from underdeveloped societies, former colonial territories. Several of these new Canadians are in a developed society, principally because Canada cannot progress economically without the presence of steady immigrant streams. The Canadian Federal Government, through its Citizenship and Immigration Commission, (CIC), makes available, to all immigrants, on a nationwide basis, a communicatively based programme of second language acquisition known as Language Instruction for New Canadians (LINC). LINC is clearly traceable, via the L or linguistic approach in communicative language teaching, to the influence of early work from the Council of Europe.

Let me deal with LINC, as a way of making the Freireian case. Several of the intended beneficiaries, members of the oppressed masses, are residents of a capitalist society whose current government is an aggressive promoter of globalisation, one of the most powerful indices of socioeconomic inequity as well as, cultural imperialism. The new immigrants, once victimised by oppression in their own societies, must now face a different version of domination. One very relevant issue for promoters of LINC programmes across Canada is whether there are efforts in the programmes to grapple with oppression.

The response to this query is emphatically negative. On the face of it, a national administration which promotes globalisation but simultaneously integrates opposition to domination in its language programmes would be adopting a contradictory posture. There is, however, a stronger reason for the foregoing response. It can be found in the inextricable connection between LINC programmes and multiculturalism. The latter has been criticised by Price (1978), Bannerji (1997), and Walcott (1997) for reproducing white superiority in Canada. What is the connection between LINC and multiculturalism? My response shall be followed by critical remarks about this social arrangement.

A Canadian Standing Committee of 1987 claims that the goal of multiculturalism is the integration—not assimilation—of racial and ethnic groups. This is a position offered explicitly by the originator of this policy, none other than Pierre Elliot Trudeau, late Canadian Prime Minister. In October, 1971, he stated publicly that there cannot be one cultural policy for Canadians of French and British heritage and another for members of other groups.

He added that despite the existence of two official languages, English and French, "...there is no official culture, nor does any ethnic group take precedence over any other...A policy of multiculturalism within a bilingual framework commends itself to the government as the most suitable means of assuring the cultural freedom of Canadians." Of vital importance to me are Prime Minister Trudeau's statements about the bilingual framework, two official languages, English and French. It is this framework which must be considered in the foreground of what is contained in the Canadian Multicultural Act of 1988.

According to the Act, the Canadian Constitution recognises the significance of maintaining and expanding the multicultural heritage of Canadians. The Canadian Government also recognises the racial, national, ethnic, and religious diversity of citizens as a basic feature of the society. It is committed to a multuiculturalism policy aimed at the preservation and enhancement of cultural heritage which is consistent with accomplishing the equality of all citizens within economic, social, cultural, and political spheres of life.

I cannot see how equality can be accomplished in a climate of official bilingualism associated with languages whose historic dominance has been a major feature of cultural and linguistic imperialism. It is not irrelevant for me to note that within the mainstream national Canadian media—both print and audio-visual—Canadian culture is typically presented as white Anglophone and Francophone culture. Discourse about other cultures is a poor distant relative to the Eurocentric focus. This peripheral presence is not divorced from a continual battle between strident Francophone separatists within the province of Quebec and their white Anglophone counterparts within the rest of the country over one Canada made of ten provinces and three territories or one Canada made up of three territories and nine provinces whose closest and newest neighbour would be the sovereign state Quebec.

The battle over difference reached one of its highest points in 1995 when a separatist government in Quebec, which had secured a provincial referendum on a sovereign state, narrowly lost. The Quebec Premier at the time, an eloquent an uncompromising separatist, Jacques Parizeau, declared, disparagingly, after the loss, that it was the "ethnic vote" which caused defeat. Monsieur Parizeau was pointing to Canadians other than Anglophones who were not Francophones. By a strange process of exclusion, these other Canadians, the ethnics, had to be differentiated from Francophones. Many of these ethnics who arrive in Canada as non-native immigrant users of English or French and wish to learn an official language under auspices of the LINC programme in Quebec are obliged to learn French. It is to LINC programmes across Canada that I direct my attention, so that I might be able to continue making a Freireian case.

LINC was instituted by a Canadian Federal Agency, the Canada Employment and Immigration Commission, for the purpose of facilitating the settlement and immigration of newcomers to Canada. Learners are currently assigned to various levels of language instruction, on the basis of their performance on assessment procedures, the Canadian Language Benchmarks Assessment tool, geared to account for their communicative competence. This competence is promoted in what are advertised as learner centered classrooms where students are assisted to participate more fully in Canadian society, to integrate successfully into a new country.

One vital basis to the assistance is a set of curriculum guidelines made up of themes, topics, and learning outcomes reflective of multiculturalism and devised in accordance with principles of communicative language teaching. What is crucial to LINC programmes is integration. This is, of course, integration within the bilingual framework of multiculturalism, a framework that is not devoid of linguistic imperialism. Further, learners, several of whom were oppressed and victimised by such practices as conquest and cultural invasion and are the objects of manipulation in globalisation, have no say in devising either the guidelines or assessment tools.

Others excluded from having any say are new immigrants from ex-communist countries in Europe. These new immigrants are not, of course, persons of colour. While they are not subject to the same discrimination as non- white learners, several of them, not unlike non-white new Canadians, are shunted to ranks of the subordinate where they labour as taxi drivers, nannies, fast food workers, and unskilled factory workers. Some of them have even returned in frustration to their home countries.

Note
1. This quote is taken from Phillipson, 1992: 144–145.

Conclusion
The Radical Democratic Multicultural Framework

I believe I have made a very strong case for a Freireian infusion to communicative language teaching. I shall bring closure to my work by offering an analysis of what Freireian foundations to communicative language teaching should look like. What is central to the examination is setting up an alternative multicultural framework for target language acquisition to a type such as the one that exists in Canada. It is within this alternative structure that European, Creole, as well as, non-European national languages will be acquired as second and foreign languages.

My reference point for setting the framework is the discourse from Marable (1996) on four versions of multiculturalism. They are racial essentialism, corporate multiculturalism, liberal multiculturalism, and radical democratic multiculturalism. It is the last which I find relevant to the goal of implementing a different approach to communicative language teaching. I am fully aware that Marable's discourse on multiculturalism is applied to the USA. I am also cognisant that the global setting is not the USA. Like the world setting, the USA is ethnically and racially diverse. Marable's discourse is also conceptually appealing.

Proponents of racial essentialism, typically Afro-American scholars, extol the virtues of African sociocultural existence to the point of viewing the virtues as superior. Further, they contrast the harmful consequences in the discrimination of Eurocentrism with the need to devise a cultural world view opposed to white domination. Several purveyors of this position have been promoters of a movement of Afrocentrism which Marable conceptualises as retreatist, in its erection of a bipolar model of race relations. For Marable, Afrocentrism constructs the dimensions of black American experience via the negative prism of whiteness. This type of framing immobilises the meaning of culture by fixating the diversity of interaction within historical rigidity.

I am in full support of Marable's characteriastion of negativity. The racial essentialism to which he refers is, to my mind, the very parallel of white superiority flaunted in the flawed epistemology which I explored earlier and did not divorce from the colonial and neocolonial settings within which target language has been taught. Racial essentialism is not the version of multiculturalism I would recommend to people who wish to implement a Freireian approach. I would also not recommend corporate multiculturalism.

Marable states that promoters of corporate multiculturalism emphasise cultural and social diversity by endeavouring to heighten the sensitivity of business executives to matters such as racial, gender, age, linguistic, and sexual differences. He notes that the principal motivating forces for this type of multiculturalism are minority markets and labour force demography. In the USA, there is great pressure on the corporate milieu to hire persons from the diverse pools of the non-white population. It is also within these diverse pools that corporate America stands to make huge profits from massive consumer spending. In the foreground of globalisation, labour force demography and consumer power are very evident.

Marable's problem with corporate multiculturalism is that its advancement is devoid of significant discussion about exploitation, racism, sexism, or homophobia. Its evasive posture can be located in celebrating diversity of all kinds without criticising anyone. Liberal multiculturalism, a broadly democratic outlook, is distinctly anti-racist. It is premised on the view that educational establishments have major obligations to deconstruct the ideology of human inequality. It is, however, inadequate in dealing with inequalities of power, privilege, and resources.

> It attempts to articulate the perceived interests of minority groups to increase their influence within the existing mainstream. In short, liberal multiculturalism is "liberalism" within the framework of cultural diversity and pluralism. (1996: 120)

The quotation above is powerful evidence of the type of multiculturalism which features in LINC programmes and, is, of course, a cogent reminder that official Canadian bilingualism is one existing mainstream. In contemporary globalisation, it is the destructive breadth of the existing mainstream in the forms of multinational manipulation, World Bank debt impositions, environmental destruction, and cultural hegemony which would emasculate liberal multiculturalism.

Unlike liberal multiculturalism, radical democratic multiculturalism is transformationist cultural critique. Discussions of culture are always connected to the issue of power, as well as, methods by which ideology is employed to control and dominate the oppressed. Proponents of radical democratic multicultural-ism stress similarities between the cultural experiences of oppressed persons around the world, strive to redefine and reorganise systems of culture and political power. It is my view that this is the type of emphasis evident in Freire's call for the oppressed to reclaim their language. What should Freireian reclamation look like from the standpoint of a communicative approach to target language teaching embedded in radical democratic multiculturalism? It should consist of an ap-proach to language pedagogy in which discourse that exposes the features of op-pression is central to the sustenance of *conscientizacao*. Such discourse must be a factor of culture and a cultural fact in communicative pedagogical practice. The practice must be evident in the teaching of European and non-European foreign languages, as well as, Creoles within ex-colonial possessions. Within the advanced industralised world where former residents of colonial possessions meet native born citizens and acquire European foreign and second languages, the sustenance of *conscientizacao* must also prevail.

Conscientizacao must not be absent from the teaching of Creoles and aborigi-nal languages in societies being dominated by linguistic and cultural imperialism, as well as, those once dominated by these two evils. The intersecting of Creolisation with *conscientizacao* offers excellent prospects for liberation. It is at the foregoing juncture that historical, cultural, educational, sporting, and scientific achievements of Creole and aboriginal users can be revealed, very powerfully.

I want to use Ebonics in classroom settings as a very important example of a non-European mode of communication which intersects with *conscientizacao*, for the purpose of highlighting just such achievements. I recognise that Afro-Ameri-can students are already highly accomplished producers of Ebonics. Thus, this mode of communication should be used as an instrument for helping them gain important foundational knowledge in classrooms. On the other hand, they should be assisted to acquire Standard English within classrooms, for the purpose of consolidating foundational knowledge. What does gaining foundational knowledge mean?

It means creating situations for affirming and reaffirming the significance of Afro-American culture among Afro-American children up to the age of ten. It means providing them with an education in, and about, Afro-American culture. And by culture I mean the various practices members in different sectors of society use for the purpose of giving meaning to their lives while they express their or-ganisational affiliations and identities. Culture encompasses ways of life, modes of existence where significant contributions from achievements in areas such as sport, education, science, commerce, economics, and politics are identified. These would, of course, be accomplishments which have led to major changes in American society, changes Cornel West has characterised as the making and remaking of America.

Providing the education in Afro-American culture means making use of the wealth and beauty of Afro-American culture for transmitting knowledge orally in a manner that is just as creative as that which exists in cultures of Standard English. I am proposing a version of education which children can use to express pride in themselves, their predecessors and heritage. It is the sort of pride which educators, jazz musicians, opera singers, writers, scientists, and poets express in the inventive genius of their improvisations.

Let me add that a principal theme of the education would be to show that artful, elegant and extraordinary performance of Afro-Americans is a strong indicator of alternate and powerful forms of self expression by creative people denied access to conventional routes of socioeconomic development, as a consequence of official and unofficial exclusion. Indeed, it would be prudent to show that the very use of Ebonics is an alternate form of self expression arising from creativity. I am also advocating a version of education, the gaining of which, should lead, neither to devaluation of a primary mode of communication, nor students' culture.

In what types of schools should such education be pursued? One important reply can be obtained by looking at:

> Immersion schools provide educators with the opportunity to develop teaching strategies, techniques, and materials that take into account the influence of the dominant American and the African-American cultures on the social environment and understandings of Afro-Americans. Educators can formulate strategies and teach techniques to African-American students to help them overcome racial obstacles. Immersion schools also provide educators with an opportunity to reduce the cultural conflict between the dominant American culture, which is enshrined in the traditional public education program, and African-American culture. This conflict is a primary reason for the poor performance of Afro-Americans in public schools. (Brown, 2000: 415)

Brown justifies immersion schools by stating that African-Americans are not free to select the impact that dominant white and Afro-American cultural ideologies have on them.

In addition, he makes sharp contrasts between voluntary migrants to the United States and those he assesses as involuntary minorities. Members of the first group, who enter the USA to improve their economic, political and social circumstances, develop positive frameworks for interpreting conditions within their host country and arrive with cultures that have not evolved in response to discrimination felt in the United States. Involuntary minorities, on the other hand, cannot use a native homeland as a point of reference to form positive frameworks. They must compare themselves to members of the dominant group. Thus, they develop negative interpretive frameworks, because the dominant group is usually better of than theirs.

I do accept that involuntary minorities do not develop positive interpretive frameworks but I do know of very significant evidence which indicates substantial numbers of voluntary migrants do not enjoy positive experiences in a host country such as the United States. There are several black persons from Africa, as well as, the Caribbean, who (very much like black Americans) are descendants of persons forced to locations, as a result of what Brown deems slavery, conquest or colonisation. These are people who are simultaneously voluntary migrants and involuntary minorities.

My amendment does not, however, mean that I reject Brown's call for immersion schools which I believe should be used as the context for Ebonics education of black American involuntary minorities and other black residents of the United States who have the dual status of voluntary migrants and involuntary minorities. Members of all groups do use, can understand, and appreciate the importance of Creoles which are not dissimilar to Ebonics.

They can also understand and appreciate the significance of being offered what Brown calls Afrocentric curricular material in immersion schools. While I do not use the term, Afrocentric, Brown's position on Afrocentric material does accord with mine about the content to be learnt by young Afro-American students. For Brown, slavery is central to an Afrocentric perspective, a perspective which resubjectivises blacks, rather than perpetuates their objectification. The Afrocentric core, very different to an Anglocentric focus which portrays the anti-slavery struggle as largely conducted by abolitionist whites, consists of infinite struggles made by African Americans and their ancestors to resist slavery: the numerous rebellions, acts of defiance (including suicide) in vessels on the "Middle Passage," and the deeds of people such as Denmark Vesey, Nat Turner, Harriet Tubman, Elijah Anderson, John Mason, Toussaint L'Overture, and Gabriel

Prosser. To Brown's list I add activities of the Maroons, Cimmarons, Bush Negroes, Cuffy, and Akara.

An Afrocentric perspective neither glorifies all actions of blacks, nor serves to celebrate mere pigmentation. Its analytical, explanatory, and evaluative application is meant to traverse pathways of upliftment and enhancement in the experiences of involuntary minorities.

> An Afrocentric curriculum provides black students with an opportunity to study concepts, history, and the world, from a perspective which places them at the centre. Such a curriculum infuses these materials into the relevant content of various subjects, including language arts, mathematics, science, social studies, art and music. Students are provided with both instruction in the relevant subject and a holistic and thematic awareness of the history, culture, and contributions of people of African descent. For example, from an Afrocentric perspective the focal point of civilisation is the ancient Egyptian civilisation (known as "Kemet" or "Said") as opposed to ancient Greece. Therefore, Egypt, not Greece, is the origin of basic concepts of math and science. This is done to show African-American students that they can maintain their cultural identity and still succeed in their studies. (2000: 423)

What I think is being put forth here is the promoting repudiation of involuntary minority sub or non-personhood via routes of owning authenticity which is genuinely emancipatory. This is not ownership which should be denied people who have been oppressed.

Education in, and about Afro-American culture should take place alongside other versions of American culture. The instrument for facilitating these other versions would be Standard English. One of the main goals of its use would be to aid language learning through implementing community and humanistic approaches which I shall examine, in detail, later.

Reference to the orality of Ebonics does not mean understanding of Afro-American culture will not occur via reading and writing. My expectation is that language skills via the approaches named will be transferred to Ebonics settings and used for accomplishing reading, as well as, writing about Afro-American culture. In addition, teaching about Afro-American and other versions of culture would continue beyond the age of ten. At this level, however, the language of instruction would be exclusively in Standard English presented with the aim of consolidating foundational knowledge.

I am proposing a version of education which Lambert (1990) a pioneer of immersion education, regards as additive, rather than subtractive bilingualism. When he speaks of additive bilingualism, Lambert is referring to situations in which second language learning does not portend slow replacement of first or home language. Lambert locates excellent examples of additive bilingualism among minorities in the USA. After having been given partial instruction in their home language, Franco-Americans in Northern New England kept French alive as their home language, although schooling also took place in English.

In the second case, he refers to studies conducted by Kessler and Quinn (1980) on Spanish speaking grade six students. Lambert (1990)reports that the students were able to learn school subjects in English and Spanish simultaneously. These students were then compared to a very privileged group of middle class, white, monolingual English speaking American pupils of the same age. Tests of both groups resulted in the Hispanic Americans generating hypotheses of much higher quality and complexity than the monolinguals. This problem solving feature was indicated also in the language produced which was exemplified by a syntactic complexity measure, so that the bilinguals clearly were using more complex linguistic structure, as well.

Tucker (1980) provides a very noteworthy assessment of additive bilingualism by identifying its cumulative and positive impact, when youngsters remain in bilingual programmes for periods beyond two or three or even five years, during which two conditions exist: efforts to provide nurturance and sustenance of their mother tongue and introducing teaching via the language of wider communication.

Additive bilingualism contrasts sharply with subtractive bilingualism, a phenomenon experienced by minority groups who—because of national educational policies and social pressures—feel forced to put aside or subtract their ethnic languages for a more necessary and prestigious national language. The subtractive experience reflects disuse of home language, its cultural accompaniments, and replacement of this language by a more necessary language. Subtractive bilingualism, so states Lambert, can be devastating, for youngsters affected by it are placed in situations where a type of semi-lingualism emerges and neither is home language, nor the more necessary language useful as a tool of thought and expression.

If English is accepted as the national language in the USA, and Ebonics as a home language, it would be reasonable to regard Lambert's position as a significant guide for assisting individuals such as Oakland children to produce the national language. My ultimate goal is to liberate, rather than maintain marginalisation of Afro-American youngsters. Should the Anglo-Caribbean look favourably to the introduction of Creole, this is the very guide I would propose be used there for providing foundational knowledge to Creole users of multiethnic and multiracial backgrounds in schools where it is necessary that they learn English.

If I am reasonable in claiming that immersion education within Canada is a form of additive bilingualism, I would also state that this mode of communicative language teaching is in need of significant curriculum content change. After a quarter century of existence in a society where the substance of cultural and racial diversity looms large among voluntary non-white Canadian migrant communities, there are, surely, strong grounds for altering topicality of immersion content to reflect such diversity against a foreground of that new socioeconomic order, globalisation.

Beyond borders of the USA, matters of employing knowledge of scientific accomplishments among Creole users within classrooms are of great significance. Many of these accomplishments, which several observers in the rich developed world associate with alternative medicine, are integral to the everyday lives of Creole users. Their massive economic significance is so paramount to the forces of domination in a context of globalisation that prominent bio- and agro-chemical multinationals have been seeking to exploit the curative values of plant life indigenous to Africa, Asia, and South America.

I do not regard my arguments as either fanciful or idealistic. When they are considered in a foreground of progressive activities conducted by the Honeybee Network, they make very good sense. This is a Network in which Freireian elements of reciprocity, humanistic values, respect for knowledge of others, and linguistic reclamation abound.

The Honeybee Network is indicative of an experiment in people-to-people learning. Participants write in English which links them globally but alienates them locally.

> We cannot reach the people from whom we have learnt. Thus while we grow in our careers and achieve recognition and professional rewards, the people often suffer silently. The ethics of knowledge extraction, its documentation, dissemination and abstraction into theories, institutions or technologies is thus our central concern.[1]

The concern signifies a philosophy of discourse which is authentic, accountable and fair. Honeybee does two things which other organisations do not. In figurative terms, it collects pollen without impoverishing flowers and it connects flower to flower via pollination. When knowledge is collected from people, collectors should ensure that people do not become poorer after sharing their insights. Persons should also link one innovator with another via reciprocation, communication, and networking in local language. The network has documented innovations, traditional practices, and collected outstanding examples of contemporary knowledge which, in 2002, formed a 10,000 strong database that has been converted to a multimedia database.

The Honeybee Network was founded in 1989 by Dr. Anil Gupta, professor, at the College of Management in Ahmedabad, Gujarat, India. Dr. Gupta is also the Coordinator, Society for Research and Initiatives for Sustainable Technologies, Institutions and the Honeybee Network (SRISTI). He was motivated by the need to locate, catalogue, and disseminate inventions and innovations devised by people in poor and remote regions of developing societies. The motivation emanated from Dr. Gupta's realisation that in publishing his papers as a conventional economist, he was exploiting ideas of other people around the world. He told Mr. Peter Day, presenter, "Global Business," BBC World Service:

> The Honeybee does what we intellectuals don't do. It collects pollen from the flower and flowers don't feel bad. They don't complain. It collects from flower to flower. Now, if we could publish and share our work in local languages, then people-to-people connections can be forged. The farmer or the artisan in one part of the world can know one another. But that is only possible in their mother tongue. Second, we realise that whenever we take knowledge of people, they must not become anonymous. We started talking about intellectual property rights of the poor people. Why? Because the only resource in which poor people are rich is their ideas. And if we take away those ideas, what is left with them!

According to Peter Day, Dr. Gupta's inspiration has led to thousands of inventions based on "age-old folk wisdom." A focus on agriculture, bio-diversity and sustainability are principal priorities of the network. These are matters of "appropriate technology" which Dr. Gupta wants protected with patents, in much the same way as ideas are protected by the multinationals.

The Honeybee Network increases the impact of local creativity by spreading its findings and enabling inventors and innovators to locate each other, as well as, communicate directly. The network also facilitates access to information in persons' local languages, as much as possible. In the words of Peter Day, members of the network, are the remarkable unsung heroes of the developing world. These are the village inventors and entrepreneurs whose ideas may change millions of lives across the developing world. Day says the network is a powerhouse of ideas, and an inspiration for all (rich or poor) wherever they reside.

The following exchange between Peter Day and Dr. Anil Gupta reaches the core of justification for the network:

Peter Day: And the message for the developing world—the message for the developed, the rich world—from the Honeybee Network is—well— none of us are too clever or too rich to learn something. And when one sees innovation in action, at a village level, then it may inspire rich and seemingly clever and educated people to have the same little explosions of insight in their own worlds that the village entrepreneur, the village inventor is having in his or her own world.

Dr. Anil Gupta: You know, you have put it very well. What has happened over the years is that when we have become very proficient, very knowledgeable, very educated, we have lost the capacity to think simply. And it is this capacity to think simply which is what Honeybee Network cherishes and celebrates. It is the celebration of creativity at its best with its simplicity at its most profound level expressed by these people. And there is no reason to complicate a solution. So, you are absolutely right that the world would be better off if technologies would also have this human value of being simple, accessible, in some sense, multi-functional, multi-purpose. And, of course, it is not without significance that large numbers of innovations by these small people—not all of them—but large numbers of them—are environment friendly, because there's the underlying value that you don't want to increase the load on the environment. You use materials which are biodegradable or which are available locally. So, I think the Honeybee Network has a message for the rich and the educated: that of a capacity, which we lost over a period of time, to relate to our roots, to think simply and to be comfortable with lots of problems of everyday life that remain unsolved for a very long period of time. I think this tremendous patience that the elite all over the world has with the inertia—the innovations are helping overcome the patience with inertia and sewing the seeds of impatience. And that's what Honeybee Network does. It sews the seed of impatience with inertia.

The pedagogical case for Creolisation can be made by looking at a discussion from Carrington (1997) on strategies for the establishment of literacy in this mode of communication. One of Carrington's main points of departure is his acceptance of this definition of a literate person: "That person is literate who, in a language he speaks, can read with understanding anything he would have understood if it had been spoken to him; and can write so that it can be read, anything that he can say" (Gudschinsky, 1968: 146). Carrington proceeds to list three strategies, all of which, are closely correlated with the historical, cultural, educational, sporting, and scientific achievements noted above.

The first strategy consists of identifying and acting in settings within the lives of Creole users where they recognise that their everyday existence can benefit from literacy in their language. The second strategy is to locate and act in contexts where the common good for the citizenry is sufficiently uncontroversial that the medium for transmission of information is not regarded as threatening by the literate social establishment. The final strategy is to find and explore routes along which Creoles have filtered into linguistic areas which are primary areas of official languages.

Humanistic Approaches in Classrooms

In his introduction to Freire's *Education for Critical Consciousness*, Denis Goulet says no contemporary writer more persistently explores the multi-faceted nature of critical consciousness than Paulo Freire, a multicultural educator with the entire world as his classroom. My position is that if the international compass of communicative language pedagogy is to have a world focus, its proponents cannot trivialise radical democratic multiculturalism. Should they so choose, they must embrace language use for the abolition of domination and can neither ignore nor exclude the Brasilian intellectual.

Within the target language classroom, adopting such a posture means maintaining the Firthian tradition. It also means locating appropriate conjunctures for methodics and humanistic approaches to language education. When I refer to methodics, I am focusing solely on limitation of topicality. It is at the meeting points of methodics and humanism that learners would be in positions to understand the relevance of choosing between a setting where globalisation within a "new world order" prevails and a world where diversity is validated in humanistic settings.

Some of the content that lies between these two worlds can be exemplified:

(a) Who are the indigenous people of the world;

(b) Recognising the ethnic and racial diversity from which persons have been making significant contributions to international socioeconomic progress;

(c) How are legal codes and organisations developed, for the purpose of guaranteeing persons' legal and human rights;

(d) Developing an understanding of ways in which significant cultural events are celebrated by members of different racial and ethnic groups;

(e) How do shades of intolerance and abuse emerge, what are effective strategies for dealing with them;

(f) Why do persons of different races and ethnicities choose to move from one country to another;

(g) What are the modes of transport used for movement;

(h) What are the climatic conditions in various regions of the world;

(i) Why do the conditions differ;

(j) What methods do people use in various regions to acquire food, shelter, and employment, and establish communication;

(k) What are private enterprise, personal investment, and public ownership of economic and financial institutions;

(l) How do governments raise revenue and use it in social programmes to help the disadvantaged;

(m) Why do countries engage in trade with each other;

(n) What trading advantages do some countries enjoy over others;

(o) Why do these advantages exist;

(p) What is free trade;

(q) What are the roles of international financial and economic institutions;

(r) Why are some of these institutions very large and powerful;

(s) How are science and technology used to improve people's health and education;

(t) Why do diseases and illnesses exist in various parts of the worl;.

(u) What types of families exist in the world;

(v) What are the different ways in which persons around the world spend their leisure time, indoors and outdoors;

(w) Why do the differences exist;

(x) What are the various threats to human, plant, and animal life from noise, water, and air pollution.

All of these choices (a–x) can be suitably integrated with reading, writing, and discourse activities grounded in a set of short passages. These are passages, the understanding of which, represents a task-oriented education which is meaningful to learners. Further, they are real and were constructed, neither by teachers nor students, but by teachers and students through the use of collaborative discourse among a group of intermediate students from multicultural, multilingual, and multiracial backgrounds in the Canadian city, Toronto. Here are passages, the presentation of which, I shall follow by ideas about how they can be introduced to students, the discourse to be featured in them, and the kind of knowledge learners should ultimately gain. Once I have dealt with these matters, I shall offer justification for my selection of teaching content, as well as, passages that can be connected to it. The passages:

Summit in Brasil

In the spring of 1992, many leaders of the world participated in a summit meeting in Rio de Janeiro, Brasil. They met in this Brasilian city to examine the enormous problem caused by pollution all over the world.

This universal problem comes in many forms: exhaust fumes emitted by motor vehicles, oil spills from tankers on the seas, jet streams from aircraft, smoke from factories and cigarettes, effluents, microwave radiation from high tension electric power lines, electrical appliances such as television sets and microwave ovens, and last—but not least—noise pollution. We, the members of the international community, would have liked our leaders to be successful at their summit meeting. We had hoped that they deliberated wisely. But when we were asked to predict the outcome of the summit, we expressed divergent views: some said the outcome would be successful; others said it would be a failure and few were unsure about the result.

Almost a decade and a half has elapsed since the summit was held and many of us are still worried about our precious environment. None of us believes that the 1992 summit was a success. So, now we wonder what will happen to the Kyoto Protocol.

Questions: Summit in Brasil

(1) Explain the Kyoto Protocol.
(2) Name three countries other than Brasil where summit meetings are held.
(3) Do you know that in 1992 there were more than 40,000,000 cars in Brasil?
(4) What was the fuel used in some of those vehicles?
(5) What is Brasil's population density?
(6) What would be the best means of reducing pollution in Canada?
(7) Why do you think the summit was held in Brasil?

(8) Why is noise pollution a major problem in big cities of the United States and Canada?

(9) Are there too many people on the South American continent?

(10) Why are some people worried about very large populations in poor countries?

Diamonds

Diamonds are the world's most precious and expensive gems. Diamonds exist in raw form far below the earth's surface in mines and are plentiful in countries such as India, Russia, Angola, and South Africa.

After extraction from the mines, the raw diamonds are cut, polished and displayed in the showcases of jewellery stores. While on display, the gems are very attractive to men and women. Many people purchase them, even though they are very costly. They purchase expensive diamond rings, bracelets, and necklaces, despite the very high prices of these items.

We believe they purchase these costly items for two main purposes. Some women want to look beautiful when they wear diamond jewellery and men want to look handsome when they wear diamond jewellery. We also think they want to look handsome and beautiful because of what they see in T.V. commercials. In many of these commercials, handsome and beautiful people who dress smartly wear sparkling and expensive diamond jewellery.

Questions: Diamonds

(1) Which country in the entire world produces the most diamonds?

(2) Which African country produces the most diamonds?

(3) Which is more expensive and valuable: gold or diamonds?

(4) Do you know that diamonds are derived from the hardest substance?

(5) Is work in diamond mines hazardous?

(6) Why do some persons refuse to wear diamond jewellery?

(7) Do you believe that women buy more expensive diamond jewellery that men?

(8) Do you think that young boys and girls should wear gold jewellery in schools?

(9) Should all jewellery stores in very large cities be protected by security guards?

(10) Why do United States legal authorities want to question officials of the Oppenheimer company?

Impoverishment

Every year purchasers of the Toronto Star newspaper are asked to share their food with some of this city's very impoverished people. Many of these people have no homes where they live permanently. They reside in temporary shelters.

We think there is a marked contrast between extremely rich and very impoverished individuals in Toronto. This great difference is invisible, sometimes, because Toronto is a wealthy city and many poor people do not sleep on the streets of this urban city. However, during a recession, we can see that there is poverty in Toronto.

We believe poverty occurs, because most people want immediate satisfaction and they acquire many expensive commodities on credit. When some of them cannot pay for the items, they become bankrupt and may lose their homes. Several persons also spend large sums of money injudiciously: they are fooled by television advertising and purchase what they do not need.

Questions: Impoverishment

    (1) Are there marked contrasts between the rich and poor in the capital of your country?

    (2) Name two impoverished cities in Asia and two impoverished cities in South America.

    (3) Which is Canada's poorest province?

    (4) Name three cities in the world with very large populations.

    (5) In which large Canadian city do most immigrants live?

    (6) Why do you think some people are not generous?

    (7) Do you believe that most advertising on television should cease?

    (8) Do you think that more immigrants should enter Canada?

    (9) Is the world population too large?

    (10) Why do Canadian women earn lower wages and salaries than Canadian men?

City Riots

In 1992, large mobs of angry people rioted in Toronto and Los Angeles. The rioters committed acts of vandalism in both urban areas. They smashed shop windows, ransacked stores, and stole expensive electronic equipment. They also set fires to buildings in Los Angeles where there was extensive property destruction.

The destruction was estimated to be over one billion dollars; some of the people who lost property after the arson were Korean proprietors whose stores were also ransacked.

Many rioters in both cities said they were angry because of racial discrimination. People rioted in Los Angeles, because four white policemen had been acquitted, after they had been tried in court for kicking a black man repeatedly and beating him several times with their truncheons/batons. The policemen were filmed on videotape but members of an all white jury decided that they were innocent and were not cruel or brutal to the black man. People rioted in Toronto after a white policeman had shot a young black male, fatally.

The Toronto police claimed that the man had been trying to sell illegal drugs and was confronted by the officer who told him to surrender. He, however, brandished a knife and threatened the officer. Although the policeman fired a warning shot in the air to scare him, he continued to brandish the knife and moved menacingly towards the policeman. The policeman then discharged two rounds and the man was fatally shot.

We do not think that mobs of people should riot and commit acts of vandalism but policemen should not be brutal or cruel to people.

Questions: City Riots

(1) What is racial profiling?
(2) Name three American cities other than Los Angeles in which people rioted, during May, 1992.
(3) Do you know that more people live in the city of Los Angeles than in Toronto?
(4) Name two illegal drugs that people in Toronto and Los Angeles use.
(5) Name two forms of discrimination other than racial discrimination.
(6) Why are some policemen cruel to civilians?
(7) Should policemen be punished for shooting civilians?
(8) Why do some people use illegal drugs?
(9) Would you like to serve as a policeman in Toronto?
(10) Should young people in high schools who carry weapons be expelled from school?

Ethnic Conflict

We have discovered that ethnic conflict occurred in the Congo, Somalia, Sudan, Ethiopia, and Yugoslavia. The conflict in those locations has been severe and several people have died in battle. Many innocent people who did not fight also died and many of those who survived suffered.

The survivors suffered because of starvation: during the time of conflict, crops in fields, vehicles that carry food, and buildings where food is stored were destroyed. Although the Red Cross tried to distribute food to starving people, it was unable to do so effectively. Sometimes, Red Cross vehicles transporting food to innocent civilians were attacked. At other times, drivers of these vehicles could not pass roadblocks set up by combatants.

In Canada, we have been able to gain information about the conflict and starvation from the press, radio, and television. All members of our class preferred to acquire their information from one—not the other two—sources. Thuyen and Keo preferred television. They said that when they receive information via television, they gain it, instantly; they feel as if they are present at locations where events are happening. They are also able to hear and see, simultaneously.

Czarek preferred to obtain his information from the press. He said he could choose to read whatever he wanted. When he watched T.V., he watched the same things on different channels. He also mentioned that he could read things repeatedly in newspapers. He could not do so when he watched T.V. William said that when he listened to the radio he did not see what was happening. He had to think and imagine and he likes doing so.

Questions: Ethnic Conflict

(1) Name four other countries in which ethnic conflict has occurred.
(2) Name six ethnic groups in Canada that come from Europe.
(3) Name five newspapers in Toronto in addition to the *Toronto Star*.
(4) What is the main purpose of a videocassette recorder.
(5) What connections exist among television and newspapers in Canada?
(6) Should every Canadian possess a television set?
(7) Why do some people refuse to talk about politics or religion?
(8) Why do you think there is ethnic conflict among people?
(9) Do you think that Canadian farmers should donate some of their food to countries where people are starving?
(10) Why do you think one race of people ruled South Africa, for a long time?

Male and Female Work

Weekend Activities	Weekend Activities
Making a Cake	Doing Laundry
House Cleaning	Preparing Breakfast
Shopping	Bathing Children

When we focus on two lists of weekend activities, we cannot locate a single domestic chore performed by our male colleague, Narinder.

William wants to find out if all men should perform domestic chores. While many of us think they should, a few think they should not. Some of us believe that if women and men should perform domestic activities, they should pool their financial resources: a man's money should not be exclusively his, a woman's money should not be exclusively hers.

Finally, we agreed that most males and females in Canada actually pool their financial resources. We think it is wise to do so, because people would be able to manage their resources well.

Questions: Male and Female Work

(1) Did you perform any domestic chores in your native country?

(2) Are married women in your country housewives?

(3) Name four different types of families living in Canada.

(4) Are many women in your country highly paid professionals?

(5) Did you know there are few female engineers across Canada?

(6) Why do some men like to earn more money than women?

(7) Why do several women in Canada and the USA work inside and outside of their homes?

(8) Do you believe that all married women work harder than their husbands?

(9) Why do some women wish to remain single?

(10) How should married couples who bear male children raise them?

Fathers' Day

In late June, every year, many people in Christian countries celebrate Fathers' Day. This is the day when children honour their male parents for being good fathers.

On Fathers Day, many Canadian husbands receive gifts from their wives and children. Every year in Toronto, we can see large numbers of people shopping at large malls such as the Eaton Centre. We believe that many of them buy gifts for their fathers and husbands.

My colleague, Zoreh, asked me two very important questions about Fathers' Day: she wanted to know when the day was first celebrated and why people celebrate it. I could not answer her. I did not know all the reasons for celebrating the day and was ignorant about the time when it was first celebrated.

However, I was able to inform her that Mothers' Day originated in the USA and was celebrated before the first Fathers' Day was celebrated. Mercedes agreed with me, fully.

All of us agree that it is appropriate to honour our mothers and fathers on two special days in May and June. We also think that many children, husbands, and wives are deceived by extensive advertising in the press, on radio, and television. Some of us even think that the audio/visual medium is responsible for the greatest deception. As a result of the advertising, several people spend large sums of money purchasing gifts before Mothers' and Fathers' Days. We think the celebration of these days has become too commercialised.

Questions: Fathers' Day

(1) Is Fathers' Day celebrated in your country?
(2) Do you know in which country Fathers' Day was first celebrated?
(3) How much money do you think is spent every year all across Canada to purchase gifts on Fathers' Day?
(4) What is the average size of the Canadian family today?
(5) Name four poor countries in which the average sizes of the family is small.
(6) Do you think mothers should be honoured more than fathers?
(7) Why do you think some husbands never abuse their wives?
(8) At what age do you think women should marry?
(9) How many children do you think a married couple should have?
(10) Why do you think some women and men never marry?

Human Differences

There is unanimous agreement among us that members of the upper class in Canada, Australia, and the USA can afford to play games such as lawn tennis, and golf. There is also no dissent among us that members of the lower class in countries such as El Salvador, India, and Kenya cannot afford to play these games. We agree, because we know there is great economic disparity between rich and poor people in all of these societies. It is also because of the disparity that the poor cannot purchase expensive sports gear used by golfers and tennis players. The poor cannot participate in other games such as polo, because they cannot purchase very costly gear.

Some of us believe that even if people could afford to purchase expensive equipment, they might not be able to play golf or polo. They might not be able to participate because of three types of discrimination against them: racial, sexual, and ethnic discrimination.

Questions: Human Differences

(1) What is your favourite sport?

(2) What is the most popular sport in your country?

(3) Which sports' personality do you most admire?

(4) Where were the games of La Crosse and golf invented?

(5) From which social class does the world's best golfer come?

(6) Which country has won the World Cup of Soccer the most?

(7) Why do you think that the sport of basketball in the USA is dominated by black Americans?

(8) Why do you think some people say professional baseball players in the USA are paid too much?

(9) Do you think Canadian and American high school students are too involved in sports?

(10) Why do some people prefer to play outdoor games?

The Twenty-Fifth Olympiad

Sport	Countries in Contention for Gold Metals
Baseball	China, Cuba, USA, Japan
Basketball	USA
Boxing	China, Cuba, USA
Cycling	Columbia, France, Germany, Italy
Diving	China, The Unified Team, USA
Gymnastics	China, The Unified Team, Romania, USA
Hockey	Germany, India, Kenya, Pakistan
High Jumping	Canada, China, The Unified Team, USA
Long Jumping	Canada, Germany, Spain, USA
Distance Races	Ethiopia, Kenya, Morocco
Rowing	Australia, Canada, USA
Rifle shooting	Australia, Canada, England, Mexico
Swimming	Australia, China, Germany, Hungary, Unified Team
Soccer	Brasil, Denmark, Germany, Italy, Spain
Volley Ball	Brasil, Cuba, Unified Team, USA
Weight Lifting	Iran, Romania, Unified Team, USA
Wrestling	Japan, Romania, The Unified Team, USA
Sprint Races	Canada, England, Morocco, USA

The Games of the twenty-fifth Olympiad began in Barcelona, Spain, on 25th July, 1992. For more than two weeks, very talented athletes from around the world competed for gold, silver, and bronze medals. Some of the field events were completed during the first few days of the Games and many gold medals were won by the best competitors.

Even before all events had begun, we completed a list of countries which we thought were in contention for gold. On our list, the USA appeared most often and some colleagues had predicted that this country would win most of the gold medals. Some predicted that China would win most of these prizes; others said there would be a tie between China and the USA for medals. We awaited the outcome of the games to determine the accuracy of our predictions.

Prior to the outcome, we had noted that Canada was not a strong contender for gold. It appeared only four times on our list. There are good reasons Canada appeared infrequently. Coaches and trainers are not very good. Canadian federal and provincial governments do not spend much money to train athletes for Olympic competition.

Questions: The Twenty-Fifth Olympiad

(1) What is the name of the person who designed the costumes displayed during the colourful opening ceremonies of the twenty-fifth Olympiad?

(2) What is your estimate of the cost of staging the twenty-fifth Olympiad?

(3) Is it true that many South Americans are fanatical about soccer?

(4) How did the English game, football, become known as soccer?

(5) Is it true that an American did not invent basketball?

(6) Why do you think the 1996 Olympic games were held in the USA?

(7) Do you think that all athletes who use illegal drugs should be banned from competition for life?

(8) Why do you think the USA assembled a team of very highly paid professionals to participate in basketball games of the twenty-fifth Olympiad?

(9) Why do you think soft drink manufacturers advertised extensively during the time when the Games were staged?

(10) Should countries compete to stage the Olympic Games?

Driving

Driving motor vehicles is very hazardous in large countries such as Canada and the USA. Some of us believe that driving in the winter is more hazardous than the summer when road surfaces are not slippery, covered with ice and snow, or visibility is good.

Summer driving may be less hazardous but we should always be alert in warm weather when we are driving. Why should we be? It is because road surfaces are clear, some drivers do not adhere to speed limits, drive very fast, and exceed speed limits. They violate traffic laws and can cause accidents.

Accidents are also caused by young male drivers who chauffeur very fast cars. Sometimes, these drivers listen to music while at the wheel and do not concentrate on the road. In addition, many of them consume excessive amounts of alcohol, become intoxicated, lose control of their vehicles and cause serious accidents.

It may not be easy to stop intoxicated drivers from endangering the lives of other people. All drivers of vehicles who care about others and want to remain sober on the streets and highways should find out what the German motor manufacturer, Volkswagen, has been doing to make driving a safe operation.

Questions: Driving

(1) What is drag racing?
(2) Name three European cities in which motor vehicles are manufactured.
(3) What are four of the busiest highways in North America?
(4) Name three means of long distance travelling in North America.
(5) How many travellers use the Toronto Subway during peak periods?
(6) Why do some people say that Sport Utility Vehicles [SUVs] are hazardous?
(7) Should penalties for drunk driving in Canada be stiffened?
(8) Why do some people exceed speed limits when driving?
(9) Which countries do you believe manufacture the most reliable cars?
(10) Are females better drivers than males?

Thuyen's Northern Fishing Trip

On Good Friday, I went on a brief fishing trip to Northern Ontario. I left Toronto at 12:30 a.m. on that Friday in one of three packed cars. After two and a half hours I reached my destination, where I and other travellers slept for a short period. After our brief rest, my companions and I caught numerous small fishes which we took with us on our return journey to Toronto. When we returned to the city early Friday afternoon, I prepared a meal by frying the fishes crisply. After the meal had been prepared, I sat with my friends and enjoyed the fried fishes, as well as, a few bottles of beer.

Although my trip was a brief one, I was happy to see many other parts of Ontario which are not heavily populated. I was also able to observe the different techniques anglers used to cast their fishing lines and catch large fishes.

Questions: Thuyen's Northern Fishing Trip

(1) Name four lakes in North America which are polluted.

(2) Name four large lakes in Canada where people do sport fishing.

(3) What are two other ways of preparing fishes?

(4) Do you know that there are fishes in Canadian rivers which are polluted?

(5) Why do several Canadians go fishing in the summer time?

(6) Why do some people prefer to be vegetarian?

(7) Why do some people choose to eat more fish than beef?

(8) Why do some people prefer to eat fishes caught from the oceans?

(9) Is the hunting of large land animals good for the environment?

(10) Why do you think that Canadians are restricted from catching unlimited numbers of cod on Canada's Atlantic coast?

Cities, People, and Customs

Chandigarh, the Punjab capital in India, Phnom Penh in Gambodia, Addis Abba in Ethiopia, and Budapest in Hungary are old cities. In order to know these facts, we must read extensively. If we read extensively, we would also gain knowledge about other old capitals in different countries of the world. Many of these countries are on the continents of Africa, Asia, and Europe.

When we look very closely at these countries, we discover that the people who live in them are of different ethnic, religious, and linguistic backgrounds: there are Hindus, Muslims, and Christians in India. These people speak Hindi, Urdu, and English. Although they believe in God, their religious customs differ. Even though Hungary is a European country, Christians and Muslims live there. Zoltan, our new colleague from Hungary, told us that his name, a common Hungarian first name, is derived from the Muslim name, Sultan.

We thus concluded correctly that Muslims influenced the development of Hungary. Zoltan told us that they influenced the development of the former Soviet Union, too. Today, we see some of that influence in the architecture of Moscow, the Russian capital.

Questions: Cities, People, and Customs

(1) Are there any very old cities in your country?

(2) How many different ethnic groups live in your country?

(3) Which of the three North American societies is the most multicultural?

(4) What does the word, 'Toronto,' mean?

(5) Do you like the architecture of modern cities?

(6) Why do you believe many modern cities are overcrowded?

(7) Do you think that all Canadians should read extensively?

(8) Why do many Americans and Canadians like to visit Africa, Asia, South America, and the Caribbean?

(9) Did Muslims rule Spain at one time?

(10) Is it true that coffee was first grown in Ethiopia?

Celebration

In 1976 and 1987 the USA and Australia celebrated two hundred years of existence. On 1st July, 1992, Canada celebrated its one hundred and twenty-fifth birthday. On that day, many Canadians waved Canadian flags and were in very happy moods.

We must remember that a few hundred years ago Europeans left their countries and settled in what we know as Australia, Canada, New Zealand, and the United States. They also settled in Africa, Asia, South, and Central America. Europeans are, however, recent arrivals in these parts of the world: indigenous people have been here for thousands of years before Europeans came. The Maoris, Aborigines, Mayas, Incas, Mohawks, and Crees had been living in these parts long before Europeans left their own countries. Toronto, Mississauga, and Oklahoma are not European names. They are names devised by indigenous people.

When some Europeans met indigenous people, they tried to conquer them. Many indigenous people were murdered and many died of diseases that originated in Europe. These people were not treated well by Europeans. Today, many leaders of indigenous people in North, South, and Central America, as well as, Australia say Europeans are responsible for high levels of illiteracy, suicide and alcoholism among their people.

So, those of us who celebrate Canada Day must not forget that some Canadians are descendants of indigenous people; these descendants and their ancestors are victims of unfair treatment by some Europeans.

Questions: Celebration

(1) Name six prominent North American actresses and male vocalists who are descendants of indigenous persons?

(2) Do you know that black people first came to the Caribbean and USA as slaves from Africa?

(3) Name four jobs early immigrants from China did, when they first came to Canada.

(4) What are English meanings of Nigeria, Nova Scotia, and Buenos Aires?

(5) Name four old cities in South America.

(6) Why did some Mohawks fight in Quebec in 1990?

(7) Why do you think that many indigenous people in North America are illiterate?

(8) Why were harmful things done to aborigines in Australia?

(9) Can alcoholism among some of Canada's indigenous people be stopped?

(10) Should indigenous people all over the world be compensated for being treated unfairly by some Europeans?

A New Home

All the members of our class are immigrants to Canada; many of us wish to reside here permanently, even though we have to live in a cold climate in Toronto. We came to Canada to enjoy more safety and a higher standard of living and we believe that these advantages outweigh the disadvantages of living in a different country.

Because we are not in our native countries, we know that we would have to adjust to new living conditions. Canada, however, is a society with diverse ethnic, religious, racial, and linguistic groups. So, we hope that we do not have to spend a long time adjusting.

We have not seen many regions of this large country but we have been impressed favourably by the clean streets and efficient means of public transportation in Toronto. We know that crime occurs in this city and in the rest of Canada, too. Much more crime takes place in some of our own countries, though. We also know that we can enjoy a high standard of living in the USA. We think we can enjoy more safety in Canada, though.

Questions: A New Home

(1) Is it true that there are several criminal gangs across Canada?

(2) How many immigrants came to Canada during the course of the last ten years?

(3) What are the main seasons in your native country?

(4) Do you know that the total population of Canada is not half the total population of India?

(5) Is the standard of living in Canada higher than the standard of living in the United States of America?

(6) Why do you believe Toronto streets are so clean?

(7) Name six locations in Canada where very poor people reside.

(8) Do you think different ethnic groups in Canada appreciate each other?

(9) Why do you think many immigrants from the Caribbean know how to speak English?

(10) Why do many native North Americans live in poor health?

A Discussion

Last month we participated in an interesting discussion about marital relationships. After we had completed the discussion, we wrote a short passage. Soon after we had written, Olga proposed that we should only converse with each other. She added that when we write we use a lot of time on the two evenings we do English. She also stated that when we converse we would be able to show our enthusiasm to each other. She was strongly supported by Czarek.

However, Thuyen, Mohammed, and Shufa disagreed with them. These three colleagues said that all of us learn more, when we converse, read, and write. Keo then proposed that we write prepared passages everyday and read them.

William listened very carefully to our contributions then offered his. He said that if we read prepared passages we might not be able to understand English very well. He also agreed with Mohammed, Thuyen, and Shufa that we can benefit more when we read, converse, and write. Finally, we accepted his compromise that we do writing, reading, and conversation on one evening and only do conversation on the other evening.

Questions: A Discussion.

(1) How many languages can you speak?

(2) How many official languages exist in the USA?

(3) How many languages do people in your native country speak?

(4) Do you like to meet new people?

(5) Do you like learning English?

(6) Why is there a Heritage Language programme in Canada?

(7) Should Every Canadian learn to speak English and French?

(8) Is it true that men speak more than women?

(9) Why do some people dislike reading books?

(10) Why do you think some students do not like to attend school?

Let me turn to the matter of teachers' engaging students with these passages. A teacher's first job is to introduce learners to each of the passages by initiating discourse about what their titles signify, e.g., the passage, "Celebration." Given that this passage has to be read, what can teachers and learners do to facilitate their understanding of this matter? The teacher can use learners' previous and current knowledge of this type of celebration as a basis to introducing the topic. The groundwork for discussion will be laid by the teacher's use of students' ethnic, racial, sexual, and national differences. The foundation will be employed to create an intergroup understanding of the title, "Celebration."

Once an understanding has been attained, the teacher introduces, and participates in, discussion of themes within each paragraph. Individual students, followed by the teacher, then read the passages. Ideally, all student reading of entire passages can be recorded on audio tape.

Once reading is completed, the ten questions can be answered, orally and in writing. The first five are factual and although the teacher may be an excellent source of expertise, s/he is not the sole source, in these times of internet searches which learners can use as important bases to reporting findings in written forms. The last five questions are what I term opinion questions, responses to which are not always expressed identically. Learners' responses should, thus, constitute fertile interactive ground for initiation and maintenance of meaningful discourse and writing in classrooms. The discourse and writing surrounding the last five questions can be used as raw material for student constructing of new passages.

This is discourse from which power plays should be absent. Its most prominent features would be formulations posed cooperatively—lists, contrasts, repetitions of previous speakers' utterances—which signify avoidance of impoliteness (Walcott, 1984), politeness strategies, intended to prevent damage and loss of face among coconversants (Brown and Levinson, 1978), and deliberate ambiguity geared to evading "socially tricky" what Weiser (1974) terms socially tricky situations. Here, I cannot resist the temptation to offer what I regard as a powerful instance of the combined significance of lists and contrasts.

I recall that during the course of the 1988 vice-presidential debate between Republican, Dan Quayle, and Democratic challenger, Senator Lloyd Bentsen in the United States, Mr. Quayle asserted: "I have as much experience in the Congress as Jack Kennedy did when he sought the presidency." I remember with intense vividness, a riveting riposte from the Senator which (today) still reverberates within political circles, something I would consider as a conversational analytical gem: "Senator, I served with Jack Kennedy. I knew Jack Kennedy. Jack Kennedy was a friend of mine. Senator, you're no Jack Kennedy.

The type of knowledge foundational to learners' speech and writing should ultimately be what Polanyi (1959) sees as unformulated or tacit knowledge, very different to explicit knowledge. He adds that persons always know tacitly that they are holding their explicit knowledge to be true. He notes that the essential logical distinction between the tacit and the explicit is that individuals can reflect on things stated explicitly in ways they cannot reflect on tacit experiences. Importantly, the structure of tacit knowledge is demonstrated via understanding disjointed parts of comprehensive wholes: in such manifestation, persons shift attention from apprehending particulars to the understanding of their joint meaning.

In making my proposal for tacit knowledge, I am not espousing a position similar to, or identical with, Krashen's, that language acquisition is either a subconscious or unconscious process. I am making statements about language use among learners as ultimately prereflective (Heap, 1979) but always grounded in consciousness.

The presentation of the passages in association with topicality which validates human diversity can now be justified. This justification has very deep roots in a conception of persons within settings of radical democratic multiculturalism which comes from ideas of Cornel West.[2] Following West, I think the topicality chosen represents a public space within which those in settings of domination are made accountable to the victims of their inferiorisation practices. West's version of victimisation is especially pertinent to the topicality I selected.

He says working people (e.g., blacks, women, gays and lesbians) would be naive not to view themselves as victims, but to remain at the level of regarding themselves as sufferers would be paralysing. Doing so would be to remain at the level of an excuse, an alibi. Such persons are agents, subjects. What they think and do can make a difference. Victimisation is to be acknowledged as just one dimension of their history and presence. Their possession of resources, traditions, communities, relationships, networks, must also be recognised as the tools which enable a transcendence of degradation. West, the Afro-American Christian, is speaking as an internationalist who does not regard things human as alien to him.

This is a position which he elaborates by pointing to the dynamism (better still the dialectical connections) between individuality and community which defines his presence. It is a presence in which there is adaptability to new circumstances. He has an understanding of individuality which is inseparable from community but he never allows community to absorb his distinctive and singular individuality. In an equally important sense, he never allows the individuality to degenerate into a selfish, rugged, and ragged individualism. This is the complex interplay between individuality and democratic community that allows for projection or the flowering of who and what he is uniquely as an individual but also contributes to a community in which ordinary people can participate for the purpose of making decisions within institutions that guide and regulate their lives.

Participation of ordinary people resonates strongly with critical pedagogy for which Freire has stood pre-eminently. It is to Pennycook (1996) and Canagarajah (1999) that I turn, with the aim of exploring the relevance of critical pedagogy, after which, I shall explain the humanistic approaches. My exploration shall be confined, via exemplification, to English language.

Pennycook views the English classroom as a site where cultures and discourses that dominate the world can be challenged and modified. For him, the subject matter which forms the foundations for challenging is made of links among matters such as popular culture, development, and capitalism. In what I see as a strong reflection of content, he makes a plea for the usefulness of English teaching via facilitating an appreciation of ways in which the language is associated with colonial history, striving for economic and political strength, divisions between private and public economic sectors. These are the very connections which should be apprehended through an understanding of global, economic, and educational systems.

What is being proposed here is no value neutral education.

> Professional competence, command of a subject or discipline, is never understood by the progressive teacher as something neutral. There is no such thing called "professional competence" all by itself. We must always ask ourselves: In favour of whom and of what do we use our technical competence. (Freire, 1987: 212)

This is education which is both radical, interrogative, and transformative. In the words of hooks (2003), it is insurrection of subjugated knowledge. In Pennycook's words, it is geared to social change. Language learning occurs in settings where various cultural, social, and ideological forms are frequently opposed to each other. As such, there is strong commitment to constructing new forms of knowledge and culture.

Pennycook's position bears close resemblance to that of Canagarajah's. Canagarajah says critical pedagogy formulates learners as subject to influences from their own contexts. Thus, language learners should gain knowledge rooted in their social practices and material settings. This is knowledge which is opposed to that emergent from needs, interests, and necessities of dominant organisations and groups which impact learning and the practices. Further, because knowledge is always changing, learners must be granted opportunities to negotiate over what knowledge should be introduced in classrooms. An important aim of the negotiation is development of a critical orientation to learning which enables learners to identify operations of dominant organisations.

My understanding of critical pedagogy is that it is aimed at self education rooted in disruption of the routine that ownership of knowledge beneficial to persons' existence is not an important feature of the everyday lives of subordinated people. More significantly, critical pedagogy stands as a rejection of essentialist assumptions, quite widespread and strongly embedded in the Western episteme, that validity of ideas about target language education flows from the West. This is the very episteme of which Luke is critical, when he points to the inadequacy and contradiction in advocacy of multiculturalism, multilingualism, language rights, as well as, anti-racist, and anti-sexist, education in target language pedagogy. For him, the inadequacy and contradiction remain deeply rooted in the connective discourse encompassing an Anglo/American/Commonwealth community of U.S. Canadian, EU, UK, New Zealand, Asian, and Australian ideology of language and literacy education.

In responding to his own query about the compelling reason for second language educators to embrace critical pedagogy, he stresses, rhetorically:

> Is it because the traditional student bodies of such programmes have historically been objects of colonial and imperial power or diasporic subjects living at the economic margins of Western and Northern cultures and economies? Is it because the work of second language education, notably Teachers of English to Speakers of Other Languages (TESOL), itself once a mixture of missionary work and orientalism, is now a transnational service industry in the production of skilled human resources for economic globalisation? Is it because the identity politics and dynamics of power and patriarchy within the TESOL classroom in so many countries typically entail social relations between teachers and students that reproduce larger social and economic relations between economically mainstream and marginal, cosmopolitan and diasporic, and white and coloured subjects? Probably all of the above. (Luke, 2004: 25)

Given my own analysis, I agree, totally. Anyone inclined to challenge my position should consider the research findings of Panreiter (2004) on Mexico City. Panreiter asks whether impoverishment and polarisation there are connected to the profound integration of Mexico into the globalised economic structure and the increasing economic significance of Mexico City as a global city.

He observes that well-placed Mexican government officials have admitted major wage reductions were decisive features in the country's move to neoliberal modernisation and globalisation, for lower production costs enabled Mexico to become more competitive, domestically and internationally. On an even more persuasive note, he adds that an indigenous woman residing in poverty within an area such as Valle de Chalco and working as a domestic (*muchacha*) in the home of a banker in Las Lomas is connected to the globalised environment in much the same way as a street vendor who sells brand name commodities. They all contribute to the reproduction of global capitalism. This is the very contribution which takes place in other global cities where numerous participants at the low end of the socioeconomic spectrum are receiving second language education.

With both of my eyes on deregulation, a major feature of globalisation, I did not miss the problem emergent from the existence of big box superstores or power centres such as Home Depot, BJ's, Target, Wall Mart, and Costco. According to the Toronto daily, the *Globe and Mail*, these are stores which entice customers by selling brand name goods at big discounts. I also know that they sell products in bulk, employ large numbers of immigrants at low wage levels, attract a huge immigrant clientele, and are staunchly opposed to unionisation. In a *Globe* Business section report of 7th October, 2004, it was observed that the growth of power centres in Canada has lagged behind those in the USA where more than over a hundred such organisations exist.

> Indeed, big box retail expansion has been so rapid south of the border that some U.S. municipalities have put restrictions on the stores because of concerns that they threaten local merchants and place too much strain on such municipal services as roads.

While the *Globe* report is factually correct about municipal services, local merchants are not just threatened, they have already been put out of business. In Canada, the Bi-Way chain of stores from which new Canadian immigrants could purchase good quality low priced consumer items and where many of them were also employed, was forced out of business by Wall Mart, the presence of which, is directly owed to the North American Free Trade (NAFTA) deal. This is, of course an arrangement implemented at a time when the global neoliberal imperatives of Presidents, Reagan, Bush (senior), Prime Ministers Thatcher and Mulroney were beginning to solidify.

The topics chosen for the passages are not intended to be exhaustive and are geared to adults. More importantly, teachers are given considerable scope for specifying what should be exemplified, when subject matter is being introduced. There is an obvious presupposition that although languages are being used, the starting point for actualising use is that information has to be exchanged among persons. It is not on every occasion that the teacher will introduce these topics. The teacher has an obligation to validate learners as thinkers who do make choices and can exercise their ability by proposing what should be introduced in class. All information can be exchanged through using approaches which are genuinely communicative. These approaches are humanistic and community language learning which are reflected through participation in publics. I shall explore the significance of such participation, after which I shall attend to the approaches.

In his discourse on publics and public opinion Mills states that the most significant feature of public opinion is the free ebb and flow of discussion. Discussion is, simultaneously, thread and shuttle linking discussion circles.

> It lies at the root of the conception of authority by discussion and it is based upon the hope that truth and justice will somehow come out of society as a great apparatus of free discussion. The people are presented with problems. They discuss them. They decide on them. They formulate viewpoints. These viewpoints are organised, and they compete. One viewpoint 'wins out.' Then the people act out this view, or their representatives are instructed to act it out, and this they promptly do. (Mills, 1956: 299)

Mills also states that out of little circles of people talking with one another, larger forces of social movement develop and discussion of opinion is the important stage in a total act by which public affairs are carried out.

He adds that in a public: virtually as many individuals express opinions as receive them; public communications are so organised that there is a chance, immediately and effectively to answer back any opinion expressed in public; and opinion formed by such discussion (a) readily finds an outlet in effective action, even against (if necessary) prevailing systems of authority, (b) authoritative institutions do not penetrate the public which is autonomous in its operations.

It is necessary for me to point out that the Mills' reference is presented as an "extreme type" which he uses as a working model to describe how modern U.S. society does not operate. I would add that other contemporary, industrialised/computerised "democratic" Western societies do not operate in accordance with it. More importantly, the model is rooted in conversation which hooks (2003) sees as a main location for identifying pedagogy of the democratic educator. She adds that discourse for the purpose of sharing information and exchanging ideas (what I designate as collaborative discourse), is the practice both within and beyond academic settings which affirms that learning can be actualised through various modes of speech.

hooks is, of course, questioning what has come to be known as advocacy of the monolingual and native speaker fallacies in target language pedagogy which service engines of power and control through strengthening norms and economic resources of societies (usually Western) from which target language emanates (Phillipson, 1992). The first fallacy refers to the view that the only permissible medium of teaching in classrooms should be the target language being learnt. What lies behind this view is thinking that exclusive concentration on the target will maximise language learning, regardless of whatever languages are familiar to learners. The impetus to monolingualism can be located in the colonial language teaching experience and assumptions that, as a consequence of discovery of phonetics, "good speaking habits" were necessary in classrooms.

The native speaker fallacy, which Phillipson characterises as ludicrous and without validity, rests on assumptions: ideal target language teachers whom all other teachers should emulate are native speakers, native speakers possess and demonstrate greater ability in producing fluent, idiomatically suitable language. These assumptions have their foundation in views that language teaching was indistinguishable from culture teaching and that learners of a target language such as English needed to familiarise themselves with a culture from which it emanates, as well as, ways of connecting with the culture. Consider this assessment of English.

> Whereas vernacular speech may seldom be used in the classroom by teachers it may be the preferred way to share knowledge in other settings. When educational settings become places that have as their central goal the teaching of bourgeoisie manners, vernacular speech and languages other than Standard English are not valued. Indeed they are blatantly devalued. While acknowledging the value of standard English the democratic educator also values diversity in language. (hooks, 2003: 45)

hooks adds that students who use Standard English but for whom English is a second language, are fulfilled in their bilingual self esteem while their first languages are appreciated. Such signification can take place as teachers implement practices which respect diversity and oppose accepted preference for preserving dominator values.

Her ideas are very powerful echoes of Freire's position on the dilemmas confronting newcomers to countries where they must learn the dominant discourse or national language of their new societies. Freire (1993) advocates command of national languages as a survival strategy for effective transformation of unjust and cruel societies where the subordinated are marginalised, insulted, and humiliated. He is, however, convinced that teaching national languages to subordinated learners should be consonant with respect of their cultural identities. Doing so entails respecting non-standard languages in the same ways as background knowledge of subordinated learners is respected. Significantly, he stresses that none of these ideas would make sense, if the question of language is separated from discussions of power or assessment of social classes and their contradictions.

The hooks position on diversity and Freire's on respect of cultural identities make good sense in the area of target language teaching. Within former British possessions, English outside target language classrooms cannot be deemed solely a colonial language, the dominator medium. In literature, film and music, for instance, English is being used transformatively to offer trenchant critiques of colonialist domination and injustice. In Africa, the writing of Chinua Achebe and Wole Soyenka, Nigerians, stands prominently. The poetry of Derek Walcott, Edward Kamau Brathwaite, and Wilson Harris of the Anglo-Caribbean is of similar importance. From India comes the work of Rohyntyn Mistry and Vickram Seth, among that of several other outstanding South Asian writers such as Arundhati Roy who made this statement about the function of literature to the World Social Forum in Brasil (2005): the point of literature should not just be the confronting of Empire, but also, laying seige to it.

Here are poems by Wilson Harris and Derek Walcott, both of which, are partially but significantly representative of what Burnett (1986) sees as thematic in Caribbean literature: tradition, language, gritty celebration of survival, festive celebration of inheriting location, discomfort over what is lost, the search for identity, and championing faith and hope within the teeth of betrayal and disillusion.

Charcoal

> *Bold outlines are drawn to encompass*
> *the history of the world: crude but naked emphasis*
> *rests on each figure of the past*
> *Wherein the golden sunlight burns raw and unsophisticated.*
> *Fires of brightness are sheltered*
> *to burn the fallen limbs of men: the green*

spirit of leaves like smoke
rises to mark the barrow of earth
and dwindles to perfection. The stars
are sparks
emblems of fire
to blacken the limbs of each god who falls:
spendthrift creation. The stable dew-drop is flame.
The dew burnishes each star in preparation for every deserted
lane.
Time lies uneasy between the paintless houses
weather-beaten and dark.
The Negro once leaned on his spade
breathing the smoke of his labour
the arch of his body banked to shelter or tame
fury and diamond
or else like charcoal to grain
the world. (Wilson Harris, 1986: 185)

A Far Cry from Africa

A wind is ruffling the tawny pelt
Of Africa. Kikuyu quick as flies
Batten upon the bloodstreams of the veldt.
Corpses are scattered through a paradise.
But still the worm, colonel of carrion, cries:
'Waste no compassion on these separate dead'
Statistics justify and scholars seize
The salients of colonial policy.
What is that to the white child hacked in bed?
To savages expendable as Jews?
Threshed out by beaters, the long rushes break
In a white dust of ibises whose cries
Have wheeled since civilisation's dawn
From the parched river or beast-teeming plain,
The violence of beast on beast is read
As natural law, but upright man
Seeks his divinity with inflicting pain.
Delirious as these worried beasts, his wars
Dance to the tightened carcass of a drum,

While he calls courage still, that native dread
Of the white peace contracted by the dead.
Again brutish necessity wipes its hands
Upon the napkin of a dirty cause, again
A waste of our compassion, as with Spain.
The gorilla wrestles with the superman.
I who am poisoned with the blood of both,
Where shall I turn, divided to the vein?
I who have cursed
The drunken officer of British rule, how choose
Between this Africa and the English tongue I love?
Betray them both, or give back what they give?
How can I face such slaughter and be cool?
How can I turn from Africa and live? (Derek Walcott, 1986: 243)

Other examples of transformative use can be found in Soyenka's radio play, "Document of Identity" and Achebe's novel, Anthills of the Savannah (1986), the second of which, I examine. Derek Cooper, host of the BBC Arts programme, Meridian, described the novel as a multilevel presentation of political intrigue, a devastating portrait of modern Africa, a morality tale in which a fictionalised nation, Kangan, bleeds to death in its search for national identity. Cooper also assessed the book as a political tract exploring the legacies of colonialism and elite groups who so often have replaced British rule.

While speaking on the BBC Arts programme, Meridian, in the nineteen eighties about this elite in his own country, Nigeria, which was plagued by military dictatorships, Achebe notes:

> We were ruled by the British for half a century or more and during this period an elite was created based on the British educational system. And it is this elite that is in power. And they have to learn that even though they may be in power they are not the people. They do not own the country. They must forge links with the vast majority of peasants and workers and women and children...who are the majority—who own the country—to create accountability. That is really the point of the leader to the led. We are not new people in the world. The fact that we were subjects of England does not mean we were created by the English. It was just a short period in our history and we must learn to go beyond that period to the long history through the millennia in which our peo-

ple were independent and self governing and had the initiative, were in control of their lives. It is from this period that the myths and the oral tradition derive. And we must again link ourselves with this heritage. And from this multiple heritage we can build a future.

I assume that it was with a very strong interest in establishing connections between people and their heritage that author Achebe offered readers, not just the English, the *Anthills of the Savannah*; he also allowed them to immerse themselves in what I term the significance of West African Pidgin.

Community And Humanistic Language Learning

The leading proponents of community and humanistic language learning are averse to mechanism and mentalism. The approaches have deep roots in what has come to be known as third force psychology, whose promoters reject Skinnerian radical behaviourism and Freudian psychoanalysis. Ideas in humanistic and community language learning are also inconsistent with the views espoused by Chomsky. These are ideas formed from unambiguous acceptance of Abraham Maslow's and Carl Rogers' thinking. They are also very consistent with Freireian views. Although they were promoted at a time when great interest in communicative language teaching was being developed, they were not integrated with either the theory or practice of communicative language teaching.

I aim to give communicative language teaching its rightful place within the realms of community and humanistic language learning. I begin with community language learning by focusing on its originator, Charles Curran, of whom Schumann (1980) correctly states: He was a clinical psychologist interested in applying counselling skills to the task of teaching foreign languages. Curran rightly observed that several foreign language learners experience anxiety and feel threatened while in the act of learning. For him, such dispositions were similar to those of individuals who find themselves at the initial stages of counselling interviews in which they attempt to account for their difficulties. Curran, therefore, applied the model of counselling to the setting of language engagement through which the student/learner was transposed to a client and the teacher to a counsellor. The principal aim of this modification was to replace barriers within the learner by warmth and acceptance.

I would say that from a Rogerian standpoint, not merely was Curran removing the conventional authoritative link between student and teacher, but he was also investing the student with real opportunities for being an equal partner in linguistic engagements pervaded by mutual security. In a Rogerian sense, Curran wanted the student's linguistic ability to be displayed in a climate where he/she is granted unconditional positive regard. Stern (1981) says community language learning aims to facilitate learning by creating a social climate where lack of knowledge of target language can be sincerely conveyed and gradually surmounted. In such a climate, he adds, the relationship between teacher and learner can change realistically from one of dependence to increasing independence in much the same way as it would, if a language learner found herself in the target language community. For Stern, the experience of gradual approximation can create for learner and student a satisfying personal connection which is necessary to genuine communication.

Curran (1978) was, undoubtedly, committed to facilitating a mutually co-operative relationship between learner and teacher. One strong basis to establishing this link was his opposition to a Cartesian view of the person. For Curran, "I" was not just some version of abstract thinking. "I" was, also, an emotional, in-stinctive, somatic being pervaded by anxiety, anger, positive feelings, and urges to learn. His target language teaching objective was to articulate a bond in which the learner and teacher were profoundly engaged in complex and creative modes of communication, the fruition of which, required their whole personalities, rather than exchanges through which they solved linguistic problems. He used the analogy of a key and lock as a way of explaining the teacher learner connection. The teacher/knower is in possession of keys to problem solving and is, thus, absolutely necessary to the learning process. The learner, on the other hand, is the individual who cooperates with the teacher, for the purpose of granting access to the keys. What the learner does is accept the intrusion of the key turning process from the knower/teacher and then, himself/herself, becomes assertive in pulling the bar in the lock. This association between learner and teacher is reciprocal and can be partially represented by the acronym, TESOL, "Teachers of English" to "Speakers of Other Languages." Here are two groups whose membership as users Curran emphasises, thereby granting expertise to both. The expertise emanates from pos-session and application of experience in users' own languages. It is not just the teacher who is experienced, the learner, user of another language is, also, experi-enced and must be considered as such by the teacher.

Curran is making a strong plea for role reversal, as well as, reflection, on the teacher's part. The adult learner is not a passive receptacle to be filled with sugges-tions, solutions, and answers offered by the teacher/expert. He/she is, also, highly emotional and deeply aware of the extent of previous knowledge in his/her own language. His/her attempts to negotiate an entirely new mode of communication are not devoid of threats to his/her confidence and ability. TESOL, therefore, suggests LESOL Learners of English as Speakers of Other Languages. The key and lock analogy, therefore, signifies a productive interaction and collaboration between LESOL and TESOL. LESOL must express a commitment to accept knowledge offered by TESOL. In turn, TESOL must be dedicated to accepting assertiveness from LESOL which precedes LESOL's familiarity with English. The ultimate goal is moving to a point where TESOL is not required.

Attainment of this goal takes place in five stages. At stage 1, the learner, who is inadequate in the target language, is completely dependent on the teacher/knower of target language. The teacher/knower thus uses his/her capability of understanding others to aid the anxious and threatened learner develop commitment to a sense of comfort in the teacher's presence. At stage 2, the learner is helped to initiate separation from teacher/knower but still displays considerable attachment. Stage 3 is characterised by ambivalence and ambiguity in the learner. For Curran, this is a delicate and decisive stage. The learner, conscious of what he/she knows, can become greatly reluctant to entering a realm of the unknown. The teacher/knower, very aware of the learner's disinclination, evidenced as pride in what is already known, may develop a tendency not to facilitate movement to the unknown. Stage 4 is attained, when the learner takes the initiative and dismantles barriers to entering the unknown. The learner's achievement here depends, very importantly, on the teacher's willingness to leave the area with which the learner is familiar.

Curran uses the lock and key analogy to explain how the teacher/knower would express such a disposition. The lock, signified by the learner's resistance, must become assertive by applying pressure to the bolt, so that the lock might be opened. This is also the point at which the learner understands what factors may prevent the teacher/knower from expressing willingness to exit the area already familiar to the learner. Possession of such understanding is a signal of the learner's entry to stage 5 where the complete learning self is involved in the complexities of learning.

In describing movement through the stages, Curran wants to create a setting in which teacher/knower and learner are beneficiaries of mutual comfort. He is quite clear that unconditional positive regard, reciprocal commitment and methodic trust, exemplified in client centered therapy, is a necessity for this movement. Further, two attitudes on the part of the teacher/knower are needed for enjoyment of the foregoing benefit. There must be complete trust and confidence in the learner. Secondly, a major factor in learner advancement is the teacher/ knower presenting himself/herself as sowing seeds of knowledge which must germinate uniquely within learners. Curran contrasts adoption of such a stance with the posture that knowledge is power which is not easily surrendered, because power confers status and security.

Three of the more important primary features of Curran's approach are: the intricacies of interaction; preference for giving priority to contexts where whole persons engage each other; and emphasising the importance of linguistic creativity by using the intricacy of interaction to promote whole person engagement. I also note that Curran's ideas first appeared, at the very time communicativists were expressing their dissatisfaction with the cognitive code learning and audiolingual approaches.

Soon after the communicativists had expressed their initial disfavour with the foregoing approaches, Moskowitz (1978) lay foundations for a distinctly humanistic view of target language learning. Not unlike the proponents of communicative language teaching, she bemoaned the fact that the language classroom was pervaded by interaction which was mechanical. She sought to replace the absence of creativity by a spirit of cooperation whose main feature was the profundity of communication. Her ultimate goal was to promote a version of humanistic education which persons greatly needed for the purpose of living. Her objective emerged from an appreciation that national and international media headlines were clearly reflective of conflict in persons' daily lives. She pointed out that humanistic education stresses self discovery, self reflection, self esteem, and understanding strengths, as well as, positive qualities in people.

This is the type of education deeply grounded in the teaching of Abraham Maslow and Carl Rogers. Moskowitz (1978) makes the link explicit in her statements that humanistic education emphasises a move from academic attainment to self-actualisation. Crucial to this drive were development of meaningful interpersonal relationships, acknowledging persons dependence on each other, expression of feelings, as well as, offering and receiving support. All of these qualities are significant features of a focus on acceptance of self and others, which emanate from education that is affective, confluent, psychological, and emotional. This is education in which subject matter is fused with feelings, emotions, and experiences of learners. In responding to a question about the relevance of humanistic education to the target language classroom, she says:

> Suppose the target language is taught so that students develop more positive feelings about themselves and their classmates and find out more about what they are really like. Such an approach will help increase the esteem and understanding students have for themselves and others, thus facilitating growth in the direction of being more self-actualised. Since self-actualisation is such a powerful inherent need in humans, as students see the subject matter as self-enhancing, it will be viewed as relevantly related to their lives. They will then become more motivated to learn to use the foreign language and, as a result, will be more likely to learn. (Moskowitz, 1978: 13)

Like Curran, Moskowitz grants primacy to contexts in which persons' deep-rooted and intricate engagement bear the fruits of linguistic creativity. She clearly has an eye on those wider social settings where self actualisation was being stifled within confines of everyday conflict, divisiveness, isolation, and loss of self worth.

Dare I ask, rhetorically, whether these are not some of the very impediments which Freire has identified? Are these not some of the same strictures which, today, burden target language learners in a setting of Western global dominance? Are these not some of the same barriers erected on foundations of dramaturgical stress? Are settings of humanistic and community language learning not very suitable areas for avoidance of "power plays"? Are these not spaces where language such as that used by London Mayor, Ken Livingstone, who evaded binary thinking can, and should, be employed?

Not merely are my responses explicitly affirmative, the Moskowitz position also constitutes a strong basis to determining how meaningful engagement among learners in settings of radical democratic multiculturalism takes place. These are the very settings where efforts can be made to ascertain ways in which Creoles, foreign, as well as, second languages are learnt by persons who benefit from what Moskowitz sees as a pedagogical objective to advance cultural pluralism. This is a goal she thinks is attainable by promoting the development of one race, the human race, through broadening students' horizons, enhancing their awareness of other cultures, other people, and other worlds.

No one should assume or conclude that my interests in humanistic and community language learning are interests heavily burdened or tainted by psychologism. My concern with matters psychological are inseparable from the sociohistorical. This is the sociohistorical, in its very negativity, which plagues the existence of persons. Several of these individuals are language learners who convey the impact of this negativity in personal terms conceptualised as anxiety, fear, powerlessness, as well as, dependence.

The conceptual basis to my claim here can be located in views of two thinkers who have made significant contributions to understanding the dynamics of domination and inferiorisation. They are the American sociologist, C. Wright Mills, and the exiled European philosopher, Herbert Marcuse. Mills notes that neither can the lives of individuals, nor histories of societies, be understood without an understanding of both. At the time of his remarkably insightful writing, he added that the history which affected every person was world history. He also pointed to the hugely transformative feature of such an association. It was that in a single generation, one sixth of humanity was changed from feudalism to what had become modernised, advanced, and fearful.

In what I deem to be one of his most profound observations, he added:

> The very shaping of history now outpaces the ability of men to orient themselves in accordance with cherished values. And which values? Even when they do not panic, men often sense that older ways of feeling and thinking have collapsed and that new beginnings are ambiguous to the point of moral stasis. Is it any wonder that ordinary men feel they cannot cope with the larger worlds with which they are suddenly confronted. That they cannot understand the meaning of their epoch for their own lives? That—in defence of selfhood—they become morally insensible, trying to remain altogether private men? Is it any wonder that they come to be possessed by a sense of the trap? (Mills, 1959: 10–11)

What is the trap? Mills viewed it as an experience in which persons feel that their private lives constitute a series of confinements. Within their daily lives, they are incapable of surmounting their troubles. Not merely did he credit these persons with being correct about their experience, he also added that private circles restricted their direct awareness of the world, as well as, their daily endeavours. Further, the greater their cognisance of their goals and threats, which lay beyond their immediate circles, the greater their entrapment.

Marcuse, (1955) was just as insightfully penetrative in his remarks about links between the personal and the sociohistorical. He was the critical theorist who dedicated himself to a Marxian/Freudian synthesis by conducting painstaking exploration of the Freudian position on what the editor of *Civilisation and Its Discon-*

tents called irremediable antagonisms between the demands of instinct and restrictions of civilisation. The thrust of the Marcusean analysis lay in locating inferiorising consequences of what he termed surplus repression on persons' everyday lives.

He made it quite clear that boundaries between psychology and political and social philosophy were useless, because of the human condition. He added that what was once recognisable as individual psychical processes have became dissolved by roles of persons in the state apparatus. The practice of psychology could, therefore, not be pursued and elucidated as a particular subject, for the psyche could not be preserved in the face of public domination which designified privacy and self direction. The upshot of these intrusive modifications was definition of the psyche via psychology conceptualised in societal dynamics. For Marcuse, psychological difficulties thus became political ones. His use of psychological categories simply meant that he saw them as political categories.

I see Paulin's position on life in Western societies as a strong echo of the Marcusean. In another part of his exchange with Christopher Hope, he asserts that there is a tendency on the part of persons residing in democracies to construct artificial distinctions between public and private life. These divisions, he adds, are inventions of bourgeoisie capitalism.

It was no accident that C. Wright Mills and Herbert Marcuse, two of the foremost intellectuals of the 20th century, were writing about the human condition, shortly after the middle of that period. It was also no accident that they offered their analyses with a particular focus on the developed capitalist world. What is very interesting about their positions is the relevance they have to that world in its contemporary form, as well as, the colonialist and current neocolonialist worlds inhabited by countless second language learners.

It is to Herbert Marcuse that I make one of my final references. His statement about preservation of the psyche is one which resonates, very strongly, with the destructive nature of globalisation, colonialism and neocolonialism used to deny numerous second language users the opportunity of pursuing the goal of self determination in their own and new societies. These users will get no closer to this goal, if they are barred from the benefits of humanitic and community language learning which nurture a cogent Freireian infusion of the communicative approach to target language education.

I bring closure to my work by stating, on a deeply philosophical note, that I think the remediation I have proposed can, and should, be buttressed by systematic efforts to determine: (1) conceptions of mind with which proponents of communicative language teaching operate; (2) differences and similarities—if they exist—among those conceptions and the Chomskyan; (3) why, given differences and similarities, do proponents use communicative competence in their teaching and learning enterprise? Issues linked to these matters cannot be separated from some very specific queries. What is the nature of affinity or difference between Stephen Krashen's subconscious or unconscious and Noam Chomsky's view that persons carry out practical activities without much conscious awareness of what is being done? Further, is Chomsky willing to see language use as practical activity? If he does, can he claim, legitimately, to repudiate the communicative purpose of language?

In a delineation of linguistic skills for the purpose of target language education, Pit Corder (1966), who depends heavily on ideas of the 17th century Moravian educator, Komensky, and greatly respected Firth's work on contexts of situation, identifies motor perceptive, organisational, and semantic skills, all of which could be subsumed by two broad aspects, the productive (generative) and receptive, (analytic) the ability to express oneself in language and understand language, respectively. Is there any validity to the argument that Chomsky's competence corresponds to reception and his performance corresponds to linguistic production?

Stern (1990) identifies the issues of balance and connections between analytic and experiential teaching. He asks whether language teaching can become entirely experiential and notes that Krashen sees analytic teaching as superfluous because it is not followed by intuitive target language mastery based on acquisition. Stern, however, notes that Krashen's view, which he terms an extreme position, is not, however, acceptable to others who have operated with combinations of analytic and experiential and deem the mix rather fruitful. Regardless of which position is accepted, close to two decades after Stern's observations, would the ghosts of acquisition, as well as, the sub and unconscious entombed within the ground of communicative competence not clash with the spirits of what Brumfit assesses as the figurative presence of communicative competence within social constructivist reality of language use?

Are power plays within institutional talk, also, integral to the phenomenon Rampton designates as identity in conversation? If so, can Rampton's claims about identity in conversation be linked validly to communicative competence? Rampton, I do recall, is quite insistent on total consideration being given to interpersonal and social meaning, when proponents of communicative language teaching examine communication strategies (CS). He also makes links between identity and stigmatisation within conversations. Given his insistence and establishment of connections, I must ask: Can he, a strong proponent of communicative language teaching, ignore Freire's ideas? Can he maintain legitimate use of the idea, communicative competence?

These projects, I hasten to state, are (all) the subject matters of another investigative effort. In the meantime, I await questions, comments, and alternative propositions, the source of which I hope is neither an Alien's Apostle, nor prelude to another Colonial Contest.

The Alien's Apostle

Why come to see all champions of the soil invoke that glossy silence of earthen treasures? A pilot's plague defiles our fading forests and raids all solar spirits of our game while the Monarch's inferno betrays its winter treat.
No: vaunt the bidders from Garrison, the seasoned square.
No: haunt the scribes from Bayland, the measure incomparable.
No: taunt the yellers from Kensington, the venue preferred.

Why purge the charge of humid hides above all howling hues with wisdom's wealth? A Princely pride anoints our jaunted juries in their fallow fields and the century's tempest bares a tale of wicket dreams.
No: crave the heroes from Kaiteur, the mystic fore.
No: brave the scions from Canjie, the vision supreme.
No: rave the mentors from Bourda, the fortune favoured.

Why bridge life's annals with the barter's blessing to braid all brawny gusts of flaxen fragrance? A builder's blight adorns the stable shadows across our bloated boundaries as the skippers' shamans preen the salty passions of oceans past.
No: deign the sceptics from Arima, the noonday trader.
No: rain the Pandits from Caroni, the wisdom forsaken.
No: feign the loyals from Queen's Park, the Antillean ruse.

Why weave those crumpled credits of the chirping quire on Issac's anthem where an Alien's Apostle treads all furrowed fathoms? A mariner's mist befriends those lunatic labours of our meagre mandarins but a dreadful drone of island demons defrocks the craft of wayward deliveries.

No: wail the herd from Carib, the flavoured sound.
No: hail the bayers from Ras, the hallowed yard.
No: bail the chorus from Sabina, the distant North.
No: rail the sages from St. John's, Alexander's arousal.

Colonial Contest

On the brightest day of our Barbary mane, we seal the greenest breach of a flightless shamrock and waive the faithful flame with our soaring falcon to singe the trading tumult in Tobal's sentries. Above the darkest swirls of our ruined remnants, we raze the migrant's musings to prize the purest tides of schooling wonders. Astride the tiers of putrid passages, we chide the Celtic craving for racing serfs and spoil his wretched runs against our tumbling torrents.

He rides the storms in misty moods of pirate passions but stays to court the teeming tools of tranquil terror. Ten thousand dramas dance upon the seasons of his tribe. Its rival warriors bathed in knightly berths of rude remembrance. From the lurking lochs of matted mentors, a sorcerer's tongue meanders to maim the rippling distance and greet all humble heroes of our graceful gazes.

Beyond the faded furrows of a ruthless rover, we hear the soulful slumber of his silent wake. Through a maze of feline forays, we snare the goaded genius who tastes all gilded glides of our searing sap. With the dreams of sheltered solace, we bare the bullish pride of lions lost to flaunt the radiance of our fallen forebears.

Notes

1. This and all other ideas of the Honeybee Network—save those obtained from the BBC World Service 24th March, 2002—were obtained from the website: Honeybee Network.
2. I heard these ideas in the summer of 1992, when Cornel West participated in a discourse with Arthur Schlesinger, author of *The Disuniting of America*, on public television.

Bibliography

Alexander, N. *Language Policy and National Unity in South Africa/Azania*. Cape-town: Buchu Books (1989).

Allen, J.P.B. "A Three-Level Curriculum Model For Second Language Education." Keynote Address. Spring Conference. The Ontario Modern Language Teachers' Association: April (1980).

Allen, J.P.B., Cummins, J. Harley, B. and Swain, M. "Introduction," in B. Harley, J.P.B. Allen, J. Cummins and M. Swain, (eds.), *The Development of Second Language Proficiency*. Cambridge: Cambridge University Press (1990a).

Allen, J.P.B., Cummins, J. Harley, B. and Swain, M. "Response by DBP Project Members to the Discussion Papers of Lyle Bachman and Jacquelyn Schacter," in B. Harley, J.P.B. Allen, J. Cummins and M. Swain, (eds.), *The Development of Second Language Proficiency*. Cambridge: Cambridge University Press (1990b).

Allen, J.P.B., and Widdowson, H.G. "Teaching the Communicative Use of English," *International Review of Applied Linguistics* XII (1974).

Ansre, G. "Four Rationalisations for Maintaining European Languages in Education in Africa,"*African Languages*. Vol., 5. No., 2 (1979): 10-17.

Atkinson, J. M. *Our Masters' Voices: The Language and Body Language of Politics*. London: Methuen (1984a).

— . "Public Speaking and Audience Response: Some Techniques for Inviting Applause," in J. M. Atkinson and J. Heritage, (eds.), *Structures of Social Action: Studies in Conversation Analysis*. Cambridge: Cambridge University Press (1984b).

Atkinson, J. M. and Drew, P. *Order in Court: The Organisation of Verbal Interaction in Judicial Settings*. London: Macmillan (1979).

Atkinson, J. M. and Heritage, J. *Structures of Social Action*. Cambridge: Cambridge University Press (1984).

Austin, J.L. "A Plea For Excuses," in V.C. Chappell, (ed.), *Ordinary Language*. New York: Dover Publications (1956/1964).

— . *How To Do Things With Words*. Cambridge: Harvard University Press (1962).

Bachman, L. *Fundamental Considerations in Language Testing*. Oxford: Oxford University Press (1990).

Bachman, L., and Palmer, A. S. *Language Testing in Practice*. Oxford: Oxford University Press (1997).

Bannerji, H. "Geography Lessons: On Being an Insider/Outsider to the Canadian Nation," in L.G. Roman and L.Eyre, (eds.), *Dangerous Territories: Struggles for Difference and Equality in Education*. New York: Routledge (1997).

Banton, M. *Racial Theories*. London: Cambridge University Press (1987).

— . "The Actor's Model of Ethnic Relations," in J. Hutchinson and A.D. Smith, (eds.), *Ethnicity*. Oxford: Oxford University Press (1996).

Baugh, J. "Linguistic Profiling," in S. Makoni, G. Smitherman, A.F. Ball, and A. K. Spears, (eds.), *Black Linguistics*. London: Routledge: (2003).

Bhattacharyya, G., Gabriel, J. and Small, S. *Race and Power*. London: Routledge (2002).

Binns, S. *The British Empire In Colour*. London: Carlton Books (2002).

Bierwisch, M. "Semantic Structure and Illocutionary Force," in J. R. Searle, F. Kiefer, and M. Bierwisch, (eds.), *Speech Act Theory and Pragmatics*. Dordrecht: Reidel Publishing Company (1980).

Blommaert, J. *Discourse: A Critical Introduction*. Cambridge: Cambridge University Press (2005).

Blum-Kulka, S. and Levenston. E. "Universals of Lexical Simplification," in C. Faerch and G. Kasper, (eds.), *Strategies in Interlanguage Communication*. London: Longman (1983).

Brathwaite, E.K. *History Of The Voice*. London: New Beacon Press (1984).

Breen, M. and Candlin, C.N. "The Essentials of a Communicative Curriculum in Language Teaching," *Applied Linguistics*: 1 (1980).

Breytenbach, B. *The True Confessions Of An Albino Terrorist*. New York: Farrar Straus, Giroux (1983).

Brown, D. "Language and Social History in South Africa: A Task Still to be Undertaken," in R. K. Herbert, (ed.), *Language and Society in Africa: The Theory and Practice of Sociolinguistics*. Braamfontein: Witwatersrand University Press (1992).

Brown, H.D. *Principles of Language Learning and Teaching*. New Jersey: Prentice Hall (1980).

Brown, I. "Who Were the Eugenicists? A Study of the Formation of an Early Twentieth Century Pressure Group," *History of Education*. Vol, 17., No., 4 (1988).

Brown, K. "Afro-American Immersion Schools: Paradoxes of Race and Public Education," in R. Delgado and J. Stefanic, (eds.), *Critical Race Theory*. Philadelphia: Temple University Press (2000).

Brown, P. and Levenson, S. "Universals in Language Usage: Politeness Phenomena," in E. Goody, ed., *Questions and Politeness*. London: Cambridge University Press (1978).

Brumfit, C. J. "Methodological Solutions to the Problems of Communicative Language Teaching," Paper presented to TESOL, Detroit (1981).

— . "Some Current Problems in Communicative Language Teaching," Opening Speech to SPEAQ Convention, Quebec City (1982).

— . *Individual Freedom in Language Teaching*. Oxford. Oxford University Press: (2001).

Burnett, P. *The Penguin Book of Caribbean Verse in English*. Harmondsworth. Penguin Books: (1986).

Burt, C. *How The Mind Works*. London: Allen and Unwin (1933).

Calvet, L. *La Guerre des languages et les politiques linguistiques*. Paris: Payot (1987).

Canagagarajah, A.S. *Resisting Linguistic Imperialism in English Teaching*. London: Oxford University Press (1999).

Canale, M. "A Theory of Strategy-Oriented Language Development," Draft paper prepared for presentation for the National Information Exchange on Issues in English Language Development for Minority Language Education, Virginia (1985).

Canale, M. and Swain, M. "Theoretical Bases of Communicative Approaches to Second Language Teaching and Testing," *Applied Linguistics*, Vol 1 (1980).

Candlin, C.N. "The Status of Pedagogical Grammars," in C.J. Brumfit and K. Johnson, (eds.), *The Communicative Approach to Language Teaching*. London: Oxford University Press (1979a).

— . "Preface," in M. Coulthard, *An Introduction to Discourse Analysis*. London: Longman (1979b).

Carrington, L. D. "Social Contexts Conducive to the Vernacularisation of Literacy," in A. Tabouret-Keller, R. Le Page, P. Gardner-Chloros, and G. Varro, (eds.), *Vernacular Literacy: A Re-Evaluation*. Oxford: Oxford University/Clarendon Press (1997).

Cassidy, F.G. "Teaching Standard English to Speakers of Creole in Jamaica, West Indies," in J. Alatis, (ed.), Report of the 20th Annual Round Table Meeting on Linguistics and Language Studies: Linguistics and the Teaching of Standard English to Speakers of Other Languages or Dialects. Washington, DC: Georgetown University Press (1970).

Catford, J.C. "J. R. Firth and British Linguistics," in A.A. Hill, (ed.), *Linguistics*. Washington: Voice of America Forum Lectures (1970).

Chappell, V.C. "Introduction," in V.C. Chappell, (ed.), *Ordinary Language*. New York: Dover Publications (1964).

Chitty, C. "Eugenic Theories and Concepts of Ability," in M. Benn and C. Chitty, (eds.), *A Tribute to Caroline Benn*. London: Continuum (2004).

Chomsky, N. A. *Syntactic Structures*. The Hague: Mouton de Gruyter (1957).

— . *Cartesian Linguistics*. London: Oxford University Press (1966a).

— . "Linguistic Theory," in *Language Teaching: Broader Contexts*. North East Conference on the Teaching of Foreign Languages. Wisconsin: George Banta Company (1966b).

— . *American Power and the New Mandarins*. Harmondsworth: Penguin Books (1967).

— . *Language and Mind*. New York: Harcourt Brace, Jovanovich (1972a).

— . *Problems of Knowledge And Freedom: The Russell Lectures*. London: Fontana (1972b).

— . "Human Nature: Justice Versus Power: Noam Chomsky and Michel Foucault," in F. Elders, (ed.), *Reflexive Water*. Souvenir Press: London (1974).

— . *Language and Responsibility*. New York: Pantheon Books (1977).

— . *Rules and Representations*. New York: Columbia University Press (1980).

— . "The Ideas of Noam Chomsky: Dialogue With Noam Chomsky," in B. Magee. *Men of Ideas*. Oxford: Oxford University Press (1982).

— . *Language and Problems of Knowledge*. Cambridge: MIT Press (1988).

Conley, J.M. and O'Barr, W.W. *Just Words*. Chicago: University of Chicago Press (1998).

Conway-Smith, E. "Garment Workers Slam NAFTA," Toronto. *Globe and Mail*, 29th May, (2004).

Cranston, M. *Philosophy and Language*. Toronto: Canadian Broadcasting Corporation Publications (1969).

Crawford, "Content in Context: Why is There a Furor Over Ebonics?," in C. Crawford ed., *Ebonics And Language Education*. London: Sankofa World Publishers (2001).

Criper, C. and Widdowson, H.G. "Sociolinguistics and Language Teaching," in J.P.B. Allen and S. Pit-Corder, (eds.), *The Edinburgh Course in Applied Linguistics*. London: Oxford University Press (1978).

Curran, C. A. "A Linguistic Model for Learning and Living in the New Age of the Person," in H. Blatchford and J. Schacter, (eds.), *On TESOL '78. Teachers of English to Speakers of Other Languages*. Washington D.C. (1978).

Daniels, J. and Houghton, V. "Jensen, Eysenck and the Eclipse of the Galton Paradigm," in K. Richardson, D. Spears and M.Richards, (eds.), *Race, Culture and Intelligence*. Harmondsworth: Penguin (1972).

Davies, A. "Review of John Munby's Communicative Syllabus Design," *TESOL Quarterly*. 15 (1981).

Drew, P. and Heritage, J. *Talk at Work: Interaction in Institutional Settings*. Cambridge: Cambridge University Press (1992).

Ellis, R. and Roberts, C. "Two Approaches for Investigating Second Language Acquisition in Context," in R. Ellis, (ed.), *Second Language Acquisition in Context*. London: Prentice Hall (1987).

Engebretson, T.O. and Stoney, C.M. "Anger Expression and Lipid Concentrations,"*International Journal of Behavioural Medicine*, Vol., 2. No., 4. (1995).

Eriksen T.H. "Ethnicity, Race, Class and Nation," in J. Hutchinson and A.D. Smith (eds.), *Ethnicity*. Oxford: Oxford University Press (1996).

Esterson, A. *The Leaves of Spring*. London: Pelican (1972).

Fairclough, N. Language and Power. London: Pearson (2001).

Finocchiaro, M. and Brumfit, C. *The Functional-Notional Approach: From Theory to Practice*. Oxford: Oxford University Press (1983).

Fisher, H.A.L. *A History of Europe*. London: Edward Arnold (1949).

Frankenberg, R. *White Women, Race Matters: The Social Construction of Whiteness*. Minneapolis: University of Minnesota Press (1993).

Freire, P. *Pedagogy of the Oppressed*. New York: Continuum (1970).

— . *Pedagogy In Process*. Seabury Press: New York (1978).

— . "Letter to North-American Teachers," in I. Shor, (ed.), *Freire for the Classroom*. Portsmouth. Boynton/Cook: (1987).

— . *Pedagogy Of The City*. New York: Continuum (1993).

— . "The Dichotomy of These Two Moments," in M. Escobar, A. L. Fernandez, and G. Guevara-Niebla with Paulo Freire. *Paulo Freire On Higher Education: A Dialogue At The National University Of Mexico*. Albany: State University of New York Press (1994).

— . *Education for Critical Consciousness*. New York: Continuum (1998).

Freund, P.E.S. "The Expressive Body: A Common Ground for the Sociology of Emotions and Health and Illness," *Sociology of Health and Illness*. Vol., 12. No., 4 (1990).

— . "*Social Performances and their Discontents: Reflections on the Historical Psychology of Role Playing*," in G.A. Bendelow and S.J. Williams, (eds.), *Emotions in Social Life: Social Theories and Contemporary Issues*. London. Routledge: (1998).

Freund, P.E.S., McGuire, M.B., and Podhurst, L. *Health, Illness, and the Social Body: A Critical Sociology*. Upper Saddle River: Prentice Hall (2003).

Galtung, J. *The True Worlds: A Transnational Perspective*. New York: The Free Press (1980).

Garfinkel, H. *Studies in Ethnomethodology*. Englewood Cliffs: Prentice Hall (1967).

Garfinkel, H. and Sacks, H. "On Formal Structures of Practical Actions," in J. C. McKinney and A. Tiryakin, (eds.), *Theoretical Sociology. Perspectives and Developments*. New York: Appleton Century Crofts (1970).

Goffman, E. *The Presentation of Self in Everyday Life*. London: Doubleday (1959).

Goodwin, C. *Conversational Organisation: Interaction Between Speakers and Hearers*. New York: (1981).

Goulet, D. "Introduction," in P. Friere. *Education for Critical Consciousness*. New York: Continuum (1988).

Graham, S. "Communication Grids: Cities and Infrastructure," in S. Sassen, (ed.), *Global Networks*. Inked Cities. New York: Routledge (2000).

Griffith, J. L. and Griffith, M.E. *The Body Speaks*. New York: Basic Books (1994).

Grillo, T. and Wildman, S. "Obscuring The Importance Of Race: The Implication Of Making Comparisons Between Racism And Sexism (Or Other -Isms)," in R. Delgado and J. Stefanic, (eds.), *Critical Race Theory*. Philadelphia: Temple University Press (2000).

Gudschinsky, S. C. "The Relationship of Language and Linguistics to Reading," *Kivung* (Boroko, Papua New Guinea) 1 (1968).

Habermas, J. *Legitimation Crisis*. Boston: Beacon Press (1975).

— . *Communication and the Evolution of Society*. Boston: Beacon Press (1979).

Halliday, M., McIntosh, A., and Strevens, P., *The Linguistic Sciences and Language Teaching*. London: Longmans (1964).

Harris, W. "Charcoal," in P. Bennett, ed., *The Penguin Book of Caribbean Verse in English*. Harmondsworth. Penguin Books (1986).

Heap, J. L. "On Recollecting the Possible: A Critique of the Repair System in Conversation Analysis," Paper prepared for presentation at the annual meetings of the Society for Phenomenology and Existential Philosophy, West Lafayette, Indiana, (1979).

Henry, F., Tator, C., Mattis, W., and Rees, T. *The Colour of Democracy*. Toronto: Harcourt (2000).

Heritage, J. and Watson, D.R. "Formulations as Conversational Objects," in G. Psathas, ed., *Everyday Language: Studies in Ethnomethodology*. New York. Irvington (1979).

Heritage, J. "Analysing News Interviews: Aspects of the Production of Talk for an Overhearing Audience," in T. van Dijk, ed., *Handbook of Discourse Analysis. 3. Discourse and Dialogue*. London: Academic Press (1985).

Hill, D. "Books, Banks, and Bullets: controlling our minds—the global project of imperialistic and militaristic neo-liberalism and its effect on education policy," *Policy Futures in Education*, Vol., Nos., 3 & 4 (2004).

Hochschild, A.R. *The Managed Heart: Commercialisation of Human Feeling*. Berkeley: University of California Press (1983).

— . *The Commercialisation of Intimate Life*. Berkeley: University of California Press (2003).

hooks, b. *Teaching Community: A Pedagogy of Hope*. London: Routledge (2003).

Hudson, R. A. *Sociolinguistics*. Cambridge: Cambridge University Press (1980).

Hutchby, I. *Confrontation Talk: Arguments, Asymmetries and Power on Talk Radio*. Hillsdale: (1996).

— . "Building Alignments in Public Debate: A Case Study from British T.V.," *Text*, Vol., 17. (1997).

Hutchby, I. and Woffit, R. *Conversation Analysis*. Cambridge: Polity (2002).

Hymes, D. "Sociolinguistics and the Ethnography of Speaking," in E. Ardener, (ed.), *Social Anthropology and Linguistics*. Association of Social Anthropologists. Monograph 10. Tavistock (1971a).

Hymes, D. "Competence and Performance in Linguistic Theory," in R. Huxley and E. Ingram, (eds.), *Language Acquisition: Models and Methods*. London: Academic Press (1971b).

— . "On Communicative Competence," in J.B. Pride and J. Holmes, (eds.), *Sociolinguistics*. Harmondsworth: Penguin Books (1972).

— . *Foundations of Sociolinguistics: An Ethnographic Approach*. London: Tavistock (1977).

— . "Communicative Competence," in U. Ammon, N. Dittmar, and K.J. Matthier, (eds.), *Sociolinguistics*. Berlin de Gruyter (1988).

Ingram, E. "Psychology and Language Learning," in J.P.B. Allen and S. Pit Corder., (eds.) *The Edinburgh Course in Applied Linguistics*. Oxford: Oxford University Press (1978).

Kachru, B. *The Alchemy of English: The Spread, Functions and Models of Non-Native Englishes*. Oxford: Pergamon (1986).

Kasper, G. "Beyond Reference," in G. Kasper and E. Kellerman, (eds.) *Communication Strategies*. London: Longmans (1997).

Kasper, G. and Kellerman, E. "Introduction: Approaches to Communication Strategies," in G. Kasper and E. Kellerman, (eds.), *Communication Strategies*. London: Longmans (1997).

Kehe, D., and Kehe, P.D. *Conversation Strategies: Pair and Group Activities for Developing Communicative Competence*. Brattleboro: Pro Lingua (1994).

Kellerman, E., and Bialystock, E. "On Psychological Plausibility in the Study of Communication Strategies," in G. Kasper and E. Kellerman, (eds.), *Communication Strategies*. London: Longmans: (1997).

Kennedy, R. "Racial Critiques of Legal Academia," in R. Delgado and J. Stefanic, (eds.), *Critical Race Theory*. Philadelphia: Temple University Press (2000).

— . *Nigger: The Strange Career of A Troublesome Word*. New York: Vintage Books (2002).

Kenny, L.D. "Doing My Homework: The Autoethnography Of A White Teenage Girl," in F. Widdance Twine and J. Warren, (eds.), *Racing Research, Researching Race*. New York: New York University Press (2000).

Kessler, C. and Quinn, M. "Bilingualism and Science Problem-Solving Ability," Paper Presented at the 14th Annual International Convention of Teachers of English to Speakers of Other Languages. San Francisco (1980).

Krashen S. "The Monitor Model for Adult Second Language Performance," in K. Croft, (ed.), *Readings on English as a Second Language*. Cambridge: Winthrop: (1980).

— . "Effective Second Language Acquisition: Insights From Research," in J.E. Alatis, P.M. Alatis, and B. Altman, (eds.), *The Second Language Classroom: Directions for the 1980s*. London: Oxford University Press (1981).

— . *Principles and Practice in Second Language Acquisition*. London: Prentice Hall (1987)

Kurath, H. "Some Aspects of the History of the English Language," in A.A. Hill, (ed.), *Linguistics. Voice of America Forum Lectures*. United States Information Service. Washington DC: (1970).

Kundnani, A. "Where Do You Want To Go Today? The Rise Of Information Capital," *Race and Class*. 40. (1999).

Laing, R.D. *The Divided Self: An Existential Study in Sanity and Madness*. London: Pelican (1965).

Lambert, W. E. "Persistent Issues in Bilingualism," in B. Harley, J.P.B. Allen, J. Cummins and M. Swain, (eds.), *The Development of Second Language Proficiency*. Cambridge: Cambridge University Press (1990).

Lankshear, C. "Afterword: Reclaiming Empowerment and Rethinking the Past," in M. Escobar, A. L. Fernandez, and G. Guevara-Niebla with Paulo Freire. *Paulo Freire On Higher Education: A Dialogue At The National University Of Mexico*. Albany: State University of New York Press (1994).

Lasch, S. and Urry, J. *The End of Organised Capitalism*. Cambridge: Polity Press (1987).

Long, M.H. "Input, Interaction and Second Language Acquisition," Unpublished PhD Thesis, Los Angeles: University of California (1980).

Long, M.H. "Input, Interaction and Second Language Acquisition," in H. Winitz, (ed.), *Annals of the New York Academy of Sciences*. New York: CCCLXXIX (1981).

— . "Native Speaker/Non-Native Speaker Conversation in the Second Language Classroom," in M. Clarke and J. Handscome., (eds.), *On TESOL '82. Pacific Perspectives on Language Learning and Teaching*. Washington DC Teachers to Speakers of Other Languages (1983).

Luke, A. "Two Takes on the Critical," in B. Norton and K. Toohey, (eds.), *Critical Pedagogies and Language Learning*. Cambridge. Cambridge University Press (2004).

Lynch, J.L. *The Language of the Heart*. New York Basic Books (1985).

Marable, M. *Beyond Black and White*. London: Verso (1996).

— . *Black Liberation in Conservative America*. Boston: South End Press (1997).

Marcuse, H. *Eros and Civilisation*. Boston: Beacon Press (1955).

— . "Dialogue: Marcuse and The Frankfurt School," in B. Magee. *Men of Ideas*. Oxford: Oxford University Press (1982).

Matoesian, G.M. *Reproducing Rape: Domination Through Talk in the Courtroom*. Chicago: University of Chicago Press (1993).

McLaren, P. "Foreword," in M. Escobar, A. L. Fernandez, and G. Guevara-Niebla with Paulo Freire. *Paulo Freire On Higher Education: A Dialogue At The National University of Mexico*. Albany: State University Of New York Press (1994).

McLaughlin, A.N. "Foreword," in C. Crawford, (ed.), *Ebonics and Language Education*. London: Sankofa World Publishers (2001).

Mills, C. W. *The Power Elite*. London: Oxford University Press (1956).

— . *The Sociological Imagination*. New York: Oxford University Press (1959).

Mills, C. W. *The Racial Contract*. New York. Cornell University Press: (1997).

— . *Blackness Visible*. Cornell University Press: (1998) .

Montgommery, M.D.J. *Talk, Media, Culture, and Society*. Vol., 8. No., 4 (1986).

Moskowitz, G. Caring and Sharing in the Foreign Language Class. Boston: Heinle and Heinle (1978).

Munby, J. *Communicative Syllabus Design*. Cambridge: Cambridge University Press (1978).

Murray, G. "The Exploitation of The Inferior Races in Ancient and Modern Times," in F.W. Hirst, G. Murray, and J.L. Hammond, *Liberalism and the Empire*. London: Johnson (1900).

Ngugi wa Thiong'o. *Decolonising the Mind: The Politics of Language in African Literature*. London: James Currey (1986).

— . "Foreword: Decolonising Scholarship of Black Languages," in S. Makoni,

G. Smitherman, A. F. Ball and A. K. Spears, (ed.), *Black Linguistics*. New York: Routledge: (2003).

Panreiter, C. "Mexico: The Making of a Global City," in S. Sassen, (ed.), *Global Networks*. Inked Cities. New York: Routledge (2000).

Phaswana, N. "Contradiction or Affirmation? The South African Language Policy and the South African National Government," in S. Makoni, G. Smitherman, A.F. Ball, and A. K. Spears, (eds.), *Black Linguistics*. New York: Routledge: (2003).

Paulin, T, (ed.), *The Faber Book of Political Verse*. London: Faber and Faber (1986).

Paulston, C.B. "The Sequencing of Structural Pattern Drills," in K. Croft, (ed.), *Readings on English as a Second Language*. Cambridge: Winthrop (1980).

Pennycook, A. *The Cultural Politics Of English As An International Language*. London: Longman (1994).

Perea, J. F. "The Black/White Binary Paradigm of Race," in R. Delgado and J. Stefanic, (eds.), *Critical Race Theory: The Cutting Edge*. Philadelphia: Temple University Press (2000).

Phillipson, R. *Linguistic Imperialism*. Oxford: Oxford University Press (1992).

Pica, T. and Doughty C. "The Role of Group Work in Classroom Second Language Acquisition," *Studies in Second Language Acquisition*. 7 (1985).

Pit Corder, S. *The Visual Element in Language Teaching*. London: Longmans (1966).

Polanyi, M. *The Study of Man*. Chicago: University of Chicago Press: (1959).

Poulisse, N. "Compensatory Strategies and the Principles of Clarity and Economy," in G. Kasper and E. Kellerman, (eds.), *Communication Strategies: Psycholinguistic and Sociolinguistic Perspectives*. New York. Longmans: (1997).

Price, J. *Native Studies: American and Canadian Indians*. Toronto: McGraw Hill Ryerson (1978).

Quine, W.V. "Two Dogmas of Empiricism," *Philosophical Review*, 60. (1951).

Rampton, B. "A Sociolinguistic Perspective on L2 Communication Strategies," in G. Kasper and E. Kellerman, (eds.), *Communication Strategies: Psycholinguistic and Sociolinguistic Perspectives*. New York: Longmans (1997).

Richterich, R. "Definitions of Language Needs and Types of Adults," in *Systems Development in Adult Language Learning*. A European Unit/Credit System for Modern Language Learning by Adults. Council of Europe (1973).

Rickford, J.R. and R.J. *Spoken Soul: The Story of Black English*. New York: John Wiley and Sons (2000).

Rickford, J. R. "Ebonics and Education: Lessons from the Caribbean, Europe and the USA," in C. Crawford, (ed.), *Ebonics and Language Education*. London: Sankofa World Publishers (2001).

Rivers, W. *Speaking in Many Tongues*. London: Cambridge University Press (1983).

Robins, R. H. *General Linguistics. An Introductory Survey*. London: Longmans (1967).

Rodney, W. *How Europe Underdeveloped Africa*. London: Bogle-L'Ouverture (1973).

Ross, A. "If the Genes Fit, How Do You Acquit?" in T. Morrison and C. Brodsky Lacour, (eds.), *Birth of a Nation 'hood*. New York: Pantheon Books (1997).

Roy-Campbell, Z. "Promoting African Languages as Conveyors of Knowledge in Educational Institutions," in S. Makoni, G. Smitherman, A.F. Ball, and A.K. Spears, (eds.), *Black Linguistics*. New York: Routledge (2003).

Sacks, H. and Schegloff, E. "Opening Up Closings," in R. Turner, ed., *Ethnomethodology*. Harmondsworth: Penguin Books (1975).

Sacks, H., Schegloff, E., and Jefferson, G. "The Preference for Self-correction in the Organisation of Repair in Conversation," *Language* LIII (1977).

Said, E. *Culture and Imperialism*. London: Chatto and Windus (1993).

Sassen, S. "Locating Cities On Global Circuits," in S. Sassen, (ed.), *Global Networks. Inked Cities*. New York: Routledge (2000).

Savignon, S. "Evaluation of Communicative Competence: The ACTFL Provisional Proficiency Guidelines," *The Modern Language Journal*. 59. (1985).

Schacter, J. "Communicative Competence Revisited," in B. Harley, J.P.B. Allen, J. Cummins, and M. Swain, (eds.), *The Development of Second Language Proficiency*. Cambridge: Cambridge University Press (1990).

Schumann, J. H. *Second Language Acquisition: The Pidginisation Hypothesis*. Language Learning. Vol., 26. No., 2: (1975).

— . "Affective Factors and the Problem of Age in Second language Acquisition," in K. Croft, (ed.), *Readings on English as a Second Language*. Cambridge: Winthrop (1980).

Schutz, A. *On Phenomenology and Social Relations*. Chicago: University of Chicago Press (1970).

Searle, J. R. *Speech Acts*. London: Cambridge University Press (1969).

— . *The Philosophy of Language*. Oxford: Oxford University Press (1971).

— . "Chomsky's Revolution in Linguistics," in G. Harman, (ed.), *On Noam Chomsky: Critical Essays*. New York: Doubleday (1974).

— . "What is an Intentional State?," *Mind*. LXXXVIII (1979a).

— . *Expressions and Meaning*. London: Cambridge University Press (1979b).

— . "The Background to Meaning," in J.R. Searle, F. Kefer, and M. Berwisch, (eds.), *Speech Act Theory Pragmatics*. Dordrecht: Reidel Publishing Company (1980).

— . "The Philosophy of Language: Dialogue With John Searle," in B. Magee. *Men of Ideas*. Oxford: Oxford University Press (1982).

— . *Mind, Language And Society*. New York: Basic Books (1999).

Singh, I. "Language and Ethnicity," in I. Singh and J.S. Pecceih, (eds.), *Language, Society and Power*. London. Routledge: (2004).

Smith, A.D. "Chosen Peoples," in J. Hutchinson and A.D. Smith, (eds.), *Ethnicity*. Oxford: Oxford University Press (1996).

Sridhar, S.N. "Contrastive Analysis, Error Analysis and Interlanguage," in K. Croft, (ed.), *Readings on English as a Second Language*. Massachusetts: Winthrop Publishers (1980).

Stern, H.H. "What Can We Learn From the Good Language Learner?" in K. Croft, (ed.), *Readings On English as a Second Language*. Cambridge. Winthrop Publishers (1980).

— . "Communicative Language Teaching and Learning: Toward a Synthesis," in J.E. Alatis, P.M. Alatis and B. Altman, (eds.), *The Second Language Classroom: Directions for the 1980s*. London: Oxford University Press (1981).

— . "Analysis and Experience as Variables in Second Language Pedagogy," in B. Harley, J.P.B. Allen, J. Cummins, and M. Swain, (eds.), *The Development of Second Language Proficiency*. Cambridge: Cambridge University Press (1990).

Stern, H.H., and Cummins, J. "Language Teaching/Language learning Research: A Canadian Perspective on Status and Directions," in J.K. Phillips, (ed.), *Action for the 80s Foreign Language Education Series of the American Council on the Teaching of Foreign Languages*. Illinois: National Textbook Company (1981).

Stern, H.H., and Swain, M. "Notes on Language Learning in Bilingual Kindergarten Classes," in G. Rondeau, (ed.), *Some Aspects of Canadian Applied Linguistics*. Montreal: Centre Educatif et Culterel (1973).

Stockwell, R.P. "Generative Grammar," in A.A. Hill, (ed.), *Linguistics*. Voice of America Forum Lectures. Washington DC (1970).

Swain, M. and Lapkin, S. *Bilingual Education in Ontario: A Decade of Research*. Ontario Ministry of Education (1981).

Tarone, E. and Yule, G. *Focus on the Learner*. Oxford: Oxford University Press: (1989).

— . "Investigating Communication Strategies in L2 Reference: Pros and Cons," in G. Kasper and E. Kellerman, (eds.), *Communication Strategies: Psycholinguistic and Sociolinguistic Perspectives*. New York: Longmans: (1997).

Thornborrow, J. "Orderly Discourse and Background Knowledge," *Text*. Vol., 11. No., 4. (1991).

— . "Questions, Control and the Organisation of Talk in Calls to a Radio Phone-in," *Discourse Studies*. Vol., 3. No., 1. (2001).

— . *Power Talk*. London: Pearson (2002).

Trexler, R.C. *Sex and Conquest: Gendered Violence, Political Order, and the European Conquest of the Americas*. New York: Cornell University (1995).

Trim, J.L.M. "Draft Outline of a European Unit/Credit System for Modern Language learning by Adults," in *Systems Development in Adult language Learning*.

A European Unit/Credit System for Modern Language learning by Adults. Council of Europe (1973).

Trudgill, P. *Sociolinguistics: An Introduction*. Harmondsworth: Penguin Books (1974/79).

Tucker, G.R. *Comments On Proposed Rules For Non-discrimination under Programmes Receiving Federal Financial Assistance through the Education Department*. Washington DC Centre for Applied Linguistics (1980).

Tudor, I. "Teacher Roles in The Learner Centered Classroom," in T. Hedge and N. Whitney, (eds.), *Power, Pedagogy, and Practice*. Oxford: Oxford University Press (1996).

Turner, R. "Utterance Positioning as an Interactional Resource," *Semiotica*. XVII (1976).

Twine, F. Widdance. "Racial Ideologies and Racial Methodologies," in F.W. Twine and J. Warren, (eds.), *Racing Research, Researching Race: Methodological Dilemmas in Critical Race Studies*. New York: New York University Press (2000).

Van den Berghe, P. South Africa, A Study in Conflict. Westport: Greenwood Press: (1980)

— . "Does Race Matter?" in J. Hutchinson and A.D. Smith, (eds.), *Ethnicity*. Oxford: Oxford University Press (1996).

Van Ek, J. "The Threshold Level in a European Language Learning System," EES Symposium 5916. Council of Europe (1977).

Wagner, H.R. "Introduction," to *On Phenomenology and Social Relations*. Chicago: University of Chicago Press (1970).

Wagner, J. and Firth. A. "Communication Strategies at Work," in G. Kasper and E. Kellerman, (eds.), *Communication Strategies*. London: Longmans (1997).

Walcott, D. "A Far Cry From Africa," in P. Burnett, ed., *The Penguin Book of Caribbean Verse in English*. Harmondsworth. Penguin Books (1986).

Walcott, R. *Black Like Who? Writing Black Canada*. Toronto: Insomniac Press (1997).

Walcott, W. "A Sociolinguistic Interpretation of Questioners' 'Repeats' and its Relevance to Politeness Strategies, Conversation Analysis, and Target Language Teaching," Unpublished PhD Thesis, Toronto. University of Toronto (1984).

Walcott, W. "The Toronto Mayor and Mombassa Natives: Canadian Ethnic Studies," *Canadian Ethnic Studies*. Vol., 35. No., 2 (2003).

Warren, J. W. "Masters in The Field: White Talk, White Privilege, White Biases," in F. Widdance Twine and J.W. Warren, (eds.), *Racing Research, Researching Race*. New York: New York University Press (2000).

Weiser, A. "Deliberate Ambiguity," in M. W. Lagaly, R.A. Fox, and A. Brack, (eds.), Papers from the 10th Regional Meeting. Chicago Linguistic Society. April (1974).

West, C. *Race Matters*. New York: Vintage Books (1994).

— . *The Cornel West Reader*. New York: Basic Civitas Books (1999).

Widdowson, H.G. *Teaching Language as Communication*. Oxford: Oxford University Press (1978).

— . "Directions in the Teaching of Discourse," in C.J. Brumfit and K. Johnson, (eds.), *The Communicative Approach to Language Teaching*. Oxford: Oxford University Press (1979a).

— . *Explorations in Applied Linguistics*. Oxford: Oxford University Press: (1979b).

Wilkes-Gibbs, D. "Studying Language Use as Collaboration," in G. Kasper and E. Kellerman, (eds.), *Communication Strategies*. London: Longmans (1997).

Wilkins, D. *Notional Syllabuses*. Oxford: Oxford University Press (1976).

— . "Learning a Language is Learning to Communicate," in *Review of Education and Culture*. Council of Europe (1978).

— . "Notional Syllabuses Revisited," *Applied Linguistics*. 2 (1981).

Williams, E. *The Negro In The Caribbean*. New York: A & B Publishers (1942).

Williams, J., Inscoe. R., and Tasker, T. "Communication Strategies in an Interactional Context: The Mutual Achievement of Comprehension," in G. Kasper and E. Kellerman, (eds.), *Communication Strategies: Psycholinguistic and Sociolinguistic Perspectives*. New York. Longmans: (1997).

Williams Krenshaw, K. "Colour-blind Dreams and Racial Nightmares: Reconfiguring Racism in the Post-Civil Rights Era," in T. Morrison and C. Brodsky Lacour, (eds.), *Birth of a Nation 'hood*. New York: Pantheon (1997).

Winant, H. *The New Politics of Race*. Minneapolis: University of Minnesota Press (2004).

Wunderlich, D. "Methodological Remarks on Speech Act Theory," in J. R. Searle, F. Kiefer, and M. Bierwisch, (eds.), *Speech Act Theory and Pragmatics*. Dordrecht: Reidel Publishing Company (1980).

Index

*A humorous, always learned, and occasionally frightening introduction
to one socialist teacher's view of America.*

HOW TO TAKE AN EXAM...AND REMAKE THE WORLD
Bertell Ollman

Authored by a famous professor who reveals the inner secrets of his trade, *How to Take an Exam...* interplays two totally disparate subjects, then brings them together in a revealing indictment of 'higher' education and the world it produces. A delightful *tour de force* that entertains while it educates.

"Funny, serious, practical, impractical, a delight to read."
—Howard Zinn, Boston University

"An invaluable tool both for taking exams and examining society."
—Dr. Michael Parenti, noted author and lecturer

"No student can afford to be without *How To Take an Exam*...don't miss this book, if you want to learn how to beat the system, that is the exam system as well as the political one."
—James O'Connor, editor, *Capitalism, Nature, Socialism*, and formerly Professor of Sociology, University of California, Santa Cruz

"Humerous, scary and angry...The tips Ollman offers about examinations are flawless, and the wisdom he presents about political economy communicates by anecdote and example rather than by programmatic analysis."
—Andrew Ross, editor, *Social Text*, and Director, American Studies Program, New York University

"A wonderful combination of Oxford scholarship, Marxist insight, Jewish humor, and revolutionary pedagogy. Ollman at his best."
—Michael Savas, University of Athens

"Ollman has done it again! He's brought together radical scholarship and a hilarious sense of humor to produce this unique book."
—Ira Shor, City University of New York

BERTELL OLLMAN, winner of the 1st Charles McCoy Life Time Achievement Award of New Political Science from the American Political Science Association (2001), has authored many books, among which is *Social and Sexual Revolution: Essays on Marx and Reich* (Black Rose Books: 1978). He is also the creator of the widely popular board game "Class Struggle." He is currently teaching at New York University in the Department of Politics.

216 pages, 70 cartoons, bibliography, index
Paperback ISBN: 1-55164-170-4 $19.99
Hardcover ISBN: 1-55164-171-2 $48.99

CRITICAL TEACHING AND EVERYDAY LIFE
Ira Shor

Critical Teaching develops teaching theory side by side with a political analysis of schooling. Written in the tradition of Paulo Freire, this book is committed to learning through dialogue, to exploration of daily themes, to creating democratic culture. It would be difficult to image anyone with an interest in teaching who would not find this book stimulating and thought-provoking, as Shor's teaching methods challenge the social limits of thought and action.

"Powerful, passionate and straightforward." —Jonathon Kozol

"Essential for those who have not given up on a bond between liberation and learning." —Dick Ohmann

"Thoughtful synthesis of experience and analysis." —Elaine Reuben

"Students, ask your teachers to read this one. Teachers, don't wait to be asked." —Bertell Ollman

"The theories presented are not new, but their milleu and methods of application are refreshingly unusual...The high quality of the student work included in the book is well worth examining." —Roger Winter, *The BC Teacher*

270 pages ◈ paper 0-919618-05-9 $19.99 ◈ cloth 0-919618-03-0 $48.99

---

send for a free catalogue of all our titles

 C.P. 1258, Succ. Place du Parc
Montréal, Québec
H2X 4A7 Canada

or visit our website at http://www.blackrosebooks.net

to order books

In Canada: (phone) 1-800-565-9523 (fax) 1-800-221-9985
email: utpbooks@utpress.utoronto.ca

In United States: (phone) 1-800-283-3572 (fax) 1-651-917-6406

In UK & Europe: (phone) 44 (0)20 8986-4854 (fax) 44 (0)20 8533-5821
email: order@centralbooks.com

Printed by the workers of

Transcontinental Printing
Sherbrooke, Québec

for Black Rose Books